Leadership in Eastern Africa

SIX POLITICAL BIOGRAPHIES

BOSTON UNIVERSITY

AFRICAN RESEARCH STUDIES

NUMBER 9

Leadership in Eastern Africa

SIX POLITICAL BIOGRAPHIES

Edited by **Norman R. Bennett**

BOSTON UNIVERSITY PRESS
1968

Library of Congress Catalog Card No. 68–21921
Printed in the United States of America

PREFACE

This collection of biographies was made possible by generous support from the African Studies Center at Boston University, and by the encouragement of its past and present directors, William O. Brown and Alphonso A. Castagno.

Alyce Havey smoothed over the usual difficulties that emerge in presenting a collection for publication. Janis Dyer, Jacoba van Schaik, Clarine Gregoire, and Andrea Mattisen typed the final manuscript. William Swanson of Yale University, Robert L. Hess of Northwestern University and Per Hassing of Boston University made helpful comments on some of the papers. Daniel F. McCall most kindly agreed to take care of some of the final details of publication during my absence from Boston. Barbara Dubins and Beverly Bolser aided in the proofreading, while Miss Dubins also performed many other services in the final stages of the preparation of the manuscript.

It is a pleasure to express my gratitude to all of the above for their help.

The quotations of Somali poetry in "The Poor Man of God" are printed with permission of the Clarendon Press from B. W. Andrzejewski and I. M. Lewis, *Somali Poetry: An Introduction* (Oxford: Clarendon Press, 1964). The photograph of Gungunhana and his wives is taken from J. Mousinho de Albuquerque, *Livro das Campanhas* (Lisbon, 1935), Volume I. The photograph of Sheikh Mbaruk bin Rashid bin Salim el Mazrui is from Mbaruk Ali Hinawy, *Al-Akida and Fort Jesus, Mombasa* (London, 1950). The painting of Lobengula is reproduced with the kind permission of the National Archives of Rhodesia.

Norman R. Bennett

Boston University
August 1966

CONTENTS

MAPS

TABLE

ILLUSTRATIONS
(following page 116)

Emperor Menilek II of Ethiopia

Sheikh Mbaruk bin Rashid bin Salim el Mazrui

Chief Gungunhana of the Shangana with two of his wives

Gungunhana in exile

Lobengula of the Matabele, 1889

INTRODUCTION

The subjects of these six biographies are all political figures, but they are of different types and played their roles in different polities. Three were kings, one a religious incendiary, and two were local leaders in the Zanzibari sphere — of these latter, one was a rebellious governor with a family grudge and the other a merchant who acquired power along with his profits. The countries in which they lived range contiguously from Ethiopia in the north to Mozambique in the south. They varied in personality, fortune, and environment, but they all shared the nineteenth century.

Period, political vocation, region (in the broad sense), and African natality (we will presently look at each of these facets, in inverse order) and resistance to European domination provide the unifying themes of the collection. For the most part their lives did not impinge on each other. The fifth (Gungunhana) and the sixth (Lobengula) were contemporary rulers of neighboring kingdoms in a regional state-system, as well as in-laws, and they faced similar outside pressures; but their stories are individual and each is worth the separate telling. The third (Mbaruk) and fourth (Kheri) may have heard of each other but apparently had no connections. Their life stories, each in its own way, tell us much of the structure of power and problems of organization in the Zanzibari state. The second (the so-called "Mad Mullah") stands out from the rest in the orientation of his career. He is more easily compared with the Mahdi in the Sudan (Muhammad Ahmad) or the many jihad leaders in West Africa in the nineteenth century than to any of the others in this book.

It would be a mistake to seek any further for common denominators. The category "Eastern African Biographies" has been left deliberately broad. Too stringent a delimitation of the traits to be used in the selection of subjects could lead to various kinds of distortion or stereotyping of the reality of the time and the area. The biographers of this collection did not, in the fashion of Plutarch, seek characters from whose lives they could draw a moral. This tradition reduced biography to hagiography in the Middle Ages and is still flourishing. On the other hand, they did not include any simply because they were "delightful stories," as Thomas Fuller did in his *Worthies of England*. Nor did they look only for individuals who could be flattered by recounting their achievements, in the manner of Tacitus' encomium of Agricola which still inspires panegyrists. And they have avoided the temptation to think of their literary portraits in terms of art. This desire leads to a delightful but dubious sort of biography of which Andre Maurois' *Ariel, ou la vie de Shelley* is an example, even though it avoids the worst excesses of the type. And, obviously, the pieces are no kin to the popular fictional biography school of which Irving Stone is the outstanding practitioner.

Our biographers are neither moralists nor aspiring litterateurs, but historians. Yet biography is one genre of writing and history is another, and our authors have been sensitive to the differences. A total merger of biography and history has been attempted elsewhere, and the result is a biography set within a succinct period history. In skillful hands and with a happy choice of subject this hybrid which treats the times as well as the individual can be particularly satisfying; but a successful marriage of this kind is rare. The life of Jack London by his daughter achieves a reasonable balance; more frequently the subject is submerged in the mass of detail of the period, as in the prolixity of David Masson's *The Life of John Milton, Narrated in Connexion With the Political, Ecclesiastical, and Literary History of His Times*. Or even more disastrously, the biography distorts the history of the period. Even rulers are not the center of *all* the events which transpire in their reigns and realms. Events in which they participate may be magnified in the telling out of proportion of their importance, while events in which they are not involved are usually reduced thereby from their true significance.

A better relationship between biography and history is maintained in the format adopted here. The individuals stand out stark, often with little background, but most readers who choose to follow the stories of these men will be able to fill in some local and temporal detail for themselves. Other historians, now and later, can find in these personal histories (and others like them that will be written) the material for new and better histories of their regions and periods. The biographers, it should be futher noted, used their training in historical research to collect data, for none of them had the advantage of a Boswell in being personally acquainted with his subject.

Many of us who are interested in African history have talked at odd times about the desirability of a dictionary of African biography. Here is a move toward that end. We hope that we may see the publication of *More Eastern African Biographies* with such subjects as Mtesa and Luwanika — to bring Uganda and Zambia into the territorial coverage — and perhaps Yusuf ibn al-Hasan ibn Ahmad, also known as Dom Hieronimo Chingulia (seventeenth century) and Muhammad ibn Uthman al-Mazrui (eighteenth century) — to enlarge the temporal brackets and, in the latter case, contribute to the documentation of a genealogical line.

A companion volume for West Africa is certainly called for and might include lives of Samory (on whom Yves Person has collected oral traditions), Uthman Dan Fodio (on whose theology Norbert Tapiero has been working), Prempeh (on whom Tordoff has already published), Rabat (about whom Nancy Bowles has collected some data), and Boatswain (on whom there is a manuscript account by Svend Holsoe).

Many opportunities exist and considerable work is being done, but the difficulties are even greater than the enormous task of duplicating the *Dictionary of National Biography*. The problems are not merely the vastness of the continental area, the multiplicity of languages, the scantiness of records. The constant problem is to penetrate the cultural milieu of the subject, to understand his outlook, his motivations, his mental horizons. Things which can be taken for granted when a biographer writes about a contemporary countryman of his own class are not obvious when one's subject, in another time and place, is part of a hierarchical system and tradition peculiar to his country. The alien observers who left the notes we must use usually did not understand the code by which the subject acted and often attributed to him motives which would have been natural to themselves. Given the universality of basic human qualities they were sometimes right, but given the multiplicity of cultures they were as frequently wrong, sometimes obviously so (i.e., from our better vantage point), and sometimes only slightly and subtly misleadingly so.

The authors of these studies are to be congratulated on the consistency with which they have sought in custom as well as in circumstance the determining factors in their subjects' decisions and actions. They empathize with their subjects, yet they are fair to all sides in the contests they recount.

Africans. Each of the six men whose biographies follow was born on the African continent but differs in race, language, and cultural background. One Amhara, one Somali, two Swahili, one Ndebele, and one Shangaan are not a single group in terms of race. Some belong in varying degrees to the Caucasoid division while the others (and the remaining degrees of the first section) stem from the Negroid division; one of the Swahili, in fact, provides the midpoint in the range.[1] Amharic, Arabic, Somali, Swahili and two other varieties of Bantu were the languages used by these men. One Christian, three Muslims, and two "pagans" is another way of dividing them.

There were many differences among them, and they shared certain traits with some individuals who were born in Europe or Asia but who nonetheless spent a significant part of their lives in Africa and influenced the development of events there. These outsiders have been excluded not because they are unimportant but because there is a greater need for information about the Africans. These African biographies are not without precedent. Sir John Gray gave us a brief biography of Ahmad bin Ibrahim, and Norman Bennett has published an account of Mirambo.[2] Some book-length studies are also in existence: Mzilikazi, predecessor of Lobengula, was the subject of Peter Becker's *Path of Blood,* and E. A. Ritter wrote a life of Mzilikazi's contemporary,

---

1. Mwinyi Kheri is an example in his name as well as in other ways of the fusion of Arab and Bantu which characterize Swahili. *Mwinyi* is a variant of a common Bantu title: *mwene, mwana, mwami,* etc., from which apparently the Portuguese had derived *Monomotapa. Kheri* is a semitic name, meaning "the blessed one," a feminine form of which is popular is Morocco.

2. *Uganda Journal,* 11:80–97 (1947); Bennett, "Mirambo of the Nyamwezi," *Studies in East African History* (Boston, 1963), 1–30.

Shaka Zulu. H. Brode has given us a life of *Tippoo Tib*, and A. Verbeken one of *Msiri, roi du Garenganze*. But these efforts are meager in number and usually in quality as well, compared with the biographies of Europeans who made their reputations in Africa: Sir John Kirk, David Livingstone, Lord Lugard, Sir Harry Johnston, General Rigby, H. M. Stanley, C. J. Rhodes, and others.

Some Asians who came to East Africa are also deserving of biographical treatment, but like the Africans typically present greater difficulties than the Europeans because of the sparsity of written sources. But although the challenge may be equal, the priority lies with the indigenous leaders because they are the indispensable ingredient to an African history. Perhaps Indian historians might research the lives of some of the "Banians" who came to East Africa.

East Africa. As used here, the region of East Africa is that part of the continent facing the east coast. This is somewhat larger than the usage common to many writers in the English-speaking world, which restricts the geographical region to the political region of former British East Africa. That practice was never wholly justifiable even when this group of dependencies had that name, and it is now less appropriate to continue such a restriction.

The area covered by this book is that which has been open historically to intercourse with the Indian Ocean. It might have been extended a little in both directions. It would not be difficult to argue that Egypt also faces the Red Sea and the Indian Ocean; Suez is a more important route than the Cape and usually has been. Only in the period between Da Gama and De Lesseps did the Cape route supresede the Sinus Arabicus or Red Sea as a commercial artery between the Indian Ocean and Europe (especially the Mediterranean). As Henri Frankfort has shown, it was via the Red Sea that the influences which resulted in the foundation of the first dynasty, i.e., the Egyptian state itself, arrived in Egypt. The Egyptians traded by this route from the beginning; this trade reached a high point in the eighteenth dynasty and subsequently passed into other hands — Phoenicians, Sabaeans, and others. In the Saitic period the Egyptians had a canal along the Wadi Tumilat from the Nile to the Red Sea. This is the canal which Darius the Persian repaired. The Ptolemies dominated the Red Sea, but by Byzantine times the Axumites had replaced Egypt. Venetians, concerned by the march stolen on them by the Portuguese, considered reopening the waterway and in 1504 proposed a co-operative venture to the sultan in Cairo.[3] The next European venture in this direction was that of Napoleon, for whom Egypt was the intended steppingstone to India; because of naval weakness he never got beyond the Nile lands. Robinson and Gallagher have recently argued, perhaps excessively, that Egypt rather than (or at least as much as) the conference on the Congo Basin precipitated the "Scramble for Africa." [4] (They were anticipated in this idea by Kautsky, which of course does not make the argument better or worse.) The perpetual importance of Egypt to the Indian Ocean trade is, I think, clear, but Egypt also faces in other directions and is best left out of this regional grouping.

To the south the kingdoms of Lobengula and Gungunhana derived from the Zulu expansion; Natal, Transvaal, and Basuto-land, which also shared its effects, could have been included. But for the same reason (i.e., that they belong primarily to another region) they are also left out.

In East Africa the Hābashā, like the Fulani in West Africa, are difficult to fit into a category with other peoples in their region. They have been important historically, not only when considered internally, but because of their influence on other African peoples. They are also set somewhat apart from their neighbors by the aura of mystique which surrounds their special origins.

If the Hābashā are unusual, the Nguni are the epitome of the typical. Their societies as well as their states fit into a continuum (which ultimately may be historical as well as typological) that includes Nyamwezi, Nkole, Ganda, and Bemba (Lozi and Lovedu are variant in important ways). The Nguni states are also interesting because, like the Akan states, we can see them coming into being during the contact period.

The group which is at the same time typical and unique is the

3. C. Diehl, *Une république patricienne: Venice* (Paris, 1915), 197; A. Toussaint, *Histoire de l'Océan Indien* (Paris, 1961), 95 (Eng. tr., London, 1966).
4. Ronald Robinson and John Gallagher, *Africa and the Victorians* (London, 1961).

Swahili. Nowhere else in Africa or other colonial areas did a mixed group comparable to the Swahili arise. The Cape Colored, formed under less auspicious circumstances, were forced down into a lower caste, as were the Anglo-Indians in another part of the British Empire. The mestizo in Latin America was more closely allied to the white ladino, the social gap being placed between the two groups and the Indian, but the distinction was still pertinent. Of all the mixed societies to which Europeans gave rise, perhaps only the Goan achieved as much integration, socially as well as culturally, with the Europeans as the Swahili enjoyed with the Arab. This unity provided what strength the Swahili states possessed, but even so it was a thin veneer; they dominated the coast but only influenced the interior. Under favorable circumstances Swahili power might have grown to match the boast that "when the flute is heard in Zanzibar all Africa east of the Lakes dances." Sir Harry Johnston colored all this area as Zanzibari territory on a map, but it did not become a reality; the claim was ephemeral and the initiative was lost to more powerful intruders. Like the Germans, the Swahili were cut short in an early stage of their colonial endeavor.

At any rate, the Swahili, aptly named, controlled the coast. Even in the nineteenth century the Swahili pattern was to seek alliances with African tribes rather than to attempt to rule them. It is interesting to compare the alliances of the Swahili magnates with the Nyika and the Digo to the seventeenth-century-European alliances on the Gold Coast. The Dutch used their African allies against all the other European settlements at one time or another; but the English alliance with the Fanti of Cape Coast was the determining factor in De Ruyter's decision not to attack the English fort in 1665 when his forces had taken every other English stronghold on the coast. At that period the European position on the west coast was strikingly similar to what the Arab situation must have been some centuries earlier on the east coast. Richard Brew, an eighteenth-century trader, married the daughter of a Fanti chief. Mwinyi Kheri, as his biographer herein relates, also married the daughter of the ruler of the country where his trading interests lay. In the seventeenth and eighteenth centuries Europeans were dealing with Africans on the west coast very much in the same fashion as the Arabs (and those *called*

Arabs) were doing on the other coast. If conditions had remained the same for a longer period, a comparable coastal society might have emerged on the western coast. Contacts were primarily around the nexus of trade. Goods came out the long distance from Europe in slow ships dependent on the winds and were exchanged for tropical commodities; and the ships slowly returned to their home ports. But trade led to the founding of settlements, tribal alliances, dynastic marriages, a racially mixed group, power and wealth for a few lucky ones, death or stagnation for the rest, and in all only a small number of aliens were involved. Except for the device of the chartered company, the relatively later date of their arrival, the difference in language and religion, the European presence in West Africa was, for about two centuries at least, quite similar to that of the Arabs in East Africa. If things had continued in that fashion, the European settlements would have remained distant outposts and probably have become more and more dominated by mulatto traders and dignitaries with names like Vroom, Brew, Swanzi, Quist and De Graaf. Bosman mentions a mulatto trader of the late seventeenth century; there had probably been earlier examples. There were to be many more, and a century later farther down the coast, Antera Duke, without the benefits of the connections of an alien father, became a big trader who kept his books in trade-English.[5] (This last fact emphasizes the difference that, whereas only literacy had to be introduced to the east coast, both literacy and a lingua franca had to be provided for the west. Bantu, despite its variety, had sufficient commonality to be the basis of the trade and cultural language of the eastern region.)

These tendencies did not coalesce; in western Africa the counterpart of the Swahili did not emerge as a coherent group. Perhaps one of the reasons that kind of stabilization could not be achieved in West Africa was that the nature and intensity of contact gradually changed because of the ferment of European society. Though apparent from Africa at first only in terms of gradually improving ships and firearms, Europe was being transformed. This can be seen more distinctly if we bring yet a third area into the comparison. As Sinologist René Grousset has pointed out, China and the West were on more or less the same

5. D. Forde, ed., *Efik Traders of Old Calabar* (London, 1956).

level of development at the beginning of the Ming dynasty (1368); but by the end of that dynasty (1644) Europe was already in possession of modern science and China was still virtually as it had been three centuries earlier. The significance for Africa is that Cheng Ho, in the reign of the third Ming emperor, started his expeditions in the Indian Ocean. Just as the Portuguese took Ceuta, his great junks reached East Africa (1417); but by the time the Portuguese had passed Cape Bajador (1434), the Chinese had ceased to come to Africa. Within a century the Portuguese had rounded Africa and reached China; the Chinese never reached West Africa or Europe.

Polity. There were three classes of rulers in the eyes of the Europeans at that time. Abyssinia, as they called it then, was a Christian state, and, since the European states from which the intruders came were also Christian, there was an immediate presumption of legitimacy which was not automatically extended to other African states and their rulers. The arms and organization of the Hābashā were as vulnerable before an experienced European army, as Napier had shown, as the Nguni states; yet the southern kings were unlucky, the northern king was not. Menilek was successful in attaining his goals. The Lion of Judah was admired for waging war on the pagan Galla to Christianize them and strengthen his kingdom; but when the Lion of Gaza tried a similar policy of aggression against the Chopi, he was "disturbing the peace." Menilek, heir to Prester John, was a Christian ruler; Gungunhana was a heathen.

The Zanzibari state, like the Hābashā state, was an emanation from Arabia, the Semitic heartland. But, whereas the latter had long since been Christian, the former was just as definitely Muslim. In the nineteenth century, the memories of the Crusades were far behind, but they had left an ambiguous residue. Barbarian Europe had been impressed by the civilization as well as the heresy of the Islamic East. Some of the respect and some of the suspicion remained, though Europe had by then far surpassed the Islamic world in power. If Barghash was not given the cordiality which Menilek received, he at least was tendered the respect due a sovereign. Under this umbrella, Mbaruk was accorded his measure of recognition.

The Nguni states were scarcely recognized as such. Their

leaders were regarded at best as chiefs, at worst as some sort of bandits. Even well into this century, a very knowledgeable anthropologist could point out that the British colonial administration treated Muslim and non-Muslim states unequally even though this discrepancy was to the disadvantage of the accepted policy of indirect rule.[6] Rattray reasoned his way to suggesting equality vis-à-vis the Muslim states and protection for the pagan states. Then, like Emmanuel Kant, who also reasoned his way to uncomfortable conclusions, he did a mental somersault and denied his suggestion.

The expectation of success for Africans, in any competition involving European power, was thus quite unequal for historical reasons; and as it happened the advantages were distributed geographically on a north-south axis. The pagan south was truly the nether end; the Christian north had the more elevated chances; and the Islamic middle zone was the median.

Although the Shangana and Ndebele states were less than a century old, and the Zulu state which had propelled them into being was scarcely older, the pagan states drew upon a tradition as ancient as the others. The lion symbolism, of which Gungunhana as well as Menilek boasted, was widely spread in Africa. Kalindi was associated with the lion, which roared at his birth, and so was the king of Dahomey, whose leonine representation in massive wooden sculpture reposes now in the Museé de l'Homme.[7] The pharaohs of Egypt had numerous lion emblems, including sphinxes, around them. Frobenius was struck by the importance of the big felines in rituals.[8] What is more pertinent is the ubiquity of lions and leopards in the royal iconography of Africa. It goes with the "divine-king," to which type virtually every African ruler belonged. In forest states the leopard often replaced the lion, as at Benin and Kongo.[9] The elucidation of the development and diffusion of this type of state and its symbols are problems for culture history.

There were some common elements in these African states.

6. R. S. Rattray, Preface, *Ashanti Law and Constitution* (London, 1929).
7. *Vide:* the translation of the Swahili chronicle, *The Kilindi,* by Abdallah bin Hemedi' lAjjemy (Boston, 1963).
8. Leo Frobenius, *Kulturgeschichte Afrikas* (Zurich, 1933), 81 ff.
9. M. Palau Marti, *Le Roi-Dieu du Benin* (Paris, 1964), 93, 171.

The troubles which the sultan of Zanzibar had with Mbaruk were not much different from those which the *negus* had with this or that *ras*, but Theodore and later Menilek were able to dominate their subordinates more successfully than their immediate predecessors. The Muslim polities in East Africa, whatever may have been the case earlier, did not at this time achieve much central control; but the system was capable of more unity, it had the symbols of legitimacy, and it might have grown in this direction if stronger European powers had not intervened.

In studying the struggles of the *negus* with his governors, Gungunhana and his rebellious province, the sultan of Zanzibar and the Mazrui insurgents, we witness the process, normal to these states, of centrifugal tendencies countering centripetal forces which often produced a kind of homeostasis, but one which easily degenerated into violence.[10] The factors which affected the outcome of the contests of outer regions with their capitals were numerous and varying. The outcome was not predictable to the participants — it was for them the great adventure — and more than other factors these struggles dominate the political history of Africa (at least when not confronted with Europe). The regional rebel had two chances for success — ultimately to dominate the capital, or to escape completely from its punitive power. The Shoan predecessors of Menilek had much earlier accomplished the first. Mzilikazi, the immediate predecessor of Lobengula had sought and attained the latter. The dynasties of Mombasa and Malindi, which the Portuguese found at loggerheads, were — according to their traditions — both derived from that of Kilwa, which then controlled neither.

The structural positions in the societies of the *negus*, the sultan of Zanzibar, and the Nguni kings seem roughly equivalent one to the other. Claims to the powers of office had to be asserted by force of a strong leadership and usually by arms. Such a state had its ups and downs: sometimes strong and relatively centralized, often weak and fragmented. Therefore, a serious problem

10. The processes of fission and fusion in African states has been discussed at greater length by I. Schapera, *Government and Politics in Tribal Societies* (London, 1956), M. Gluckman, *Order and Rebellion in Tribal Africa,* and P. Lloyd, "The Political Structure of African Kingdoms" in *Political Systems and the Distribution of Power,* M. Gluckman and F. Eggan, eds. (London, 1965).

is encountered in evaluating the observations of the first European explorers: when they report that no effective political control is exercised by any chief over an extensive area, is this state of affairs primordial or a temporary (or permanent) decline of a once substantial kingdom?

Let us look at a case where we happen to have historical evidence. In Ethiopia, from the end of the reign of Iyasu I, known as the Great (1706 A.D.), to the accession of Tewodros (Theodore) II (1855 A.D.), there was a period of considerable dissolution of power, sometimes called The Age of Princes. During this period, in the early nineteenth century, Nathaniel Pearce, who spent nearly a decade in the country, described a number of more or less autonomous polities in a contiguous area, with the rulers claiming descent from a common progenitor. The *idea* of a unified state remained, but the various claimants to the throne succeeded only in controlling different provinces.[11]

Pearce, with his limited curiosity and pragmatic approach, might have assumed that this was the normal state of political organization had he been the first outsider to arrive and had the Hābashā been non-literate. As it was, however, the more erudite James Bruce had been there earlier in the Age of Princes (1770) and had received from Ras Michael, a kingmaker of the period, copies of chronicles of earlier periods of the kingdom. The Portuguese also had been there in the sixteenth century when the country was unified. So the reality of the former unity of the Hābashā state was not in question, and there is no problem of putting Pearce's observation of the diffuseness of political authority into the perspective that is proper to the case.

What Pearce described is analogous to what Richard F. Burton found in the Nyamwezi area. He reported traditions of the Wakalaganza, precursors of the Nyamwezi, who were supposed to have disappeared as an empire about six generations before. But most modern scholars have doubted or at least largely dis-

11. *Life and Adventures of Nathaniel Pearce written by himself during a residence in Abyssinia from the years 1810 to 1819*, J. J. Halls, ed., I, 112. He found six kings still alive who had once ruled in the capital at Gondar. They were, he wrote, "related to each other and, as they boast, are descended from the true race; but the kings of Abyssinia have so many wives from far and near that it makes it difficult to decide to whom the Crown ought to descend."

counted Burton's report of this tradition of the Wakalaganza.[12]

It must be admitted that the Nyamwezi need not be explained as a parallel of the Hābashā case. To find a contrasting model, we might take the institution of *bretwalda* in Anglo-Saxon England. Each royal house in the various states, such as Wessex, Mercia, and Northumberland, was composed of descendants of the leaders in the Saxon invasion of Britain and claimed even more illustrious descent from the great god Woden. No king could admit that any other house was superior to his own. Nonetheless, the overlordship of a *bretwalda* could be established. Appearing first in the fifth century, according to the *Anglo-Saxon Chronicle,* with Aella of Sussex, the title and the powers were claimed intermittently by strong kings. Under Offa of Mercia and then Egbert of Wessex the central authority was made more effective. But the position was not inheritable; it had to be won. To be a candidate, one had to be a legitimate king. (Only three times before the Norman conquest did a man not of a royal house even obtain temporary occupancy of a throne, and each time he came to a violent end. None of these usurpers ever tried for the title of *bretwalda*. The task accomplished by Albert the Great of bringing about the permanent unification of England was made rather easier by the disappearance of competing royal lines in the wars between the English states, as Alcuin observed, and this diminution increased with the invasion of the Danes, so that the House of Wessex alone had the symbols of legitimacy.

The Saxon experience was a gradual development from diversity — independent small states of similar dialects and culture — to a final achievement of unity, while the Hābashā experience was a devolution from unity to virtually independent small states of similar dialects and culture. Both the Hābashā and the Saxon were literate societies. Most of the societies of Africa were nonliterate. Into which category of development then shall we place the Nyamwezi?

Lacking written historical evidence we might turn to anthropology for evidence. However, even careful study by an anthropologist is not proof against missing the cues of past political

12. Burton, *The Lake Regions of Central Africa* (London, 1860), II, 4. See Oliver in R. Oliver and G. Mathew, eds., *History of East Africa* (London, 1963), I.

cohesion, unless — as is seldom the case — special pains are taken to investigate diachronic evidence. The Tallensi, for example, are presented in the exemplary social analysis of Professor M. Fortes as a stateless people, with the implication that they always have been so. Traditions of certain Tallensi lineages and of neighboring Mamprussi and Mossi states, as Professor Skinner points out, indicate otherwise.[13] Compare similarly *The Chiga* by May Edell (the Chiga were an acephalous people at the time of her field work) with the *Kingdom of Mpororo* by H. F. Morris.

The traditions which Burton, Skinner, and Morris noted cannot be ignored. But oral traditions are not, of course, to be taken at face value; they must be evaluated, as any other evidence must; but if they are to be discounted, we must have reasons for doing so.[14]

If we consider the relationship of African states to interregional trade, we find an additional reason for supposing the Wakalaganza tradition to contain some plausibility. The problem of how the trade of the coastal cities of East Africa was carried on in the interior is a perplexing problem. The Zanzibari traders did not penetrate into the far interior until the nineteenth century. European activities and European firearms helped stimulate this surge into the continent as they did Muhammad Ali's thrust into the Nilotic Sudan.

How then was the trade of the coastal cities carried on in earlier centuries? The hypothesis that simple societies passed goods from tribe to tribe until they reached the Indian Ocean ports is scarcely creditable as an explanation of the economic growth of these numerous port cities. It is an inadequate basis for a continuing trade of any volume. Perhaps Swahili traders in pre-Portuguese times ventured inland, but we have no documentary evidence for it. Perhaps inland peoples carried their goods to the coast or at least to rivers which flowed to the sea. But, if so, who were these peoples who were organized to collect and transport the goods and who were sufficiently adept at trade to be able to maintain their enterprise?

13. E. Skinner, *The Mossi of Upper Volta* (Stanford, 1964), 6.
14. It is probably no longer necessary to remind any reader interested in this kind of problem that J. Vansina's *Oral Traditions* (Chicago, 1965) is indispensable.

If the Wakalaganza empire ever existed, it would have been prior to the end of the seventeenth century, six generations before Burton's visit. It may not be mere chance that the reported Wakalaganza collapse was coincident with the Omani conquest and the consequent disruption of the coastal cities. If trade with the interior was interrupted for an extended period, then loss of trade revenues and the inability of the king to distribute largesse — so important in African states — may well have precipitated a decline; if the dynasty could not recover and it lost power to regional subordinates and distant relatives, a series of smaller states would arise. The Wakalaganza were probably already divided into two main provinces, one of which corresponded with the Sukuma groups and the other with the Nyamwezi.

Somewhat more hesitantly, one might suggest that the Chwezi kingdom — which declined and was superseded about five centuries ago, it seems, by states which developed into the present interlacustrine kingdoms — may have had contacts with the Swahili towns. The devastation of the coast by the Portuguese may have had the same consequence for the Chwezi as we have postulated that the Omani intrusion may have had upon the Wakalaganza. Further, we might suggest that the Wakalaganza state grew up, when trade revived, in the vacuum left by the decline of the Chwezi.[15] While this interpretation lacks substantiation at this time, its merit is that it provides a potential solution to the quandary of how trade with the interior was carried on prior to the nineteenth century.

What we learn from the observation of various travelers in the nineteenth century is that the interior trade had just begun (or been resumed?). It is to be expected that the coastal interests and the inland interests would contend experimentally, and at times violently, until relationships could be systematized to some common agreement. Perhaps this contest had had its precursors in previous centuries, but firearms, then less efficient and less numerous, would have played a smaller part. Increased fire power in the nineteenth century caused not only higher mortality in each clash of armies, but was more exhaustive of the resources on which the trade was based: ivory and population. Lesser rates

15. On the Chewzi, see the brilliant treatment of Roland Oliver in Oliver and Mathew.

of exploitation of tusks and slaves in the earlier period had permitted regeneration of the numbers of elephants and people. The later, unsystematized and wasteful trading with the interior became one of the excuses for European intervention.

The weakness of the Zanzibari was that they were better organized for trade than for military protection of their trade routes. The weakness of African states which could provide this protection was not that their tolls on the trade diminished profits too much, but that when the military organization was kept in prime condition there was a tendency to continual *razzias,* which were disadvantageous to trade.[16] In time, either the traders or the kings might have stabilized the situation, but, as the nineteenth century came to an end so did their autonomy to seek such a solution.

Conflict between states probably arose more frequently from issues relating to the control of trade than from attempts to extend power over alien neighbors. Conflict within states was more purely political. Both contributed to the further diffusion of the idea of state-building.

The process of fission accounted for perhaps the larger number of the African states. The circumstances were often only vaguely recalled, but the connection was preserved in the royal traditions (e.g. that the Lovedu derived from Monomotapa).[17] Sometimes kingdoms arose through other forces (not excluding imitation) but usually adapted their emblems of royalty (as in the Galla kingdoms' borrowing of Kaffa and Amhara devices). In these ways much of the continent became filled with states of varying sizes and stability. A few hunting peoples survived and eluded the dominance of their neighbors, and a somewhat larger number of food producers remained in segmentary societies with simple organization and no central control; but the most effective resistance to the state-building idea was in the societies with age-grading systems. South of the Hābashā, west of the northern Swahili, east of the interlacustrine Bantu states, north of the Nguni extensions, there was a massive cluster of peoples for whom age-grades were the most important element of social or-

16. K. Ingham, *A History of East Africa* (London, 1962), 61; N. Bennett, *Studies in East African History* (Boston, 1963), 7, 8.

17. E. and J. Krige, *The Realm of the Rain Queen* (London, 1943), chap 1.

ganization.[18] It is probably no coincidence that we have no biography from any of these peoples. Unlike the state organization, the age-grading system did not emphasize individual achievement and status. It is not easy to find an individual on whom to focus a biography at this remove of time, and a social history of these peoples is perhaps all we will ever have.

Although we cannot appreciate the full flavor of life in that period, we can in some ways comprehend the realities better than those nineteenth-century travelers who were on the spot. The Europeans all considered Mwinyi Kheri, a Swahili, to be under the power of the sultan of Zanzibar; in fact he was far less amenable to control by the ruler of the Swahili than he was to influence from the king of Buha, who was ignored by the Europeans. Now, because of Bennett's research, we can see the relationships as they were.[19] This case is curiously opposite to that of Asameni, whom the Europeans considered to be acting on his own, when in actuality he was the minion of the king of Akwamu.[20] Appearances were deceiving. One who exercised power might be doing so only by delegation from one who remained obscure; a second, who had actual power, might seem to be in the shadow of a nominal ruler; still another, who had the symbols of power and seemed to exercise them, might be narrowly constrained by the real powers of other dignitaries who gave willing performance of the ceremonials of subordination but not always obedience to the nominal ruler.

If our subjects are largely political men and important primarily to political history, they are not for that reason irrelevant to the social history which we must ultimately obtain; for the political history is the skeleton of a social history. It is within the polity that communication is most effective, culture grows, and social stability or change is intimately entwined with political conditions.

18. H. Fleming, "The East African Age-Grading Culture Area" (unpubl. diss., University of Pittsburgh, 1965).

19. Bennett, "The Arab Power of Tanganyika in the Nineteenth Century" (unpubl. diss., Boston University, 1961) 40 ff.

20. W. E. F. Ward, *A History of Ghana* (London, 1958), 93 ff.; I. Wilks, "The Rise of the Akwamu Empire," *Transactions of the Historical Society of Ghana*, III, part 2 (1957), 120 ff.

Nineteenth century. During the nineteenth century, Henry Adams decided, "man had translated himself into a new universe which had no common scale of measurement with the old." The forces which Western man controlled after a century of the industrial revolution were certainly on a different "scale of measurement" than those which nineteenth-century Africans could command. Africans were still in the old universe — only the Euro-Americans were in the new — but Adams, like most of the West, paid scant heed to Africans; or in fairness we might say that they simply did not fall within his ken.

African leaders and their peoples were caught suddenly in a rapidly shrinking world in which white men in steam-driven iron ships came more frequently and in greater numbers to the shores of Africa. Machine-made textiles from Lancashire and Lawrence were brought in great quantity to exchange for ivory and gold to the mutual benefit of native and foreign populations. Guns with interchangeable parts, such as Eli Whitney had made popular, were also in demand. But when Africans confronted Europeans in battle instead of in trade, they found that Maxim had gone Whitney one better.

Not only were Europeans better armed, but despite the length of their supply lines, their communications and logistics were infinitely superior. General Wollesley, for example, in 1874 could string a thin metal wire from the battlefront to the coast, whence a fast ship could race to the nearest point of Europe where telegraphic communication could again be resumed, this time direct to London. The demands for supplies of munitions, tinned foods, and medicines were then amply provided from factories and warehouses. Extensive and well-organized political, industrial, and military systems meshed. The African leaders had no such advanced message system and nowhere to send their requests for materiel of such types, in such quantities. The size of the African realms, the numbers of their populations, their economic and other institutions were miniscule in comparison with their European opponents'.

Lobengula and Gungunhana had some appreciation of the odds against them, yet they had to face them with old means and methods no longer adequate, outmoded by the innovations of the invaders. Menilek, no doubt remembering Theodore's experience, took a diplomatic rather than a military stance toward the Europeans, reserving his armed efforts for his Galla and Sidamo neighbors, until forced to confront a European army; then he was fortunate in that he faced only inexperienced Italians commencing on their (modern) colonial ventures. The more-committed British would have come back from a defeat at Adwa, as they did from Isandhlwana, with fresh forces and ample supplies and reversed the score. The sultan of Zanzibar also relied on diplomacy and eschewed armed conflict. He avoided war but did not manage, as the *negus* did, to hold his territory intact.

Whatever the type of state, the nineteenth century, with its new alignment of forces, superseded earlier arrangements between Europeans and Africans. The seventeenth-century Europeans, as we noted, were dealing with Africans on a basis of near equality; and if it had not been for the vastly increased potential in the nineteenth century of European commercialism and militarism derived from the new technology, European settlements might have been drawn more closely into the African polities. Instead, all African regions were pulled more closely into economic and social relations with Europe, and Europe made another assault, this time more effectively than the Portuguese prelude, on the independence of the old Swahili society; and this time they also penetrated to the interior. Thus, as much as of any individual, this book is a portrait of the nineteenth century — as manifested in East Africa.

In summary, these biographies, in addition to the tales of individual doings and undoings, give us some raw material for regional histories, they help delineate the characteristics of the nineteenth century and to demonstrate political processes in East African societies. All of these are great boons, and this collection is most welcome.

Daniel F. McCall

Wollaston, Massachusetts
May 1966

Menilek II

by HAROLD G. MARCUS

Associate Professor of History
Michigan State University

Menilek II of Shoa and Ethiopia was a direct descendant of the wellborn military leader, Negasi, an Amhara from Menz, who ruled until 1705 as the first modern independent sovereign of Shoa.[1] Negasi was succeeded by his son, Meridazmach Sebstyanos, who reigned from 1705 to 1720, only to be assassinated by his son and successor, Abie, who held the throne from 1720 to 1745.[2] Abie was followed by Meridazmach Amha Yesus, who conquered Ankober during his thirty-year rule, "which gave him access to the high plateau of Shoa and allowed the sovereigns of this state to gather under their scepter all the territories of southern Ethiopia, which had been occupied by the Galla after the invasion of Mohamed Gran." Amha Yesus's successor, Asfa Wossen, can be considered the true founder of the kingdom of Shoa. He married a lady said to have had Solomonic blood, and he united by conquest or alliance the various states which were to constitute Shoa when Menilek came to power. In 1808 he was succeeded by his son, Wossen Seged, who seems to have taken the title of *ras,* or duke, during his four-year rule. He was followed by his eighteen-year-old son, Sahle Sellasie, Menilek's grandfather, who reigned thirty-three years and seems to have first taken the title of *negus,* or king. Both Wossen Seged and Sahle Sellasie seem to have appropriated their titles without imperial approval.[3]

Menilek's father, Haile Melekot, acceded to the throne upon

1. Some Ethiopian traditions suggest, in retrospect, that Negasi was a descendant of the famous Emperor Lebna Dengal (1508–1540), who was of the Solomonic dynasty. This point of view is well represented in the work of the contemporary Ethiopian author, Tekle Sadik Mekuria, *Ye Itiopia Tarik ke Atse Tewodros iske Kedamawi Haile Sellassie* (Addis Ababa, 1946 E.C.), 65.

2. *Meridazmach* was a title given to princes who ruled kingdoms but had not been named *negus* or king.

3. Paul Soleillet, *Voyages en Éthiopie* (Rouen, 1886), 272; see also Donald N. Levine, "On the History and Culture of Manz," *Journal of Semitic Studies,* IV:208–209 (1964).

Sahle Sellasie's death in 1846. Several years earlier at a palace
feast he had encountered one of his mother's Gurage slave girls,
Ejig Ayyehu, who, in the prince's drunken state, "appeared
prettier than she really was." [4] When the girl was discovered to
be pregnant, she told the queen where the responsibility lay,
and, after some hesitation, Haile Melekot admitted his involvement and begged his mother's forgiveness. Far from being upset,
however, the queen was delighted that the girl was pregnant
by Haile Melekot and decided that, if the baby were a boy,
Haile Melekot would marry Ejig Ayyehu and Sahle Sellasie
would be told he had a grandson. Menilek was born on August
17, 1844. The old king was delighted, and it is said that he
conferred upon the baby the name of Menilek, after the legend-
ary and glorious first Solomonic emperor of Ethiopia, and
prophesied that he would have a long reign which would see
the reestablishment of the ancient empire of Ethiopia. After the
child's parents were married, Menilek was baptized Sahle Mariam
in the Church of Kidassie Mehret in Ankober.[5]

The Formative Years

Very little has been recorded of the first ten years of Menilek's
life, but it was a period which saw momentous political changes
within Ethiopia, and one from which the boy emerged as a
distinct political entity. In 1844, Ethiopia did not have a centralized government, even though an emperor did keep court at
the old capital of Gondar. This emperor was the puppet of Ras
Ali, who controlled central Ethiopia; but Ras Wobie ruled in
Tigre; Gojjam was autonomous and governed by Ras Goshu and
his descendants; Wollo was an independent, though uneasy,
federation of seven clans; and Shoa was a sovereign principality.

4. Menilek's chronicler, Gebre Sellasie, writes that Ejig Ayyehu was wellborn and owned much land. This seems to be an exaggeration but is expli-
cable because, as Gebre Sellasie's editor, Maurice de Coppet, points out, the
chronicler "composed his work with constant care to justify all the acts of his
master and to conceal what would be prejudicial to his glory." Guèbre Sellasié,
Chronique du Regne de Ménélik II, Roi des Rois d'Éthiopie (Paris, 1930), I,
73.

5. Antonio Cecchi, *Da Zeila alle Frontiere di Caffa* (Roma, 1886), I, 249–
250; Henry de Monfreid, *Ménélik tel qu'il fut* (Paris, 1954), 45–49; Soleillet,
Voyages, 86.

This anarchic, almost feudal state of affairs was revolutionized by the emergence of the Emperor Theodore, an upstart military genius with no authentic claim to the Solomonic throne. Theodore fought his way to the control of central Ethiopia by 1854, and two years later, after defeating Ras Wobie, he had himself crowned emperor on February 5, 1856. The new emperor was determined to obtain permanent control over all the political

Ethiopia

units of the highlands by disestablishing their hereditary and traditional rulers and creating a centralized state whose administrators would be totally dependent upon the will of the imperial crown.[6]

Since Shoa was one of the strongest of the hereditary principalities, and because its ruler had been implicated in a plot against the imperial power, the new emperor soon challenged King Haile Melekot. At the beginning of the rainy season of 1856 Theodore set out for Shoa to force the king's submission.[7] Haile Melekot refused, hoping that the imminent rains would impede Theodore's army and force him to withdraw. Contrary to the usual practice, however, Theodore continued his advance during the rains and, in October 1856, arrived at the Shoan frontier.

Haile Melekot, weakened by dissidence among his chiefs and by an illness that was shortly to claim his life, was unable to prevent Theodore's progress. Concerned about his son's safety in face of the emperor's advancing army, he asked a group of loyal Shoan chiefs, headed by his brother, Ato (Esquire) Darghie, to safeguard Menilek in the event that "God wished that the Kingdom of Shoa should be reconstituted." [8] At the end of 1856, the king died and his demoralized army collapsed. Darghie fled with Menilek toward Minjar, a fertile plateau between the Kessem and the Awash rivers. Theodore sent Ras Ingeda and his troops after the fugitives, fearing that his victory would remain temporary as long as Menilek continued at large to provide a rallying point for the Shoans. Ras Ingeda therefore applied constant pressure to Ato Darghie's weak retinue until it appeared better to surrender than to see the whole party, including Menilek, annihilated.[9] The emperor appointed Haili, Haile Melekot's bastard half-brother, *meridazmach* of Shoa, and had Menilek,

---

6. Rev. Henry A. Stern, *Wanderings among the Falashas in Abyssinia* (London, 1862), 63, 68–76; Clements R. Markham, *A History of the Abyssinian Expedition* (London, 1869), 55, 61–66.

7. In the highlands of Ethiopia the long rainy season starts in late June and continues until late September.

8. Cecchi, *Da Zeila*, 254.

9. Afeworq Gebreyesus, *Dagmawi Menilek* (Roma, 1901 E.C.), 10–13; Guèbre Sellasié, *Chronique*, 86–92; Cecchi, *Da Zeila*, 251–255; De Monfreid, *Ménélik*, 70–81.

his mother, Ato Darghie, and other important Shoans brought to his court, where he received Menilek "with honor and joy," and treated him like a prince.[10] Theodore was more than kind to the young heir to the Shoan throne; while reminiscing about his days of captivity, Menilek once said, "[Even though] he killed my father and took me to his court, he always loved me as a son; he educated me with the greatest care, and almost showed for me greater affection than for his own son." Theodore even told Menilek "more than once . . . [that he] would rule after him." [11]

While acting as a page and a courtier at the imperial court, Menilek gained valuable experience in statecraft. Being "quick, gentle, and unpretending . . . [Menilek] propitiated the tyrant's favour, and was honoured with the hand of a royal princess, a daughter of the invincible conqueror." [12] Furthermore, Theodore gave him the title of *dejazmach*.[13] But Menilek never forgot who he was, and that he belonged on the Shoan throne. The province had been in an almost constant state of insurrection for several years, and as Theodore's political difficulties in Shoa mounted in 1864 and 1865, Menilek began to give serious consideration to the possibility of escape. He received several offers of support from the Shoan priests and military chieftains with whom he maintained secret contacts. When he finally decided to flee Theodore's bastion at Mak'dala, certain courtiers sensed his plans and voiced their suspicions to the emperor, who, however, took no action because he trusted Menilek fully.[14]

On June 30, 1865, "during a dark and auspicious night," Menilek and some of his followers, Shoans also imprisoned with him at Mak'dala, "guided by a few glimmering stars, quitted the camp. Afraid to disturb the sleeping hosts, they noiselessly threaded their way across the wide chasm which forms a most

10. Cecchi, *Da Zeila*, 255; Guèbre Sellasié, *Chronique*, 87; Alaqa Walda Maryam, "The History of King Theodore," *The Journal of the African Society*, XXI:15 (October 1909).
11. Fra Guglielmo Massaja, *I Miei Trentacinque Anni di Missione nell'Alta Etiopia* (Tivoli, 1928), IX, 28.
12. Henry A. Stern, *The Captive Missionary* (London, 1868), 219.
13. *Dejazmach*, literally "the general at the door," is roughly equivalent to earl; it is the rank immediately below *bittwodded*, or best-liked, which is second only to *ras*.
14. Menilek later regretted this decision and breach of faith with Theodore. Massaja, *Etiopia*, IX, 28.

formidable barrier between Amba Magdala and the [Wollo] Galla country, and then, pursuing their tortuous path up a steep bank to the south-east, they arrived by dawn of day on the high table-land of the Wollo Galla." [15] Their plan was to reach Shoa and reconquer the land of Haile Melekot.

Prior to his escape Menilek had apparently been assured that Queen Wirkit of the Wollo Galla, a mortal enemy of the emperor, would provide him with immediate refuge. It seems, however, that the queen's actual plan was to hold Menilek captive and exchange him for her son, the Imam, who was also held at Mak'dala. But Theodore heard of Menilek's escape in time to watch from his mountain fortress as Wirkit's troops met the fugitives and started to escort them in apparent friendship across the Wollo border. "Conscious that this desertion involved the irretrievable loss of a kingdom," he concluded that "Worket has found a son who is free; she can dispense with the one who is chained." At Theodore's court such a statement had the effect of a death sentence, and the "Imam and his companions . . . were instantly dragged out of the prison compound, and, in the presence of the King and his nobles, hacked and chopped to pieces." [16] Having nothing further to hope for from Menilek's presence in her country, the queen provided him an escort to the Shoan frontier, where he was welcomed enthusiastically by his late father's supporters.

Many Shoans rallied to Menilek's cause, and, in August, on a plain in eastern Shoa, with the nucleus of his new army around him, Menilek proclaimed himself king of Shoa. The new king quickly turned to the task of defeating Ato Bezabeh, Theodore's most recent governor of Shoa and an old slave of Menilek's father. Bezabeh's army defected as soon as the men realized who was marching against them, and, in a short time, Menilek was in military control of Shoa. Ato Bezabeh fled to an *amba* (a flat-topped mountain) and, in traditional style, begged Menilek's pardon, which he received along with the governorship of an important part of Shoa. Pardoning Bezabeh was a shrewd act of politics for Menilek. Although regarded as a symbolic leader by Shoan nationalists reacting to northern political con-

15. Stern, *Captive Missionary,* 219.
16. *Ibid.,* 220–221.

trol, Menilek still had to work with the appointed officials of the previous administration until he could consolidate his authority. Had he brought the Bezabeh episode to a state of crisis, he might have made incumbent Shoan administrators and politicians uneasy about his future intentions and, perhaps, have caused their political alienation. Accordingly, Menilek "did not punish any of the chiefs, nor any of the prisoners [of war], and left them [in] their positions, even though he could have reproached them." [17]

During the first year of his rule Menilek was completely engrossed in safeguarding his newly conquered political base. The Galla on the borders of Shoa mounted several attacks which were repulsed vigorously; any sign of weakness would have invited more raiding. Furthermore, the recent political events had left a residue of disorder and insecurity in Shoa, and Menilek had to provide convincing evidence of his abilities as a leader and protector of men. "To reorganize the administration, to make his subjects again respect the laws . . . to protect them from every external danger and especially from the revenge of the Atze [Emperor], Menilek started [by] . . . expanding, disciplining, and gaining the affection of the army." [18] He also revoked many of Theodore's reforms and reverted to the "mild and paternal laws" by which his forebears had governed Shoa, thus gaining support among the conservatives by stressing the continuity between his reign and that of his father.[19]

Menilek was twenty-one years old when he returned to Shoa, an extreme youth in Ethiopian terms and an untried political leader. A glimpse of his personality, described in the invaluable memoirs of Fra Guglielmo Massaja, emerges from his response to the situation presented to him three years later by the Napier expedition of 1868.[20] The Napier expedition was designed to free British missionaries held captive by Theodore at Mak'dala, as well as to demonstrate that British power could protect British subjects anywhere in the world from abuse and insult,

17. Guèbre Sellasié, *Chronique*, I, 104.
18. Cecchi, *Da Zeila*, 265.
19. Massaja, *Etiopia*, IX, 74.
20. Fra Massaja (later Cardinal Massaja) was a missionary who arrived in Shoa shortly before this period. He had his first meeting with Menilek on March 6, 1868.

even though the insult and abuse may have resulted from British incompetence and lack of tact. The British governor of Aden had sent Menilek a letter requesting Shoan assistance in the expedition and explaining that "we do not come to conquer her [Ethiopia], nor to submit her to our rule, but solely to free our brothers, unjustly held prisoner by Theodore." The letter also warned that Menilek would run the risk of British retribution should he decide to aid the emperor. In his first meeting with Fra Massaja, Menilek asked him his opinion of the result of the coming encounter and was told that the British would probably win, even "if the country unites with Theodore and sincerely defends him." Menilek replied that Theodore no longer enjoyed the support of most Ethiopians, but that the British maneuver might rally them to support their emperor, and that he, like any Ethiopian prince, would have to defend himself with all his power against anyone violating his frontiers.[21] Menilek nevertheless responded affirmatively to the British governor's request and led Lord Napier to believe that he could expect active assistance from Shoa. In fact, Menilek did not aid in the destruction of the emperor who trusted him as a son and for whom Menilek had the highest regard and affection. On the other hand, Menilek was not dismayed by the news of the fall of Mak'dala and the emperor's suicide since these events eliminated the threat of Theodore's revenge. Indeed Menilek went so far as to order a holiday and to attempt to regain British favor by sending a mission to Mak'dala with letters to Lord Napier and a great quantity of provisions for the British army. When the commissioners arrived at the fortress, however, they found that the British were already well on their way back to the coast.

A short time later Menilek discussed this episode with Massaja. He told the missionary that he was personally saddened by the death of the emperor who had been like a second father to him. Surprised by this admission, Massaja asked him why, then, he had ordered a holiday to celebrate Theodore's defeat and death. Menilek replied that it was to "satisfy the passions of the people . . . as for me, I should have gone into a forest to weep over the untimely death of that man . . . I have now lost the one

21. Massaja, *Etiopia*, VIII, 172–173.

who educated me, and toward whom I had always cherished filial and sincere affection." He claimed that when he had taken up the British proposal with his advisers, he had felt "a great repugnance" at the thought of playing a role against Theodore, and that he and his government had chosen not to ally themselves with the British, although they had written the British that they would. To a certain extent, however, he was still not happy about the decision: "if I should have fallen in with the British army, not only would I have been consigned the fortress of Mak'dala after the victory, and been presented with rifles and cannons, but I probably would have been elected and acclaimed Emperor by the victors and by the people. Now all is lost, and perhaps another . . . will sit upon the throne which belongs to me by right . . . Don't I have reason, consequently, dear Father, to be sad and melancholy?" [22]

The outcome of the contest at Mak'dala opened several new possibilities for Menilek. First, many Shoan chiefs held in captivity at Mak'dala were freed. Among these were several of Menilek's relatives to whom he could give important governmental positions; Ato Darghie, his earlier adviser and teacher, was an especially trustworthy man. Second, no one had as yet won the newly vacated imperial throne. Menilek believed his claim to the Solomonic throne to be better, and his chance for success as good, as that of any other pretender in the country. When he heard, soon after the fall of Mak'dala, that Wagshum Gobesie of Tigre had occupied Gondar and named himself Emperor Tekle Giorgis, Menilek in turn proclaimed himself Emperor Menilek II of Ethiopia.[23] To strengthen his position, he left Shoa under Darghie's supervision and invaded the now unfriendly province of Wollo, conquering a large part of that country in a short time. He founded the strategic town of Wara Ilou and left a garrison there and in a second strategic area. Thus provided with a buffer state between Shoa and Tigre, Menilek embarked upon a slow, continuous expansion among the Galla tribes northwest and southwest of Shoa.

22. *Ibid.*, IX, 15–16, 24, 26, 27–28.
23. *Ibid.*, 34. As neither Gobesie nor Menilek had been consecrated and anointed by the *abun* (Metropolitan) of the Ethiopian Church, their behavior was irregular.

In the meantime Dejaz Kassa of Tigre had become a third competitor for the throne and had the advantage of an army well equipped with modern weapons because he had supported the British at Mak'dala.[24] Gobesie attempted to raise support against Kassa by demanding submission and tribute from various Ethiopian chiefs, including Menilek who responded by delegating a representative to make his act of submission. Gobesie scornfully rejected this improper form of submission and prepared to attack Shoa. Before he had time to carry out this plan, however, he was challenged by Kassa, and in July 1871, their two armies met at Adwa, where Gobesie was defeated, captured, and later imprisoned. Kassa thereupon took the title of emperor and, on January 21, 1872, was crowned Yohannis IV of Ethiopia at the Church of Mary in Axum.[25]

Imperial Ambitions, 1871–1878

Meanwhile, Menilek had completed his Wollo campaign and had received the submission of its ruler, Abba Watto, and his agreement to govern the country under Shoan sovereignty.[26] According to one authority, Menilek's sucess with Wollo stimulated his ambitions and gave him the "idea of pushing forward to Gondar and, ejecting the Emperor from there, have himself proclaimed King of Kings of Ethiopia." [27] While this may be an exaggerated point, Menilek did, doubtlessly, have glorious ideas about his future role. The fact that he did not at this time officially recognize Yohannis as *negus negast* (king of kings, or emperor) is indicative of his plan to dispute the crown, and in 1871, while Tekle Giorgis and Yohannis were at each other's throats, he had sent an army composed of Wollo Galla and Shoans toward Gondar. Menilek apparently decided that what-

24. William M. Dye, *Moslem Egypt and Christian Ethiopia* (New York, 1880), 124.

25. Had Yohannis followed the custom of the previous few centuries, he would have been anointed in Gondar, the most recent religious and political capital of Ethiopia. Many political leaders in central and southern Ethiopia, Menilek among them, used Yohannis' deviation from custom as an excuse to withhold recognition of his accession to the throne. They also did not recognize the authority of the new *abun*, Athanasius, who had been appointed solely at Yohannis' request. See Massaja, *Etiopia*, IX, 101.

26. Afeworq, *Menilek*, 22.

27. Cecchi, *Da Zeila*, 267.

ever the outcome of the battle between the two contenders, the victor would be left in such a weakened state that his forces could easily be defeated by the relatively stronger Shoan army. Unfortunately for Melinek, however, Abba Watto, the general of one-half of the army, seems to have chosen this time to revolt. He proclaimed Wollo's independence anew and led his army into the nearly impregnable position of Mak'dala. This defection so weakened Menilek's expeditionary army that it was forced to return to Shoa for reinforcements. Menilek then advanced once more into Wollo where he devastated the land, but try as he might he could not dislodge Abba Watto from Mak'dala.[28]

With his military strength dissipated by this rebellion, Menilek lost the opportunity to gain the imperial throne before Yohannis was actually anointed emperor, thus greatly changing the political situation. It was never easy to overthrow an anointed monarch; Menilek knew the problem would grow the longer he waited, and he therefore formulated a new and dangerous policy, one which assumed the active cooperation of an outside imperialistic power.

The central feature of this new approach was the utilization of Egyptian territorial ambitions in northern Ethiopia. Menilek planned to lure Yohannis into central Ethiopia by moving into Wollo and threatening Tigre, Yohannis' home province, from the south. At the same time the Egyptians in Massawa would advance to the eastern frontier of Tigre and attack Yohannis as he moved against Menilek; meanwhile, the Egyptian forces stationed in the Gulf of Tajurah area, in cooperation with the army of the friendly sultan of Aussa, would march into Wollo near Lake Hayk and effectively threaten Yohannis' flank. The emperor would thus be trapped in a triangle and be defeated, allowing Menilek to accede to the imperial throne and the Egyptians to take possession of the territories they coveted.

The Egyptians accepted this scheme, and, in 1873, Menilek raised a mammoth army to implement the plan as well as to put down Abba Watto's revolution in Wollo once and for all.[29]

28. Cecchi, *Da Zeila*, 268–269. Massaja says nothing about Wollo's revolution but suggests that inexperience and youth caused Menilek to miss this opportunity to become emperor. Massaja, *Etiopia*, IX, 103. Cecchi's story seems much more reasonable since Menilek had already shown his ability as a general.

29. Augustus Wylde, *'83 to '87 in the Sudan* (London, 1888), I, 329.

The *abba* almost seemed to cooperate with the plotters when, after about a year of war, he turned to Yohannis for assistance against Menilek's overwhelming forces. Yohannis, who had by 1875 consolidated his rule in the northern heartland of Ethiopia, regarded Abba Watto's request as an opportunity to force Menilek's recognition and moved into Yejju with his army. But when he received word that the Egyptians were moving against him from Massawa, he retired, leaving Abba Watto to fend for himself. Menilek was able finally to recapture Mak'dala, and, in July 1876, Abba Watto was put in chains and imprisoned on an *amba;* his brother was appointed chief of the Wollo Galla under Menilek's suzerainty, and the Wollo chiefs were forced to come to Wara Ilou to make an act of submission and to take an oath of fealty to Menilek.

By this time, however, the strategic situation had changed considerably. First, in the fall of 1875, the Dankali of Aussa had treacherously led the unsuspecting Egyptians into a trap, and Munzinger Pasha, the leader of the Egyptian force and the governor of Massawa, a key personality in the plot against Yohannis, had been killed along with all his troops.[30] Second, contrary to expectations, Yohannis won a smashing, although in the long run indecisive, victory at the battle of the Mareb on November 17, 1875, and captured numerous rifles, six artillery pieces, ammunition, baggage, and twenty thousand thalers.[31] Thus, two parts of the planned triangular trap had collapsed, and Menilek was left in a precarious and exposed position.

At first he did nothing but enlarge his army while congratulating Yohannis on his victory. The war was not over, however, and he still hoped that his Egyptian allies might succeed. This hope evaporated with the news of Yohannis' decisive victory over the Egyptians at the battle of Gura-Kaya Khor on May 8 and 9, 1876.

Left to carry out his plans alone, Menilek decided to act while the emperor was still involved in the last stages of the Egyptian war, before he could resume steps to make Shoa submit to his authority and recognize his legitimacy. To allay Yohannis' sus-

30. Herbert Lewandowski, *Ein Leben für Afrika* (Zürich, 1954), 210; Gerhard Rohlfs, *Meine Mission nach Äbessinin* (Leipzig, 1852 [?]), 58–60.
31. Dye, *Moslem Egypt,* 138–141.

picions, Menilek used a border encroachment by Ras Adal of Gojjam as a pretext for mobilizing his army and embarking on a campaign. Instead of going directly north into Gojjam, Menilek moved northwest into Wollo, crossed into Yohannis' territory, passed Mak'dala and Debre Tabor and arrived at Gondar. The emperor, who was still occupied in Tigre, could not respond to this challenge, and, almost as if he were unwilling to insult Yohannis unless he were there in person, Menilek did not enter the capital but moved on to Gojjam. Ras Adal, in the face of Menilek's superior army, retired into his fortress at Gibella and sent requests for military assistance to Yohannis.

While Menilek was besieging Ras Adal, a divisive rebellion had begun in Shoa, instigated by Menilek's consort, Bafana. Bafana was a resident of Ankober, where Menilek organized his first government. She was apparently very attractive and had a reputation for being astute and ambitious. Before becoming Menilek's consort in 1865, she had been married several times and had given birth to several children, some of whom had died. Menilek treated here as his queen, even though their liaison appears to have been only of a civil nature.[32] Bafana sought the throne for one of her sons by her first marriage and also wished to establish in Shoa the form of Ethiopian Christian observance which was generally practiced in the regions controlled by Yohannis. Thus, for religious and political reasons, Bafana easily interested the emperor in her plans to overthrow Menilek, and she found ready supporters among the considerable number of Shoans who shared her religious views. To provide a front of legitimacy to her revolution, Bafana used the royal ambitions of Merid Haili, a bastard son of Menilek's grandfather, King Sahle Sellasie.[33] Bafana's scheme was very clever: Merid Haili would raise the banner of rebellion and have himself acclaimed king during the rainy season, a time when it would be impossible for Menilek to return from Gojjam. Meanwhile, Yohannis, in conjunction with Ras Adal, would defeat

32. Paul de Lauriber, *Douze Ans en Abyssinie* (Paris, 1898), 375; Massaja, *Etiopia*, IX, 31–32.

33. This is the same Meridazmach Haili whom Theodore had appointed governor of Shoa after the death of Haile Melekot and the capture of Menilek. He had proved to be an inept administrator and was removed from that office after two years. Cecchi, *Da Zeila*, 255.

Menilek in Gojjam. Yohannis, who did not want the Shoan
dynasty to continue in Menilek's family, would then force Merid
Haili to cede his sovereignty to a son of Bafana, who would
formally submit to the jurisdiction of the imperial crown. Bafana, who would act as regent until her son attained his majority,
would also make an act of homage to Yohannis.

In order to put this scheme into operation, Bafana had been
the strongest voice in advising Menilek to move against Yohannis, and she had followed him to Gojjam, ostensibly to provide
wifely affection, but actually to spy and keep Yohannis informed
of her husband's activities. In the spring of 1877, when Menilek
received reports of Merid Haili's premature and abortive revolution, he did not suspect Bafana's complicity. Indeed, he sent
her, at her own suggestion, to straighten out affairs in Shoa and
gave her a written edict naming her regent until he returned.
Bafana's continued intrigues might have been successful, had
the army remaining in Shoa not rebelled against her authority.
Menilek received confused reports, and for the first time several
trusted subjects informed him of Bafana's treachery. But Menilek, still trusting her, attributed the negative reports to the
jealousy of his informants. Though he soon returned to Shoa,
it was because of his growing doubts about his exposed strategic
position in Gojjam.

In April, Menilek had heard reports that Yohannis was advancing toward Gondar and intended to cross into Gojjam to
help Ras Adal. Menilek knew that the approaching rains might
leave him surrounded by his enemies with no means of escape
across the flooded Abbai River. Moreover, his army was weakened by sickness and desertion, and many of his exhausted soldiers did not want to winter in Gojjam with the threat of fighting two armies at once. For these tactical motives, then, and
not because of any suspicions of Bafana, Menilek returned to
Shoa toward the end of April.

It took him some time to straighten out the internal situation
that he found in Shoa, and in the process the council of officers
and chiefs forced him, much against his will, to exile Bafana
to a faraway village. With the collapse of Bafana's plot, Yohannis, who had arrived in Gojjam only to find Menilek gone, did
not know whether his army was strong enough to challenge

Menilek in Shoa. Nonetheless, it was clear that he must either invade Shoa or retire to Tigre, since Menilek's troops had thoroughly pillaged Gojjam of food.[34]

Yohannis felt compelled to repay Menilek for his audacious invasion of the north and decided not to move into Shoa from Gojjam, but from the Shoan dependency of Wollo. By so doing, he must have felt that he could always retreat into Tigre in case of danger, or, perhaps, gain the allegiance and help of one of the two constantly warring political factions in Wollo; certainly, food supplies would be much easier to obtain there than in impoverished Gojjam. As soon as Yohannis came into Wollo in January 1878, Menilek moved his troops into the area around Litché and prepared for battle. At the same time, Europeans in Shoa heard rumors that he had sent ambassadors to Yohannis to treat for peace but had been rebuffed by the impossibly harsh conditions set by the emperor. Negotiations continued, but Yohannis' advance into the Shoan province of Menz on January 23 nearly brought matters to a crisis. Menilek ordered a general mobilization and, on February 3, moved toward Menz. Between February 6 and 10, there was some sporadic and probing fighting between the two armies, but sometime thereafter Menilek retreated toward Litché. On February 12, a council was held to discuss the crisis and appraise the military situation. On the basis of the limited military clashes that had taken place, and of some eyewitness intelligence, the council "unanimously rejected war" in face of the "preponderant force of the enemy." [35]

This belated admission of Menilek's military weakness raises the important question of why he originally ordered the advance into the north. Cecchi and Dye argue that he marched when he received incorrect intelligence that Yohannis had been defeated by the Egyptians. This seems unlikely, however, since the final Egyptian defeat occurred on May 8–9, 1876, and Menilek did not leave Shoa until early 1877, late enough to have received accurate reports. Massaja, on the other hand, argues that Menilek's ambitions and his youthful inexperience led him into this strategic blunder. Aside from the fact that in 1877 Menilek was

34. The information in the last four paragraphs has been drawn from Massaja, *Etiopia*, X, 148–163.
35. Cecchi, *Da Zeila*, 419, 431.

thirty-three and had ruled in Shoa successfully for twelve years, Massaja's conclusion appears unreasonable because, even granting him his point about youth and inexperience, Menilek at this time took no major decisions without the advice of capable and experienced councillors who certainly must have known the dangers involved in a direct challenge to the power and pride of the emperor. One possible explanation seems to be that Menilek hoped to foment a large-scale revolution in Ethiopia to offset Yohannis' military superiority. Both he and his advisers apparently felt that the people, as well as many chiefs and officials, would rally to the Shoan monarch because his genealogical claim to the throne was better than Yohannis' and they probably believed, for a number of reasons, that Yohannis had not yet consolidated his rule in the northern highlands. This analysis, admittedly imperfect, would at least explain Menilek's strangely meandering route into Gojjam, a province directly accessible from Shoa. When Menilek failed to receive the acclamation he had expected in Tigre, he quickly moved on to Gojjam, hoping to reduce Ras Adal to submission, and quite possibly hoping to turn that province into another buffer zone such as Wollo.

Meanwhile the Church had become increasingly involved as a mediator between the king and the emperor. Through the good offices of the clergy, representatives of the two parties opened serious negotiations on February 15; almost immediately, a truce resulted. Hostages were exchanged as a sign of good faith, and a preliminary convention, the Peace of Dembaro, was negotiated which stipulated that Menilek should render periodic homage and tribute to Yohannis, although it did not apparently require him to appear personally before the emperor. The convention further provided that Menilek must give the emperor military assistance whenever necessary and that he must renounce his sovereignty over Wollo.[36] Yohannis then promulgated an edict announcing his reconciliation with Menilek and ordering his army not to pillage the country. Upon the conclusion of these preliminaries, the emperor sent a negotiating team headed by his confessor, Abba Germa Sellasie, to discuss the details of a formal treaty.

The cession of Wollo was very painful to Menilek. Bafana,

36. Guèbre Sellasié, *Chronique,* 143.

who had returned from exile,[37] informed Antonio Cecchi, an Italian explorer in Shoa, that the king was "already very contrite" about this action, and that it was "certain that he will write the Emperor asking him to return Wollo, in compensation for which he will make an act of complete submission." [38] Apparently Yohannis agreed to this plan, as the final agreement of March 14, 1878, returned most of Wollo to the king with the stipulation that he build churches there and Christianize the Galla population. The other conditions of the agreement were that Menilek renounce the title, king of kings, and be called only king of Shoa; that he pay periodic tribute to Yohannis; that he provide supplies for Yohannis' army whenever it passed through Shoa; and that he and Yohannis aid each other in times of need. In what appears to have been a supplementary agreement of March 20, the boundaries of Menilek's domain were defined as the Bascilo River on the north, the Abbai to the west, and the Awash to the east and south; and Menilek agreed that the Shoan Church would adopt the Tigrean Church dogma of Christ's double birth.[39]

Cecchi found Menilek "sad and pensive" on the morning of March 20 before making his submission, and he seemed like a victim dressed up for a sacrifice. As he went to Yohannis' camp, "his dignitaries followed him at a short distance, silent as if they were participating in a funeral cortege." Behind them marched an escort of twenty-five thousand Shoan troops.[40] Guebre Sellasie reported that "the manner in which the King came to make his submission was truly astonishing, because the decorations of his chiefs and of his army were so varied that from the king up to the last soldier all had a marvelous splendor." [41] Menilek approached Yohannis on foot, carrying a rock on his neck and with his face down in the traditional form of submission. As soon

37. Menilek was deeply attached to Bafana, and had, immediately after exiling her, begun a campaign for her return. By the time the preliminary peace was decided, she had returned to his side. He did, however, divorce her after Yohannis specifically warned him of her continued subversive activities. See Lincoln de Castro, *Nella Terra di Negus* (Milano, 1915), I, 130.

38. Cecchi, *Da Zeila*, 438.

39. Implementation of the religious settlement was put off for approximately one year to prepare the Shoan population for the change.

40. Cecchi, *Da Zeila*, 441.

41. Guèbre Sellasié, *Chronique*, 145–146.

as he set foot on the cloth of the imperial tent, Yohannis' cannons "thundered twelve times, announcing to the two armies the downfall of Shoan independence." Yohannis received Menilek with signs of great respect, careful not to hurt his damaged dignity further. He invited him to sit at his right on the imperial sofa, and, asking his dignitaries to retire, he had the door to the tent closed. He and Menilek talked privately for two hours and apparently ironed out the final details of the treaty. When affairs were brought to a satisfactory conclusion, Yohannis offered to crown Menilek *negus* of Shoa, thus further regularizing their relationship. After the coronation ceremony six days later, Yohannis said, "you are accordingly King and master of a land conquered and possessed by your forebears; and I shall respect your sovereignty if you will be faithful to the agreements decided between us." Some days later Menilek delivered a tribute so munificent that the emperor could only cry, "Only today am I aware of being Emperor!" [42]

Imperial Ambitions, Empire, and Trade, 1878–1889

The agreements with Yohannis temporarily thwarted Menilek's attempts to change the political balance in the Abyssinian highlands. But, although the way to the north was closed, southern and eastern expansion could still change the strategic balance within Ethiopia as a whole and could, thus, provide Menilek with an enlarged and strengthened base of power from which to take advantage of any future opportunities to gain the Ethiopian crown. It was at this stage that Menilek embarked upon a new policy which was characterized by a large-scale geographic expansion of Shoan power into southern and eastern Ethiopia and the consolidation of his political position through the purchase of modern arms and the opening of diplomatic relations with several European powers.

Menilek realized all too well that his challenge of Yohannis had failed in part because of the inferiority of his army's weapons. He had long ago learned the value of modern arms, and he had attempted on several occasions to increase the supply of rifles and munitions coming into Shoa from the coast. In 1871 he had

42. Massaja, *Etiopia*, XI, 10, 46.

sent Abba Mikael, a priest with some earlier European experience, on a mission to open relations between the kingdom of
Shoa and France and Italy with a view, mainly, to expanding the
arms trade. While the expedition was not notably successful,
Abba Mikael did have an opportunity to speak to various Italians
who were so stimulated by the priest's descriptions of Ethiopia
and its peoples that they organized a movement to sponsor a
geographic expedition.

In 1872, Pierre Arnoux, a French businessman in Alexandria,
originated a grandiose scheme:

> Nothing less than to open a European route toward central Africa
> via Obock and Shoa . . . to furnish in the markets of Marseilles
> an entrepôt for Ethiopian products without any Egyptian interfer-
> ence, to found on the high plateau a French colony, to introduce to
> Shoa our industry and our civilization, to assist King Menilek by all
> moral and material means to rejuvenate Ethiopia, to facilitate to
> explorers and scholars entrance into the heart of the African con-
> tinent [and] finally to thwart the slave trade by our presence and
> our efforts.

Menilek was very impressed by many of Arnoux' ideas and invited him to Shoa to implement his plans. Arnoux' caravan arrived in the last part of 1874 and presented gifts to Menilek, who
was most interested in the rifles, steel-coated cartridges, and re-
volvers. Arnoux told the king that "from Shoa . . . will arise the
signal for the regeneration of Ethiopia; it is from your reign that
will date . . . a new era, more glorious and brilliant than that of
old King Caleb whose power extended to Yemen." France, Arnoux stressed, would act as the catalyst in this national rejuvena-
tion. Menilek responded to these ideas with great emotion, telling
Arnoux, "You have fathered my most secret desires. It is God,
without doubt, who has sent you to me. I am happy to listen to
your counsels . . . The French are my friends; it is upon them
that I shall base the hope of my reign." [43]

By May 13, 1875, Menilek, with the agreement of the council,
had decided to organize a caravan to carry samples of Ethiopian
products to the coast for transshipment to Europe. Arnoux was

43. M. L. Louis-Lande, "Un Voyageur Français dans l'Ethiopie Méridionale," *Revue des Deux Mondes,* 3rd series, XXX (Dec. 15, 1878), and XXXI:
879, 887, 888 (Jan. 15, 1879).

authorized to act as Shoa's representative in Europe, where it was hoped that the samples would stimulate a trade by which means Menilek could obtain arms and munitions.[44]

Even though Arnoux had received no cooperation from the French government in the realization of his plans, he intended to make Obok, on the Gulf of Tajurah, the Shoan entrepôt instead of using Zeila where he would have to deal with the devious and grasping governor, Abu Bekr, and the intrigues of the Egyptian government.[45] When Abu Bekr learned of Arnoux' plans, he quickly concluded that a French success in Obok could mean the economic ruin of Zeila and called a meeting of chiefs and dignitaries who decided unanimously to take appropriate measures to stop Arnoux. In Shoa, meanwhile, the preparations for the caravan were completed and Arnoux was given documents to deliver on behalf of Menilek to various European chiefs of state. The French merchant took leave of Menilek on June 6, 1875.

Arnoux' chief of caravan, Muhammad, was one of Abu Bekr's many sons and had been instructed by his father not to take the caravan to Obok as Arnoux and Menilek wished, but to follow the route to Zeila. When Arnoux realized what was happening, and objected, he was told bluntly, "There is no route marked out for Obock, nor are there guides to take you there; the drivers will not follow you [since] they prefer to return to Zeila where they have their families and interests; finally, at Obock you will find neither boats nor provisions." [46] Helpless, Arnoux resigned himself to the situation; the caravan arrived in Zeila on August 21. Arnoux' enforced visit there has all the elements of a Kafka story. It was a continuing nightmare during which his world collapsed through treachery, falsehood, duplicity, and insinuation. He ultimately lost control of the caravan goods, which had been stored in one of Abu Bekr's warehouses, and at the same time, through the duplicity of his two trusted Ethiopian assistants, serious doubts were cast upon the various diplomatic documents

44. *Ibid.*, 889–898.

45. Obok had been purchased for ten thousand thalers in April 1862 by M. Shaefer, who was Napoleon III's chief Oriental interpreter. The French government made no attempt to exploit the area until 1883. See Sir Rawson W. Rawson, "European Territorial Claims on the Coasts of the Red Sea and its Southern Approaches in 1885," *Proceedings of the Royal Geographical Society,* VII:108, 110 (1885).

46. Louis-Lande, "Voyageur," 405.

he carried. Thus, Arnoux' idealistic dreams and Menilek's plans for a European trade were thwarted by the entrenched economic interests of the coastal governor.

On his trip to the coast Arnoux had met the Italian geographic expedition to Shoa, led by Marchese Orazio Antinori, who had also been seriously victimized and harassed in Zeila by Abu Bekr.[47] Indeed, one member of this mission, Sebastiano Martini, had to turn back to the coast with Arnoux to return to Italy for more supplies and money. The rest continued toward Shoa and arrived there on August 28, 1876. They were received by Menilek at Litché in October.

Around this time the king was described as being

> of ordinary height, rather corpulent, with large muscles . . . a face pockmarked by smallpox, a high forehead . . . lively and intelligent eyes, the expression of which, like that of his mouth, indicated gentleness and inspired sympathy. He has a regular nose, rather a large jaw, [and] . . . his teeth . . . are regular and very write.[48]

Marchese Antinori wrote that at the audience the king was seated upon a type of divan, "head and feet naked, his body covered by a pair of white trousers, by a shamma [toga-like garment] of white cotton bordered in red, and . . . upon his shoulders a cloth cape . . . with hood." To the Marchese, Menilek appeared an imposing man, and he seemed to be kind and open. "He is a great friend of Europeans, a fanatic for weapons, about whose mechanisms he appears to be most intelligent." [49]

Menilek was delighted with the modern arms which the expedition gave him, and he wanted more. By the time Martini finally arrived in Shoa in September 1877, Menilek had made plans to obtain arms by sending one of the Italians to Europe as his agent. He chose Martini because he was a military officer, because he had not yet settled down to life in Shoa, and because he was the Italian most experienced in shipping goods from Europe via the Ethiopian Red Sea coast to Shoa.

Menilek called a council on the arms problem, inviting the

47. "Spedizione Italiana in Africa," *Bollettino della Società Geografica Italiano* [hereafter *BSGI*], Series II, XIII:460 (June–July 1876).

48. Cecchi, *Da Zeila*, 162–163.

49. "Spedizione Italiana nell'Africa Equatoriale, Relazione della Commissione," *BSGI*, XIII:669, 671 ff. (Nov.–Dec. 1876).

grandees and councillors of the court, the Catholic missionaries, the military, and the members of the Italian expedition. He pointed out his need for arms in the face of the emperor's military threat, and explained how easy it would be for Martini to obtain the weapons for him in Italy. Martini and Antinori tried hard to extricate themselves from the potentially awkward situation, but Menilek stubbornly held to his resolve, and an agreement was reached whereby Martini would again return to Italy as Menilek's agent and at his expense, while the king would assist an Italian expedition to Kaffa and other southern areas, supplying the money, servants, mounts, escorts, and letters necessary for the journey, and giving the Italian Geographical Society the village of Let-Marafia as a permanent station. Martini left Litché on December 1, 1877, with "the acclamation of the court and of the whole population of Litché." [50] Menilek fulfilled all his promises to the Italian expedition, but Martini did not arrive back in Shoa until the crisis of 1878 had passed.

Thus, these hasty, makeshift methods did not obtain for Menilek the regular supply of arms which he felt he needed. Only after France and Italy effectively took control of the large areas of the Ethiopian Red Sea coast could the arms trade which Menilek wanted begin to grow. Only then could new routes into Shoa be found that would not cross the territories of Yohannis, the Khedive of Egypt, or Abu Bekr, all of whom, for one reason or another, wished neither to see Menilek supplied with modern weapons nor the Europeans firmly entrenched on the coast. In 1880, the Italian government finally annexed Assab and its environs which had, since 1869, been more or less under the control of Mm. Rubatino and Co. Between 1882 and 1884 the French government began taking an interest in the strategic and economic possibilities of the Gulf of Tajurah and made a contract with a Marseilles steamship company to establish a packet service to the Persian Gulf; the ships would refuel at Obok, where the company would ultimately organize an establishment for refitting French vessels.[51]

At this time Menilek was opening diplomatic relations with Italy upon the recommendation of his chief foreign adviser, Al-

---

50. Massaja, *Etiopia*, X, 115–120.
51. G. Angoulvant et Sylvain Vignéras, *Djibouti, Mer Rouge, Abyssinie* (Paris, 1902), 1–3; Rawson, "Territorial Claims," 110–114.

fred Ilg. Ilg believed that Italy was the weakest and most harmless of the major European powers and that it was potentially less dangerous to involve this nation in Shoa in an advisory capacity than Great Britain or France.[52] Negotiations between Shoa and Italy ensued, and an eighteen-article treaty of amity and commerce insuring the close cooperation of Shoa and Italy was signed on May 21, 1883.[53]

In a very short time, two new routes into Shoa were in operation. By 1884, the Assab route, which crossed the domains of the sultan of Aussa and part of Dankalia before climbing the plateau into Shoa, was becoming popular. In 1882 Paul Soleillet opened the Obok route, which was physically one of the most dangerous approaches to Shoa because of the fierce Dankali and Issa tribesmen who regarded caravans as fair game for plunder. Nonetheless, it was the shortest route, and by 1883–1884 many French travelers were using it. With the opening of these two routes, trade between Shoa and Europe grew rapidly and an ever-increasing amount of war materials reached Menilek while a stream of ivory, civet, hides, coffee, and gold were sent to Europe.

European traders, among them the French poet Arthur Rimbaud, bought weapons in Europe from any available source; often they were obsolescent military weapons which the European governments sold at an extremely low price and which could be resold at a handsome profit in Ethiopia. By 1884–1885 the demand for weapons, both by the central Shoan government and among the less important provincial officials, was so great that the traders could no longer keep up with it, and the price of the weapons was bid up so high that Menilek's treasury became depleted and payment had to be deferred for several months. By 1886, however,

52. In 1877, Menilek wrote to the Aden branch of the Swiss firm of Furner and Escher requesting the services of a Swiss engineer. Alfred Ilg, a young engineer who had studied at the Polytechnicum in Zurich, arrived in Shoa in April 1879, accompanied by the mechanic Zimmerman and the carpenter Appenzeller. While Ilg was often to act in his professional capacity, he rapidly became Menilek's chief adviser on all European questions and was ultimately appointed minister of state. For a resumé of Ilg's activities in Ethiopia see Georges Montandon, "Alfred Ilg," *Le Globe, Organe de la Société de Géographie de Genève*, LV:83 (1916); see also Conrad Keller, *Alfred Ilg, Sein Leben und Seine Werke* (Frauenfeld and Leipzig, 1918), 65.

53. Carlo Rosetti, *Storia Diplomatica dell'Etiopia durante il Regno di Menilek II* (Torino, 1910), 7 ff; see also Francesco Crispi, *La Prima Guerra d'Africa* (Milano, 1914), 66 ff.

Menilek's military supply requirements were sufficiently filled that he could afford to bargain with merchants and diplomats for better and more modern weapons. Accordingly, he imposed enormous price reductions on the merchants, raised duties, delayed payments, and harassed them in other ways.[54]

What Menilek was doing with his well-armed military force was obvious to all observers. Soleillet put his finger on the touchstone of Menilek's external policy in 1882 when he wrote: "The kingdom of Shoa is small by itself, but in reality Menilek had conquered all the Galla country to Kaffa." [55] Between 1878 and 1882 Menilek had conquered an empire piece by piece and had created unity from the ruins of twenty petty states; he had moved Christian Semitic power back into areas where it had not existed since the sixteenth century. Gebre Sellasie's chronicles are full of tales of the more successful expeditions, and other sources describe Menilek's expeditions into parts of Arussi, Soddo, and Wollega.[56]

In 1882, Yohannis became alarmed at Menilek's increasing successes in the south and attempted to balance his growing power by appointing Tekle Haimanot of Gojjam ruler of Kaffa. On his way to take over his new kingdom, Tekle Haimanot passed through and laid claim to some Shoan territory. In the ensuing battle, Menilek's forces badly beat the Gojjami army and took Tekle Haimanot prisoner. Yohannis thereupon decided it was time to make a new arrangement with the king of Shoa. In the height of the rains, he moved into Wollo where Menilek, still anxious to indicate peaceful intentions, met him to negotiate a new relationship.

In the agreement which resulted, Yohannis officially confirmed Menilek's conquests as dependencies of Shoa as well as recognizing the Shoan's claims to Kaffa. Menilek agreed to free Tekle Haimanot, probably after Yohannis promised to rescind the latter's title of *negus* of Kaffa and give it to Menilek. Further-

---

54. Enid Starkie, *Arthur Rimbaud in Abyssinia* (Oxford, 1937), 91–95; Jules Borelli, *Ethiopie Méridionale* (Paris, 1890), 109; Jean-Marie Carré, "Arthur Rimbaud en Ethiopie, Lettres inédites," *La Revue de France*, XVI:469 ff. (June 1935).

55. Soleillet, *Voyages*, 6 ff.

56. Guèbre Sellasié, *Chronique*, 164 ff.; Docteur Mérab, *Impressions de l'Ethiopie* (Paris, 1922), II, 32.

more, Yohannis recognized Menilek as his immediate successor to the Ethiopian throne. In return Menilek promised to hand on the succession to Yohannis' son, who was to be married to Menilek's daughter, Zauditu. As a dowry the girl received the province of Wollo and the title of queen, while Yohannis' son was given the province of Tigre and the title of king. The two were married amid regal splendor on October 24, 1882, at Wara Ilou, but, as the groom was twelve and the bride only six, it was agreed that they should live apart for three years.

Thus, Menilek's enlarged base of political power and his new weapons had forced the emperor to give him considerable recognition. His territory was bounded by Wollo in the north, the Bascilo and Abbai rivers on the west, the Awash river, Gurage Mountains, and Gibbi river in the east, and by Arussi and Kambatta to the south. If he could continue his expansion into Kaffa and Borana, "Shoa, thus enlarged, will incontestably . . . be the richest jewel in the crown of Abyssinia." [57] Arthur Rimbaud wrote in 1887: "Menilek dreams of a continuous extension of his domains to the south, beyond the Awash, and thinks perhaps to emigrate from Amhara country to the middle of these Galla countries with his guns, his warriors, [and] his wealth, [and] to establish a southern Empire far away from the Emperor." [58]

The period 1882 to 1886, marked by several unsuccessful attempts to subdue the southern Arussi Galla, was otherwise relatively calm. By then, Menilek felt the time was ripe to annex Harar, the capital of the rich eastern province which he had always coveted. Its control would provide Shoa with the best and easiest route to the coast and its lucrative trade revenues. When the Egyptians had found it necessary to evacuate their garrison at Harar after their Sudanese debacle of 1885, they had left as sovereign the Emir Abdullahi Ali Muhammad Abdel Shakur of the city's ancient ruling family. A fanatic Muslim who hated all Europeans and Christian Ethiopians, he killed several British subjects shortly after the Egyptians left and, on April

57. Henry Audon, "Voyage au Choa," *Le Tour du Monde*, LVIII (1889), 130.

58. Jean-Marie Carré, *Lettres de la Vie Littéraire d'Arthur Rimbaud* (Paris, 1931), 212.

18, 1886, had the members of an Italian expedition massacred. Menilek decided to take action before the Europeans, who also wanted Harar, intervened to avenge these deaths. He had laid the groundwork for this attack by constructing a fortress in Chercher, the mountain massif which runs from the Awash to Harar. When the news came that the British were massing troops at Zeila, Menilek was on an expedition in Arussi. He immediately proclaimed his intention of taking vengeance upon the emir for killing Christians and ordered the fifteen thousand troops stationed in Chercher to challenge the emir's army of five thousand. At the same time, Queen Taitu at Entotto was directed to organize a strong army and send it to Menilek in Arussi.[59] When the emir's Turkish general succeeded one night in surprising and routing the Ethiopian forces, Menilek hurried to Harar and camped about fifty kilometers from the city at Chalanko. He sent the emir a letter stating: "I have come to bring your country under subjection, but not to ruin it. If you submit, if you become my vassal, I shall not refuse you the government of the country. Reflect upon this so that you will not be sorry about it later." [60]

The emir refused the offer and attacked Menilek's camp on Ethiopian Christmas day, January 7, 1887. After a fifteen-minute battle he was decisively defeated and fled, leaving behind his weapons and army. From behind the city walls, the emir then sent a letter of submission, but, despite Menilek's magnanimous acceptance, he and his wives and children fled that night into the Somali country to the east of Harar. A few days later Menilek triumphantly entered Harar; and although he imposed a large indemnity upon the town, confiscated the goods of those slain in battle, and took items from various foreign shops, he did not permit any looting by his troops. He named an uncle and former slave of the emir, Ali Abu Bekr, as civil governor,

---

59. Taitu became Menilek's wife in 1883 after he had divorced and exiled Bafana. Taitu came to Menilek after several marriages. She was reportedly attractive in her youth, although in later life she bcame quite obese in the style of Ethiopian noblewomen. She had great energy, an iron will, and was always in control of her emotions. She was highly intelligent and politically astute, and she often acted as one of Menilek's advisers. He apparently consulted her on all major matters. See De Lauribar, *Abyssinie*, 573–578.

60. Guèbre Sellasié, *Chronique*, 242–243.

left behind a three-thousand-man garrison under Dejazmach Makonnen, and returned triumphantly to Entotto.[61] Makonnen found it difficult to control the garrison troops who, after Menilek's departure, carried on a series of minor lootings and other acts against the local population. It is also possible that Makonnen was angry that Menilek had not named him full governor and actively provoked a rebellion to provide an excuse to take over the civil power. The Harari became increasingly disturbed and uneasy and finally rebelled. Whether correctly or incorrectly, Ali appears to have been strongly implicated in the rebellion, which was quickly squelched when Makonnen marched into town with his troops, cowed the population, and imprisoned the civil governor, who was sent in chains to Menilek. Once in the town, the troops went wild, demolished and looted homes, tyrannized the population, and killed several people. While Menilek probably had not authorized this retaliation, he used the opportunity to send more troops to Makonnen to carry on a military campaign in Harar province to impose and consolidate Shoan rule over the population.

Thus, by 1887, Menilek controlled an area which was almost as large as the northern Ethiopian heartland, an area with excellent natural resources and a large population from which to draw an enlarged army. To gain further strength, Menilek signed a treaty of amity and alliance with Italy on October 20, 1887; Italy virtually recognized Menilek as a sovereign power in Ethiopia and assured him "military aid and otherwise to make good his rights" in return for a promise "to aid the Government of His Majesty the King of Italy in all circumstances" (article 2). Menilek was also granted five thousand Remington rifles (article 4), probably his real reason for signing the treaty.[62] As Italy at this time was near to a state of war with Yohannis, there can be little doubt that this treaty represented an act of insubordination by Menilek against the authority of the emperor. Furthermore, he constructed a defensive alliance with Tekle Haimanot of Goj-

61. *Ibid.* Makonnen was the father of Haile Sellasie I.
62. Text of the treaty of October 20, 1887, as quoted in Rosetti, *Storia Diplomatica*, 23–24. Menilek never fulfilled the promise he made in the treaty to march with the Italians against Yohannis. Nor, on the other hand, did he send troops to the emperor when the latter requested military reinforcements.

jam who in 1887 had futilely requested the emperor's assistance against the Mahdists of the Sudan who were attacking his domains. The alliance was a direct insult to the emperor, and, late in 1888, Yohannis moved against the two rebellious leaders. The *negus* of Shoa and the *ras* of Gojjam met the emperor on the banks of the Abbai. Menilek, now the strongest political figure in Ethiopia, forced Yohannis to encamp and open negotiations. Faced externally by the threats of the Mahdists and the Italians and internally by the recalcitrant behavior of his major chiefs, the emperor was in a difficult position. For three months he carried on futile negotiations. Then the Mahdists attacked in the northwest and Yohannis was forced to retire, "leaving his rebellious vassals in triumphant possession of the field." [63]

Menilek and the Italians, 1889–1896

On the verge of a brilliant victory over the Mahdists, the Emperor Yohannis was mortally wounded at the battle of Metemmah of March 9 and 10, 1889. As he lay dying he called together his chiefs and "in their presence solemnly acknowledged young Ras [then *dejazmach*] Mangasha as his natural son by the wife of his own brother." He commended Mangasha to the care of his followers and especially to Ras Alula of Asmara, an old comrade-in-arms. Though this admission was tantamount to declaring Mangasha heir to the throne, only Ras Alula remained true to Mangasha when they returned to Tigre, the base from which he would have to make good his claim to the throne.[64] The rest of the Tigre chiefs, along with most other major Ethiopian leaders, tentatively accepted Menilek as the new emperor because of his imposing military strength and the legitimacy of his claim as established in 1882.

Nonetheless, while Menilek was deeply involved in the preliminary consolidation of his position as emperor, Mangasha succeeded in establishing himself as autonomous ruler of Tigre,

63. George F. H. Berkeley, "The Abyssinian Question and Its History," *The Nineteenth Century and After*, LIII, CCCXI:94 (Jan. 1903).

64. George F. H. Berkeley, *The Campaign of Adowa and the Rise of Menelik* (Westminster, 1902), 3–4.

acknowledging no other suzerain. As Tigre bordered on the Italian colonial holdings on the Red Sea coast, Menilek feared that Mangasha might try to use the Italians to further his imperial claims, just as Menilek had used them in his political struggle to gain the throne. So, to neutralize Mangasha's pretensions as well as to regularize his own status, Menilek made use of the means he had at hand to gain formal Italian recognition of his accession to the imperial throne.

Earlier, in September 1888, Count Pietro Antonelli, the Italian plenipotentiary in Ethiopia, had drafted a treaty which would have given Menilek increased Italian support in return for the cession of certain highland areas adjacent to Massawa, which the Italians needed to ensure the security of their colony.[65] Antonelli was the main architect of Italy's so-called Shoan policy which aimed at assisting Menilek to become king of kings in hope that, out of gratitude, the new emperor would feel obliged to accept an Italian protectorate over his country. Menilek, motivated largely by the demands of internal Ethiopian politics which required Mangasha's isolation, and probably not foreseeing the ultimate aims of Italian policy, signed and sealed the suggested treaty on May 2, 1889, at the town of Wuchalé (also known as Ucciali or Wichelé).[66] Thereby he gained official Italian recognition of his accession to the imperial throne, as well as the important right to import military supplies duty free through the Italian port of Massawa. In return, Menilek ceded to the Italians the strategic areas they coveted in Tigre — although these happened to be a part of Ras Alula's domains — and granted them special privileges in commerce, industry, and justice.

Article 17 of the treaty aimed at implementing Antonelli's policy of turning Ethiopia into an Italian dependency. The Italian text of the article read: "His Majesty the King of Kings

65. Sven Rubenson, "The Protectorate Paragraph of the Wichalé Treaty," *Journal of African History*, V:273 (1964).

66. Here I disagree with Professor Sven Rubenson, who feels that Menilek had little further need of Italian support after his accession to the throne, and that Ras Mangasha and Ras Alula were more dangerous to the Italians than to Menilek. If this analysis were correct, then there would have been no real reason for Menilek to sign the Treaty of Wuchalé. I cannot believe that a politician and diplomat as shrewd as Menilek would have signed a treaty which gained him nothing. See Rubenson, "Wichalé Treaty," 278.

of Ethiopia consents to use [*servirsi*] the Government of His Majesty the King of Italy for all the business he has with other powers or governments." [67] Menilek approved this article because its Amharic version merely suggested that he *might* make use of the Italian government in diplomatic matters if he wished, and because Antonelli insisted that such a statement would indicate the emperor's good will and sincerity toward the Italian government.

Italy immediately implemented the Treaty of Wuchalé. General Baldissera occupied Keren, the capital of Bogos, on June 2, 1889, and Asmara on August 3. In order to obtain a defensible frontier along the Mareb, Belessa, and Mai Muni rivers, the Italians then went beyond the agreement and occupied the rest of Alula's province of Hamasien and the provinces of Oculie-Cusai and Serae. These moves, coupled with the occupation of the important commercial and political Tigrean city of Adwa on January 26, 1890, proved to be a damaging strategic blunder. Italy's actions forced Mangasha to seek good relagtions with Menilek in order to save at least a part of his patrimony, and they provided Menilek with the first clear evidence of Italy's greedy intentions toward Tigre and possibly toward the rest of Ethiopia.

The pattern of Italian imperialistic aims became even more clear when Dejaz Makonnen returned from a trip to Italy with the text of a supplementary convention to the Treaty of Wuchalé, signed in Rome on October 1, 1889. Articles 5 and 6 of this convention granted Menilek a loan of four million lire, but Article 3 stipulated that a rectification of territorial boundaries would be made on the basis of *uti possidetis* to date.[68] Menilek understood Article 3 to mean territories controlled as of the date of signature of the convention and ratified it over the opposition of certain of his advisers because he needed the loan to buy armaments. Later he wrote King Humbert that he had accepted the supplementary agreement out of friendship, despite the "many articles which are not advantageous to our country." Regarding the original territorial concessions he had made in the Treaty of Wuchalé, Menilek contended that Antonelli had claimed that Italy "only desired a site with a cool climate for the

67. Rosetti, *Storia Diplomatica*, 41 ff.
68. Text of the convention, as quoted in Rosetti, *Storia Diplomatica*, 45 ff.

soldiers at Massawa, as a refuge in the hot months." Menilek also explained that he and Antonelli had been unable to agree on a satisfactory frontier during a meeting in March 1890, because of his conviction that, "If I call myself King of Kings of Ethiopia, it is because I have added Tigre to my kingdom; and if, then, you will take [land] up to the Mareb, what is left for me?" [69]

In this same letter, Menilek informed the Italian king that he had been severely criticized by Shoan and Tigrean notables for giving up so much territory in the original Treaty of Wuchalé. When Count Augusto Salimbeni, the new Italian plenipotentiary, arrived in Shoa on July 1, 1890, he quickly discovered that Menilek was indeed in an extremely vulnerable position on the frontier question. Not only did his chiefs claim he had "sold" the country, but the empress herself had vituperatively asked Menilek: "How come King John never wanted to cede an inch of territory; he battled the Italians [and] he battled the Egyptians for this [principle]; he died for it; and you, after such an example, wish to sell your country? Who will [want to] tell your history?" [70] To avert the increasing opposition, Menilek had to stand firm against further Italian territorial claims. Salimbeni quickly concluded that if Italy wished "to maintain the Mareb frontier, we must rely only upon bayonets and cannon."

In the meantime, the controversy about Article 17 had begun. On October 11, 1889, the Italian government, "in conformity with the General Act of the Conference of Berlin of February 26, 1885," sent a circular to the major foreign powers informing them of the contents of Article 17.[71] On December 14, however, Menilek, who did not feel obligated by the article, sent several letters directly to the heads of state of Great Britain, France, and Germany. The British government replied:

> Inasmuch . . . as the Italian Government have notified us that by a Treaty concluded on the 2nd of May last between Italy and Ethiopia, "it is provided that His Majesty the King of Kings of Ethiopia consents to avail himself of the Government of His Majesty the King of

69. Menilek to King Humbert, Sept. 27, 1890, as quoted in *ibid.*, 81.

70. Carlo Zaghi, ed., *Crispi e Menelich nel Diario Inedito del Conte Augusto Salimbeni* (Torino, 1956), 110, 124–125.

71. Rosetti, *Storia Diplomatica*, 60–61.

Italy for the conduct of all matters which he may have with other Powers of Government," We shall communicate to the Government of our friend His Majesty the King of Italy copies of Your Majesty's letter and of our reply.[72]

Menilek was surprised by the implications of the British reply and instructed Alfred Ilg to compare the Italian and Amharic versions of the treaty. When the mistranslation was discovered, Menilek immediately concluded that Antonelli and the Italian government had deliberately tricked him.

On August 18, 1890, Menilek wrote Salimbeni that Ethiopia had been humiliated in Europe as a result of the inaccurate translation of Article 17, despite the specific stipulation in Article 19 that the Italian and Amharic versions of the treaty were equally faithful and valid.[73] On September 27, 1890, he wrote King Humbert, spelling out his basic position:

> Having studied anew the said Article, we have established undeniably that the terms written in Amharic and the translation in Italian do not conform . . . I said in friendship that our affairs in Europe could be handled with the assistance of the Kingdom of Italy, but I did not make any agreement which therein obligated me . . . I did not accept, at that time, any obligatory statement, and today I am still not the man to accept it.

He hoped that Humbert would "rectify the error committed in Article 17 and announce the mistake to the friendly powers to whom you have communicated the said article." [74] In the event that the Italian king chose not to communicate the error, Menilek ensured, through independent communication, that Europe would know of the imbroglio.[75]

Because of Menilek's unyielding position regarding his northern frontier and Article 17, Salimbeni's situation became increasingly difficult. In late August 1890, he confided to General Gandolfi that "according to my point of view, war is the only possible solution to the Ethiopian problem." He believed that the crux of the problem was that "in Italy they confuse, and

72. As quoted in Zaghi, *Crispi*, 405.
73. *Ibid.*, 148.
74. As quoted in Rosetti, *Storia Diplomatica*, 78 ff.
75. See, for example, Menilek to Queen Victoria, Aug. 24, 1890, as quoted in Zaghi, *Crispi*, 409.

disgracefully continue to confound, the poor King of Shoa . . . with the Emperor, who is another thing entirely." [76] Crispi was, however, unable to accept Salimbeni's analysis of the change in Menilek and decided to send Antonelli, the architect of the Shoan policy, to Addis Ababa to solve all the outstanding difficulties.

Antonelli arrived on December 18, 1890, with authority to grant Menilek the boundaries he demanded if he would only accept the Italian version of Article 17. Salimbeni felt that "Antonelli counts too much upon his influence with the King and hopes to persuade him [too] easily"; and indeed, Antonelli's high expectations were dashed the first time he raised the issue of the mistranslation with Menilek and tried to place the blame on the Ethiopian interpreter, Gerazmach (count) Joseph: "The King and the Queen sustained the attack and responded with equal violence, the King scolding [*imbriscola*] so much that he lost his voice." [77] The following day Antonelli attempted to introduce a compromise which would still have treated Ethiopia as less than sovereign. This time "the Queen was more upset than the King," saying, among other things, "I am a woman and I do not love war; but rather than accept this, I prefer war." At still another meeting she exclaimed: "The Italian Government has made article Seventeen known to the powers. We have also let the powers know that this article, as it is written in our language, has another significance. Like you, we also have to respect our dignity . . . You want . . . the other powers to consider us . . . as your protectorate, but that will never be." [78] That all Ethiopia supported the emperor and empress in their fight to maintain their rigid positions was made clear to Antonelli when Ras Mangasha and Ras Makonnen were included in the negotiations.

By late January 1891, Antonelli realized that his attempts were futile and sent Crispi a long dispatch which Salimbeni smugly described as "an ample confirmation of information I reported by letter and telegram on the actual situation in Shoa."

76. Salimbeni to Gandolfi, Aug. 31, 1890, in *ibid.*, 157; Salimbeni to Traversi, Sept. 6, 1890, in *ibid.*, 161.

77. *Ibid.*, 253.

78. *Ibid.*, 254; Report of Antonelli to Crispi, Jan. 29, 1891, in *ibid.*, note 31, 285.

Although Antonelli could not bring himself to admit the real reasons for his conclusions, he recommended that Article 17 be abrogated. He pointed out that the bases for Italian policy in Ethiopia were primarily "economic and peaceful"; since Italy had already accomplished a great deal in Ethiopia, Article 17 was not essential for safeguarding Italian interests in the country. Furthermore, although the "article has, it is true, some advantages to determine the extent of our sphere of action . . . it has . . . [always] create[d] troubles for us with other powers . . . [With the abrogation of Article 17] it will be easier to come to an accord with those powers . . . in delimiting our spere of influence in Africa." [79] He added, almost as an afterthought, that the abrogation of the article would also make it easier to maintain friendly relations with Menilek. On February 2, 1891, recognizing the futility of further discussion, Antonelli instructed Salimbeni to leave Addis Ababa as soon as possible and requested instructions from Italy regarding his own departure.

On the night of February 3, 1891, Ras Makonnen unexpectedly transmitted to Antonelli the draft of a series of accommodations which appeared to represent a significant softening of the Ethiopian government's position. In exchange for the territories which Italy had unilaterally absorbed, the draft stated that Menilek would accept Article 17 as it stood in both the Italian and the Amharic texts. The emperor claimed that these concessions demonstrated his long-standing friendship for King Humbert, for whose sake he was ready and willing to transact all his European business "with the assistance [*appoggio*] of Italy." [80] Antonelli, surprised and delighted at this completely unexpected *volte face,* willingly accepted the proposed accommodations. On February 6, he was called to the palace, where he accepted the invitation of Menilek and Ras Makonnen to sign the agreements immediately, even though they were as yet only partially in formal treaty form and the agreement regarding Article 17 was only in Amharic. Antonelli was assured "that it was as had been fixed in the letter," and that as soon as the Italian translation had been made, it would be transmitted to him.[81] When it had

79. *Ibid.,* 289.
80. *Ibid.,* 294.
81. Antonelli's report to Crispi in *ibid.,* note 10, 306.

not arrived by February 8, however, Antonelli asked Salimbeni to translate the Amharic text for him. Salimbeni discovered that the Amharic text included one word which, in effect, canceled Article 17. Antonelli rushed to the *gibbi* (palace) where, in a stormy interview with Ras Makonnen, he pulled the seals off the documents to indicate that he considered them null and void. Shortly thereafter, he saw the emperor and in another heated discussion demanded that all the signed documents, particularly the frontier agreements, be returned to him immediately. That evening, Antonelli sent a letter to the *gibbi* announcing the withdrawal of all Italian diplomatic personnel from the country, because he regarded the change in the text not as "an offense against me, Pietro Antonelli, but against my King . . . [whom] I represent here." Salimbeni and Antonelli left Shoa on February 12, 1891.[82]

The failure of the Antonelli mission provided an opportunity for several important Italian military and civil administrators in Eritrea to set forth a Tigrean policy which aimed at setting Mangasha and other Tigrean chiefs against Menilek in the classic manner of divide and rule. These men felt that "since Tigre had become weak, to continue to support Menilek was merely to render him all powerful and independent." Furthermore, they considered Menilek "a myth created by the imagination of Antonelli" and "preferred the more modest and secure advantages of agreements made with local chiefs" to the expensive policy of supporting an independent Ethiopia. After the obvious failure of the Shoan policy, a new Italian government under the Marquis di Rudini chose to expedite the Tigrean policy to obtain the amity of the Tigrean chiefs in hopes "of forming a buffer between us and Shoa and establishing a permanent division between the north and south of Abyssinia, a division which is in the historic order of things in Ethiopia, and which could very much be considered necessary to the security of Eritrea." [83]

Italian authorities in Eritrea immediately opened negotiations for an alliance with the important Tigrean chiefs and especially with Mangasha, who, after his earlier failure to gain Italian

82. *Ibid.,* 295–301.
83. Berkeley, *Adowa,* 22; Zaghi, *Crispi,* xxii; O. Baratieri, *Memoires d'Afrique (1892–1896)* (Paris, 1899), 17.

support, must have been delighted with the prospect of another chance to gain the imperial throne. The negotiations came to a successful conclusion on December 8, 1891, when General Gandolfi exchanged a pledge of friendship with Mangasha and several other chiefs who further agreed to the Italian annexation of Serae and Oculie-Cusai.[84]

Menilek realized that the new Italian policy was aimed at undermining his position, and he must have foreseen the possibility of war with Italy when he formally denounced the Treaty of Wuchalé as of May 1, 1893. In a letter to the president of France, he explained his action:

> Always seeming to be moved only by friendship, in reality [Italy] tried by strategem to monopolize my country. God, having given me the Crown and the power, I intend to safeguard intact the heritage of my fathers . . . My Empire has an importance sufficient not to desire any protection and [to be able to] live independently.[85]

The French government, which had never recognized the Italian claim to a protectorate over Ethiopia, responded through its president that

> France, which has for Ethiopia only sentiments of very sincere and disinterested friendship, follows with profound sympathy Your Majesty's constant efforts to develop the grandeur and the prosperity of that proud nation which for centuries had defended so courageously its independence and its Christian faith.[86]

More encouraging to Menilek than this sympathetic reply, however, was the continuing stream of munitions from France and from its ally in Africa, Russia, which came through French Jibuti into Ethiopia.[87] While bolstering Menilek's strength and morale, these arms shipments caused growing concern to Italy.

84. *Ibid.*, 18.
85. Menilek letter in Develle to Billot, July 1, 1893, Ministère des Affaires Etrangeres, *Documents Diplomatiques Français* [hereafter *DDF*], 1st series (Paris, 1945), X:515.
86. Carnot to Menilek, Sept. 22, 1893, *DDF*, XI:6.
87. For information on the flow of Russian, French, and other armaments into Ethiopia, see Richard Pankhurst, "Fire-Arms in Ethiopian History (1800–1935)," *Ethiopia Observer*, VI: 152–173 (1962). See also Sven Rubenson, "Some Aspects of the Survival of Ethiopian Independence in the Period of the Scramble for Africa," *University College [of Addis Ababa] Review*, 1:21–23 (1961).

The Italian government did not, of course, admit that Menilek's unilateral denunciation of the Treaty of Wuchalé had abrogated its claimed protectorate.[88] Italy never stopped hoping for Menilek's recognition of Article 17 and, in February 1893, sent a special mission to try again to gain his acceptance. It is ironic that the two million cartridges the mission presented to the emperor seem to have so strengthened his position that he was able to denounce the treaty all the sooner. Furthermore, the mission and its bolstering gift constituted a serious diplomatic blunder in regard to Italian-Tigrean relations, which were further damaged when General Baratieri, the governor of Eritrea, was instructed to obtain from Mangasha a letter that would include a statement in the following sense: "Obedient to the supreme will of His Majesty the King of Italy, I declare my readiness to recognize Menilek, King of Shoa, as Negus Negast and Emperor of Ethiopia." Thus, Mangasha was once again robbed of his hope of using Italian support to gain the imperial throne, or even to remain independent. The Italians now appeared as treacherous to the Tigreans as they did to Menilek, and a nationwide feeling against white men — giving rise to the saying "one recovers from the bite of a black snake, but . . . never . . . from the bite of a white snake" — developed in Ethiopia and "stimulated the fear of conquest." [89]

"Tired of his profitless alliance with Italy" and pushed by the growing national revulsion against the Italians, Mangasha could follow no other course but to resubmit to Menilek if he wanted to save himself from becoming a complete pawn in the misguided Italian policy of chasing "the phantom of Uccialli." On the morning of June 9, 1894, Mangasha appeared at the palace in Addis Ababa, carrying "upon his shoulder a rock . . . to place, as a sign of submission, at the foot of the Negus." [90] Menilek accepted the submission and apparently intimated that the *ras* might later become *negus* of Tigre if he assisted in the impending struggle against the Italians. Spurred by his ambitions, Mangasha had concentrated enough forces in Tigre by

88. Note from the Italian Embassy, Jan. 10, 1894, *DDF*, XI:11.
89. Baratieri, *Mémoires*, 37–38, 75.
90. *Ibid.*, 77; J. G. Vanderheym, *Une Expédition avec le Négous Ménélik* (Paris, 1896), 130.

December 1894, to cause Italy grave concern. On December 17, General Baratieri ordered Mangasha to disband his men, and, when Mangasha refused to do so, the Italians marched across the Mareb frontier on December 30.[91]

During the following month's campaign against Mangasha, the Italian colonial army established garrisons at the towns of Senafé and Saganeiti and at the strong points of Addis Adi and Adi Kayyeh. General Baratieri was then faced with two alternatives: to advance farther into Tigre and risk war with Menilek, or to retire from the areas conquered, although retreat "would not have satisfied the aspirations, or befitted the dignity of the Italian people."[92] By March 1895, however, there was no longer any choice. Mangasha had raised new forces, and in order to forestall him, Baratieri was forced to occupy the strategic Tigrean town of Adi Grat which commanded the "natural route of invasion for Shoa." When for reasons of prestige he then occupied the important military, political, and commercial city of Adwa, war with Ethiopia could no longer be avoided.[93] The ease of these early Italian victories caused "the Italian Government and nation . . . [to form] too low an estimate of the difficulties to be overcome during the campaign against Menilek."[94]

With war imminent, Menilek issued a mobilization proclamation declaring:

> Enemies have now come upon us to ruin the country and to change our religion . . . Our enemies have begun the affair by advancing and digging into the country like moles. With the help of God I will not deliver up my country to them . . . Today, you who are strong, give me of your strength, and you who are weak, help me by prayer.[95]

In response to this call, "every tucul [hut] and village in every far-off glen of Ethiopia was sending out its warrior."[96]

91. Baratieri, *Mémoires*, 106–108.

92. Berkeley, *Adowa*, 88.

93. Harold G. Marcus, "A Background to Direct British Diplomatic Involvement in Ethiopia, 1894–1896," *Journal of Ethiopian Studies*, I:125 (July 1963).

94. Berkeley, *Adowa*, 82.

95. Quoted in Richard K. P. Pankhurst, *Ethiopia Observer (Special Issue on the Battle of Adowa)*, I:346 (Dec. 1957).

96. Berkeley, *Adowa*, 126.

On December 7 and 8, 1895, Ras Makonnen opened the war with a victory over the Italians at Amba Alaji. While this defeat was not a major military disaster for Italy, it did cause "the whole political edifice, indispensable to our colonial defense . . . [to be] shaken to its foundation, and, to some extent, to fall to the ground, increasing the boldness, confidence, strength, and pretensions of the enemy." [97] Many chieftains who had had doubts as to the war's outcome now joined Menilek's forces.

Ras Makonnen followed the retreating Italians and beseiged them at the fortress of Mek'ele from December 8 until they surrendered on January 23, 1896. He then allowed them to evacuate the fort with the full honors of war and to join General Baratieri at Idaga Hamus. The Italian forces then crossed the Mareb and took up defensive positions from Adi Grat to Inticho and Adi Kwala.

Meanwhile, the Ethiopian army had grown to nearly one hundred and twenty thousand men, and, in late January 1896, the emperor began his advance to Hawzen and Adwa to take advantage of Makonnen's victories. On March 1, the Italian army attacked the Ethiopian positions near Adwa and was beaten so severely that it was forced to retreat, abandoning all its artillery. This was the definitive struggle of the war; five days later, the Italians started negotiations for peace.[98]

Two Italian officers, Major Salsa and Lieutenant Roversi, traveled to Menilek's camp at Adi Kwala to open the discussions. Roversi wrote of the trip across the battlefield: "I have never seen anything so terrible . . . Our poor dead had still not been despoiled by the victors nor touched by the hyenas; as far as the view extended, one only saw soldiers stretched out dead; the bodies were so close to each other that it was necessary for us to guide our mules with dexterity to avoid stepping upon them." [99]

---

97. Baratieri, *Mémoires*, 281.

98. Completely surprised by the size of Menilek's forces, the king of Italy remarked: "Had we known what was going to happen, we should have made very different arrangements." When the gravity of the situation was recognized, Italy sent one of its leading officers, General Baldissera, to take over Baratieri's command; but Baldissera did not leave Italy until February 23 and was still at sea when the Battle of Adwa was fought. See Needham to Ford, Public Record Office, London, F.O. 403/239, Feb. 26 and 28, 1896. For a more detailed account of the Battle of Adwa, see Wylde, *Abyssinia*, chap. II.

99. De Lauribar, *Abyssinie*, 599.

Still upset by this dismal scene, the two officers took for flippancy Menilek's polite attempts to put them at ease by avoiding all discussion of the war during the first meeting. But the following days of negotiations, from which they returned on March 19 with the basis for a peace treaty, showed the two men that the emperor's purposes were serious, although not vindictive.

The prime condition he demanded for peace was the complete abrogation of the Treaty of Wuchalé, although he conceded the need for the negotiation of a new treaty and allowed the Italians to retain the Mareb-Belessa-Mai Muni frontier. The problem of repatriation of Italian prisoners of war was postponed until the negotiation of the formal treaty, but Salsa felt that this "difficult question . . . [would] not [be] impossible to resolve." [100] Menilek apparently wished to leave the prisoner problem open in order to be in a better bargaining position during the final negotiations, and because he wished to consult with his advisers in Addis Ababa before making any binding commitments. The Italian government also found it impossible to obtain from Menilek a preliminary statement which would pledge him to refuse the protectorate of any other European power. These problems were resolved in the final negotiations for the treaty, which were completed in Addis Ababa on October 26, 1896.

The Addis Ababa Treaty affirmed Ethiopia's historic independence and represented a major victory for Menilek's foreign policy. Article 1 declared that the state of war between Italy and Ethiopia was over. Article 2 stated that "the Treaty concluded at Wuchalé on . . . May 2, 1889, is and will remain definitely annulled with its annexes." By Article 3 "Italy recognizes absolutely and without reserve the independence of the Ethiopian Empire as a sovereign and independent state." Articles 4 and 5 stipulated that "until these frontiers have been delimited, the two contracting powers agree to observe the *status quo ante* . . . determined by the course of the Mareb, Belessa, and [Mai] Muna Rivers." The remaining four articles facilitated commercial and industrial intercourse between the two nations, provided for the transmission of the treaty to the powers, stipu-

---

100. In Baldissera to Ricotti, March 19, 1896, in Governo Italiano, Ministero Degli Affare Esteri, Commissione per la Publicazione dei Documenti Diplomatici, *I Documenti Diplomatici Italiani* [hereafter *DDI*], 3rd series (Roma, 1953), I, 22.

lated the ratification procedure, and stated that the official texts in Amharic and French agreed absolutely.[101]

Diplomacy, 1896–1898

Menilek's victory over the Italians established him as an important power in eastern Africa. After 1896, therefore, the major European nations and their literate public became increasingly interested in Ethiopia as a political entity and in Menilek as a leader and a personality. Diplomats, travelers, and journalists came to Ethiopia and recorded their impressions of the emperor, descriptions which make it possible to construct a picture of Menilek during the years of his greatest power — 1896 to 1908.

The middle-aged emperor usually received foreigners seated or reclining on the royal *alga* (couch), which was "covered with silks and carpets and [stood] under a canopy ornamented with silken hangings. He wore on his head . . . [a] white muslin handkerchief, fastened across the brow with ribbons of pale greenish blue, with streamers hanging down the back; a purple velvet cloak, richly ornamented with large silver plaques on each side, was thrown across his shoulders." [102] He had "charming manners and a particularly pleasant voice" that hinted at his good sense of humor and great intelligence.[103] One observer was struck by the emperor's open and frank attitude, and an Ameri-

---

101. There is a complex of possibilities why Menilek accepted this frontier and did not, instead, try to drive the Italians out of Ethiopia entirely: first, if he had pressed the Italian government into a position from which it might feel compelled by national pride to mount a larger military effort against him, he could not be certain that his ill-disciplined men would win against defensive and fortified Italian positions, and he did not wish to risk his new reputation as an astute military leader and his army's hard-won prestige; second, he did not wish to lead his army, short of rations as it now was, through the agriculturally poor country south of Eritrea, especially with the imminence of the long rainy season; third, he probably felt that the incorporation of further Tigre-speaking areas into the empire would unnecessarily strengthen the position of Ras Mangasha, whose loyalty to Menilek was opportunistic and remained questionable. Treaty as quoted in Rosetti, *Storia Diplomatica*, 181 ff.

102. Count Edward Gleichen, *With the Mission to Menilek* (London, 1898), 128–129.

103. Herbert Weld Blundell, "A Journey through Abyssinia to the Nile," *The Geographical Journal*, XV:100 (Feb. 1900); Prince Henri d'Orléans, *Une Visite à l'Empereur Ménélik* (Paris, n.d. [1897?]), 123.

can traveler observed that Menilek's "manner toward strangers is kindly, [and] unostentatious; his interest in all things new, and to him understandable, is ever keen." [104] Ever ready to try things for himself, Menilek even made an unsuccessful attempt at learning to ride a bicycle.

Practically all observers were amazed by the emperor's wide interests and his knowledge of world affairs. He carefully questioned an English sportsman regarding British political parties, the war in South Africa, and European rivalries; and he discussed archaeology with the first German ambassador to Ethiopia, who was greatly impressed with Menilek's potential as a patron of the arts and sciences.[105] He was particularly interested in new weapons, and, when a new stock-loading pistol was explained to him in 1899, he grasped "the intricacies of the mechanism with a readiness which amazed" the donor, who remarked that, regarding "mechanical contrivances," Menilek "has almost the knowledge of a specialist." [106] Some years later, when the mechanism of the automobile was described to him, "Menilek proved to be an attentive and intelligent listener, not allowing a single part to be left until he fully comprehended its functions." The same writer noted that the emperor's interests encompassed "traction engines, railways, guns, engines, phonographs, and other novelties," but "he was too honest to pretend knowledge that he did not possess, and too anxious to learn to hide his child-like inquisitiveness into the working of each . . . serious toy." [107]

Menilek's normal day began at three in the morning when he would spend two hours at devotions in his private chapel. He would then receive courtiers, administrators, government officials, and diplomats until ten, when he would breakfast with the queen, at the same time discussing major affairs of state and diplomacy with his other chief advisers. After breakfast, Menilek and the queen retired and were generally unavailable for

---

104. Oscar T. Crosby, "Personal Impressions of Menelik," *The Century Magazine*, LXIII:899 (April 1902).

105. A. E. Pease, *Travel and Sport in Africa* (London, 1902), III, 83; Felix Rosen, *Eine Deutsche Gesandtschaft in Abessinien* (Leipzig, 1907), 266–267.

106. Herbert Vivian, *Abyssinia* (London, 1901), 198, 209.

107. Clifford Hallé, *To Menelik in a Motor Car* (London, 1913), 262, 272, 292.

public business until two o'clock, when the emperor would de-
vote about four more hours to business and judicial affairs, or
to pleasure if the pressure of events allowed. At six o'clock, the
emperor dined with high military officials, whereupon he retired
for conversation to his rooms, accompanied by the queen and a
select group of courtiers. At ten the emperor and the queen
retired for the night.

A painstaking administrator, Menilek "made time to attend
personally to every detail of administration in a country constituted of many heterogeneous elements. Accessible to all his subjects from the highest to the lowest, he succeeded in universal
respect and affection." [108]

While Menilek liked to think of himself as an enlightened
ruler, he was realistically aware of the state of social evolution
in Ethiopia and governed accordingly. When Alfred Ilg once
complained about the severity of Ethiopian justice, Menilek
retorted:

> You speak like a European, as if I have to govern people trained
> in the ideas of your country. I have no prisons; I do not wish the
> people who work to have to feed thieves. Besides, the people would
> not see them hidden behind walls. The people would forget them.
> While in this manner, mutilated, wandering, abandoned, they walk
> to the ends of their lives an example of punishment.

All the same, Menilek had a keen sense of justice; once, when
an irate public was goading him to take capital action against
the captive king of Kaffa, he told the prisoner that he was "less
guilty than these people who wish to have you judged by an
angry man," and punished him only with house captivity in
Addis Ababa.[109]

Menilek also had a shrewd appreciation of international relations and politics. The chief of the first American diplomatic
mission to Ethiopia in 1903 found it "doubtful whether any
practical statesman, certainly none laboring under the disad-
vantages of the Emperor Menilek, has any keener appreciation
of the relative forces of the earth." [110] A British diplomat wrote

108. James Rennell Rodd, C.G.E., *Social and Diplomatic Memories, 1884–
1901* (2nd series; London, 1923), 162–163.
109. Cited in Hughes le Roux, *Ménélik et nous* (Paris, n.d.), 212, 218.
110. Robert P. Skinner, *Abyssinia of Today* (London, 1906), 86.

that "Menilek was a man of quick and keen intelligence capable of appreciating political situations with a clearness of apprehension which I had hardly anticipated." [111] When Menilek discussed politics, his "expression changed with extraordinary rapidity. The smile died away, the easy carelessness was no longer to be seen, and his eyes lit up with a shrewd, strong expression." [112] The emperor used his grasp of the eastern African power situation and his shrewdness in foreign policy and diplomacy to their best advantage in the years after 1896 when he conceived and carried out the policy which enlarged his empire to its present proportions and sustained its hard-won independence.

With the Italian threat eliminated, Menilek's first interest was to gain more formal recognition of his independent status from the European colonial powers which surrounded his empire. British territory was adjacent to Ethiopia in the east and south, and it seemed possible that British authority would soon establish itself in the Sudan. Before Adwa, British policy makers had considered Menilek's empire an "Italian Sphere of Influence" [113] and had relied upon Italy to act as their "watchdog" in northeastern Africa against a possible French sally into the Nile Valley from the east. British reaction to the Italian defeat had, therefore, been swift; on March 12, 1896, British troops marched on Dongola "to relieve the pressure upon the Italians" because Lord Salisbury's cabinet felt "that the collapse of Italy . . . and Dervish success would jeopardize British interests." [114] Menilek and his advisers must have been aware that this act represented the first step in a plan to conquer the Sudan and the Nile Basin. It was not at all certain, however, that Great

111. Rodd, *Memories*, 173.

112. Vivian, *Abyssinia*, 203.

113. Until 1896 official British maps called Ethiopia "The Italian Sphere of Influence"; later, however, this designation was lined out and replaced by "Abyssinian Boundaries." See F.O. 1/32, map of East Africa.

114. William L. Langer, *The Diplomacy of Imperialism* (New York, 1956), 537; J. A. S. Grenville, *Lord Salisbury and Foreign Policy* (London, 1964), 118. The latter study clearly proves that fear of a French thrust into the Nile Valley was not a significant factor in the decision to mount the Egyptian advance on Dongola.

Britain would attain its ultimate object. The British were faced by the military strength of the Mahdist state under the Khalifa Abdullahi whose political and military posture, although declining in 1896, still appeared strong enough that the possibility of a British defeat could not be discounted.[115] Another factor which tended to make Menilek uncertain about the Nile Valley situation was the existence of a French policy to gain control of the upper Nile Valley as a lever to force British concessions in Egypt. France hoped to gain Ethiopian cooperation and assistance in this plan and had dispatched a mission under the leadership of Major Marchand into the Nile Valley from the west in mid-1896.[116] It was altogether possible for Menilek to conceive of a French success in the Sudan even if he provided no assistance.

Considering that his long-term interest in the Nile Basin was derived as much from the need to protect his empire as from the desire to expand it westward, Menilek did not care to risk the alienation of any one of the three powers who might soon control that area. All his diplomatic skills would be required just to guarantee, and perhaps benefit from his position, regardless of the outcome of the Sudanese struggle. Open failure to support French plans could result in the enmity of the country which had been Menilek's main foreign support against the Italian threat, and whose assistance he might well need again to checkmate Great Britain in its drive to secure the Nile Basin for Egypt. On the other hand, if Menilek openly supported either France or the Sudanese, Great Britain could regard him as a potential enemy and, if successful in the Sudan, might extend her campaign to secure the Ethiopian sources of the Nile. Finally, open support of either one of the European powers could alienate the *khalifa,* who could then be a most dangerous neighbor should he be successful in retaining his country's independence.

115. The British themselves did not exclude the possibility. See G. N. Sanderson, "Contributions from African Sources to the History of European Competition in the Upper Valley of the Nile," *Journal of African History,* III:71 (1962).

116. France had always considered Ethiopian assistance necessary for the success of its policy in the Nile Basin. See C. Maistre, "Le Président Carnot et le Plan d'Action sur le Nil en 1893," *L'Afrique Française,* 42:156 (March 1932).

To solve his diplomatic dilemma, Menilek began by establishing cordial relations with the Mahdist state on the basis of
their common interest in withstanding the challenges of European imperialism and guaranteeing the security of their common
frontier. Menilek and Abdullahi exchanged some information
and assured each other of their good intentions, but apparently
this affair of convenience did not result in any formal agreement. From the emperor's point of view it was politic merely
to buoy up the *khalifa*'s morale without making any entangling
commitments.[117]

To assure the friendship of France, through whose port of
Jibuti flowed his major arms supply, proved somewhat more
difficult. After the battle of Adwa, French authorities felt the
time had come "to reap the fruit of our policy by attaching
ourselves with durable connections to the sovereign of an Empire which in the future, by reason of its geographic location,
will be of interest both to our establishments in the Gulf of
Tajura and the regions of the upper Nile Valley, to which we
have access from Ubangi and which could shortly pose political
questions of great importance." [118] The French cabinet therefore decided on November 24, 1896, to send a special mission
led by M. Leonce Lagarde, the governor of French Somaliland,
to negotiate a treaty. On January 29 and 30, 1897, Lagarde and
Ras Makonnen signed two agreements which specified, respec-
tively, that Menilek would consider Jibuti as the official outlet
for Ethiopian commerce, and that armaments for the Ethiopian
government would pass through Jibuti duty free. Two more
important treaties were signed by Menilek and Lagarde on March
20. The first, a frontier treaty, ceded to Ethiopia a large section

117. Sanderson, "European Competition," 70, 84–86. It is interesting
to note that Menilek rushed to safeguard his claims as soon as the authority
of the Mahdist state broke down in its border regions. This is particularly
evident in the case of Beni Shangul, and might also explain why Menilek
ordered Dejaz Tesemma to mount an expedition to the area of the Nile-
Sobat confluence, although fear of the MacDonald Mission of 1898 also
played a role in the latter case. See Marcus, "Western Border," 86; G. N.
Sanderson, "The Foreign Policy of the Negus Menilek, 1896–1898," *Journal
of African History,* V:92 (1964); and Sanderson, "European Competition," 87.

118. Menilek had suggested such a treaty in March 1895, when he sought
French aid against the Italian claim to a protectorate over Ethiopia. Note
from the Political Director, Sept. 30, 1896, *DDF,* XIII:62, n.; Menilek to
Félix Fauré, March 1895, *ibid.,* XIII:133.

of what France considered part of its Somaliland holdings, thus reducing that colony to its present small size.[119] In return for this important concession, Menilek signed the agreement described by French authorities as "a real treaty of alliance." [120] This "Convention for the White Nile," effectively kept secret by both parties, pledged Menilek "to complete and well-nigh unconditional support of the French political aspirations on the upper Nile." [121] Article 1 stated that "His Majesty, the Emperor of Ethiopia, establishing his authority on the right bank of the White Nile from 14° south, will aid, as much as possible, the agents of the French Government, who will be on the left bank between 14° and 5°30′." [122]

While the first three agreements with France gave Menilek major territorial, political, and economic concessions, the secret treaty pledged him to actions which would damage his *détente* with the Sudan, and might even bring him into direct conflict with Great Britain. To retain the advantages he had gained, without damaging his diplomatic poise, required the subtle evasion of some of the obligations undertaken in the Nile Convention. Menilek therefore allowed the French to use Ethiopia as a jumping-off place for several expeditions sent to meet the Marchand mission. At the same time he issued his men "ambiguous instructions . . . [provided] guides who misled the French, and . . . [permitted] Tassama and his agents to frustrate the missions by every possible means, not excluding arrest and internment." [123] When the French complained about this obstructionism, the emperor apologized for the "imbeciles" who disobeyed his instructions and prepared new letters of authorization. Nonetheless, so much time and human resource had been expended that the ill-equipped French missions ultimately failed. By these tactics, Menilek had once again protected himself against all eventualities: he had shown enough good will toward France that, "had the French succeeded in their schemes for the upper

119. Agreements of Jan. 29 and Jan. 30, 1897, *ibid.*, XIII:147; Frontier Treaty, March 20, 1897, *ibid.*, XIII:277.
120. Pierre-Alype, *L'Empire des Négus* (Paris, 1925), 94.
121. G. Sanderson, "Emir Suleyman Ibn Inger Abdullah," *Sudan Notes and Records*, XXV:63 (1954).
122. Convention for the White Nile, March 20, 1897, *DDF*, XIII:278.
123. Sanderson, "Foreign Policy," 88.

e, he would doubtless have found ways of turning their success to his advantage";[124] he had not weakened the position of the *khalifa*, who had no way of knowing about the secret Nile Convention; and he had avoided placing himself in an awkward strategic and political position vis-à-vis Great Britain.

Meanwhile, the British had become uneasy about Ethiopia's relations with France and with Mahdist Sudan. In December 1896, they learned that Ethiopian envoys had recently been in Omdurman and that the travel routes between Ethiopia and the Sudan via Gallabat and Gedarif had been reopened. The British knew that Menilek and the *khalifa* had long had contacts, but the London government viewed this latest mission as particularly ominous and decided to take steps to head off a possible arms trade between the two countries.[125] Furthermore, it was then becoming evident to Great Britain that her military operations in the Sudan would require the administration of the upper Nile region; and Ethiopian infiltration into the hinterland of the British Somaliland protectorate was becoming serious. There was no doubt that these problems could only be solved by the opening of direct diplomatic relations with Ethiopia.

Because of Britain's position as a neighbor with a very real strategic interest in Ethiopia, Menilek was necessarily anxious to lessen British suspicions about his relations with the Sudan and France; at the same time, he needed to preserve his present and future good standing with these powers. He was able to attain his objectives without great difficulty because, fortunately for him, British policy aims in Ethiopia proved to be defensive rather than offensive. The British mission to Menilek, headed by Rennell Rodd, Lord Cromer's chief lieutenant in Egypt, had three major goals, none of which was objectionable to Menilek. First, Rodd sought Menilek's agreement not to assist the Mahdists in the Sudan; second, he hoped to regularize the British Somaliland–Ethiopian border; and third, he wished to obtain a commercial treaty embodying the most-favored-nation principle.[126]

In a treaty signed on May 14, 1897, Menilek promised "to halt to the best of his ability the passage across his Empire of

124. *Ibid.*, 93.

125. For a listing of diplomatic contacts between Sudan and Ethiopia, 1895–1898, see Sanderson, "European Competition," *passim*.

126. F.O. 403/255, Salisbury to Rodd, Feb. 24, 1897 and Feb. 25, 1897.

arms and munitions to the Mahdists, whom he declares the enemies of his empire." [127] His ready willingness to sign such a statement seems to indicate that Menilek had never actually intended to give material aid to the *khalifa* and, therefore, felt that he could afford a pledge of non-intervention in the Sudan in return for the favorable concessions in British Somaliland he would receive in return. Furthermore, in exchange for a statement enough like a most-favored-nation treaty to satisfy Lord Salisbury, Menilek forced Rodd to concede the duty-free transit of all goods passing through Zeila. The most difficult negotiations were in regard to the Somaliland border and took place at Harar between Rodd and Ras Makonnen after the actual signing of the treaty. The results of these talks were then annexed to the main body of the treaty. The annex ceded to Ethiopia 13,500 square miles of Somali territory, thereby giving Menilek control of the Gadabursi and Zeila-Jildessa trade routes and putting him in good strategic position to march on Berbera. There was little the British could have done to avoid this large cession since "Abyssinians have been in more or less effective occupation of the greater part of this tract for many years, and we have not been more than momentarily successful in driving them out of one or two of the disputed localities." Rodd felt that "It would . . . have been impossible to dislodge the Abyssinians from posts which they had occupied, without recourse to arms." Furthermore, he concluded that "failure to reach a settlement would have prejudiced our certainty of securing friendly neutrality on the western side." [128]

It is therefore easy to agree with G. N. Sanderson when he says that "Menilek was . . . a subtle and far-sighted diplomatist with, at times, an almost Bismarckian capacity for keeping several irons in the fire." It is difficult, however, to agree when he suggests "that down to the collapse of the Mahdist state itself, the Mahdist alliance was the central feature of Menilek's diplomacy." [129] The *détente* with the Sudan clearly appears as one feature of a carefully constructed foreign policy conceived to consolidate the victory over the Italians at Adwa, to safeguard

127. Governo Italiano, Ministero degli Affari Esteri, *Tratatti* (Roma, 1906), I:556; see also F.O. 403/255, Rodd's draft treaty and Menilek's counter draft.

128. F.O. 403/274, Memo. by J. C. Ardagh, Director of Military Intelligence, Feb. 28, 1898; Rodd, *Memories*, 182–183.

129. Sanderson, "Foreign Policy," 93

Ethiopia's position on all sides, and to obtain concessions from both France and Great Britain. That Ethiopia emerged unscathed and strengthened from a situation which could have weakened its entire external posture is a measure of Menilek's statesmanship.

Innovation, the Railway, and Consolidation of the State, 1896–1908

With his diplomatic position firmly established, Menilek was able to turn his attention to Ethiopia's modernization. With his interest in machinery and modern technology, he helped to bring about numerous innovations in his country. At his invitation foreign workmen constructed modern buildings in Addis Ababa; in 1886, the first modern bridge over the Awash was erected, followed by numerous other spans throughout the empire. Menilek pioneered the first real postal system of the country, enabling Ethiopia to be admitted to the International Postal Union in 1908. Other innovations in the field of communications were the installation of two telegraph and telephone systems which, when they worked, provided Ethiopia with rapid communication with the outside world and facilitated administration and the dissemination of information within the country. In 1894, Menilek issued Ethiopia's first national currency and, in 1903, installed a mint in Addis Ababa. These monetary reforms were capped in 1905 when he granted a charter for a Bank of Abyssinia to be affiliated with the National Bank of Egypt. Advances in the fields of education and health were made with the opening of hospitals and schools and the establishment of a government printing press.[130] The most significant feature of Menilek's policy of modernization, however, was the construction of the Jibuti–Addis Ababa railroad.

The complex story of the Ethiopian railroad began in 1879 when Alfred Ilg constructed a model railway to show Menilek, then king of Shoa, what modern transportation could mean for the future of Ethiopia. Remembering the small railway which the British had built for moving troops during the Mak'dala expedition, Menilek felt that at this time he should not uni-

130. Richard Pankhurst, "Misoneism and Innovation in Ethiopian History," *Ethiopia Observer*, VII:300–305 (1964).

laterally build anything so strategically dangerous and that the Emperor Yohannis would never agree to a project which would so greatly strengthen Shoa. When Menilek became king of kings in 1889, however, Ilg again suggested that the possibilities for a railroad be studied, and, because Menilek was then anxious to enhance his strategic position vis-à-vis the Italians, he issued a decree on February 11, 1893, authorizing Ilg to carry out a feasibility study. Late that year, Ilg reported that his projected plans were workable and that funds could be obtained in France. Accordingly, on March 9, 1894, the emperor granted Ilg a ninety-nine year concession allowing him to form a company to build a railway in three stages: Jibuti to Harar, Harar to Addis Ababa, and Addis Ababa to Kaffa and the White Nile. The concession, however, dealt in detail only with the first part of the line and guaranteed, among other things, that no competing lines would be built from the Indian Ocean or the Red Sea.[131] In January 1896, a contract for the railway construction was signed with a Paris firm. It was not until a year after the Battle of Adwa, however, that the French government granted formal permission to the Imperial Railway Company of Ethiopia to lay the line to Harar over French Somali territory and to build the necessary appurtenances in Jibuti.

Because the railway company too "casually assumed that they could procure with ease the large sum required" for the construction, it soon ran into serious financial difficulties and, in 1899 and 1900, was forced to invite British capital to invest heavily in the venture.[132] As a result, a British holding company, the International Ethiopian Railway Trust and Construction Company, Ltd., gained control of the French railway company by the middle of 1901. This takeover caused concern in French colonial circles, where a vigorous campaign was immediately begun to secure the French government's intervention in the building of the railroad.

Meanwhile, the British government was concerned that the

131. Keller, *Ilg*, 131–134; F.O. 403/299, Railway Concession, Oct. 1900; F.O. 403/334, Law Officers of the Crown to Foreign Office, Feb. 16, 1903; Governo Italiano, *Tratatti*, 415.

132. J. B. Christopher, "Ethiopia, the Jibuti Railway and the Powers, 1899–1906," (unpubl. diss., Harvard University, 1942), 26; T. Lennox Gilmour, *Abyssinia: the Ethiopian Railway and the Powers* (London, 1906), 18; Leonard Woolf, *Empire and Commerce in Africa* (London, n.d.), 206.

"French should not occupy the predominant position in Abyssinia, which the construction of the railway will probably give them." [133] Sir John Lane Harrington, the British plenipotentiary in Ethiopia, took this concern a step further and suggested to the emperor that the railway "had placed practically the whole future commercial development of his country in the hands of the French." [134] While the emperor denied this accusation, Harrington's action did effectively arouse Menilek's suspicions of France whose motives he had not hitherto questioned. That Britain's concern and Menilek's suspicions were not unfounded became clear on February 6, 1902, when the French government and the railway company signed a convention which was

> a very remarkable document. It embodies an agreement between a European Government and a company domiciled in Europe, by which the Government agreed to financial assistance to the company for the purpose of constructing and subsequently working, a railway in the territory of an independent foreign state, the sovereign of which had granted a concession for the construction of a railway to the company as a commercial enterprise. [135]

As a result of this convention "a private enterprise suddenly became the official protégé of one state, operating in another equally sovereign state, but without the consent of the second party." [136]

When Menilek learned of the convention, he was furious. If the French expected to have total control over the railway, he felt "they might as well tell me to prepare for war at once . . . Why don't they say they will buy Abyssinia?" The emperor recognized that the final article of the convention, which required his agreement before construction of the Ethiopian section of the line could be begun, was only "to smooth it all over." Had the French really wanted his consent, he knew they would have shown him the convention before signing it; "this is only to cover our eyes." [137] To counter this French maneuver, Menilek turned to Great Britain for assistance. In view of the con-

133. F.O. 403/298, Crowe to Foreign Office, May 15, 1900.
134. F.O. 403/299, Harrington to Salisbury, May 30, 1901.
135. Gilmour, *The Railway*, 22.
136. Christopher, "The Railway," 140.
137. F.O. 1/40, Harrington to Boyle, April 5, 1902.

cern that Harrington had expressed about the convention, the emperor expected that Britain would rapidly commit itself to his support. But the London government felt from the very beginning that "King Menilek's proposals are of a nature which require careful examination before they can be entertained. They would involve us in heavy expenditure and in far-reaching responsibilities." [138] After further study, the London government concluded that "the issues are scarcely of sufficient gravity to warrant expenditure of millions." [139] Thereafter, try as he might, the emperor could obtain no British financial support in his political struggle against the French-dominated railway. He continued, however, to enjoy considerable British diplomatic support, and with its help he proceeded to take unilateral steps to block railway construction under the terms of the 1902 convention. He had earlier shown his displeasure with the railway company by refusing to attend the inauguration of the Jibuti-Dirre Dawa section of the line (the first 310 kilometers) — an event he would have thoroughly enjoyed — which was finished in December 1902. He then damaged the company's borrowing power by withdrawing the privilege of collecting a 10 per cent levy on merchandise in transit, a privilege granted in the 1894 concession "to a private company and not to a foreign Government." [140] He also withdrew his original agreement to channel all goods shipped between Jibuti and Dirre Dawa through the company, thus causing railway traffic to drop below the level where the company's receipts could cover expenses and pay interest on its bonds. Finally, the emperor refused to sanction the construction of the second section of the railroad from Dirre Dawa to Addis Ababa and the company was forced to stand by, idly eating up its capital.

The railway company now faced a second financial crisis. The 1902 convention had freed it from the domination of British capital, but the subvention granted by the convention had been discounted to obtain the cash necessary to buy out British interests and to finish the first section of the line. The company had expected to be able to find the further financing it would need in the Paris money market; but, faced with Menilek's refusal to

138. F.O. 403/322, Lansdowne to Cromer, April 14, 1902.
139. F.O. 1/43, Sanderson to Cromer, March 17, 1903.
140. Cited in Christopher, "The Railway," 210.

recognize the convention and with his obstructionist behavior, it could procure no further funds in Paris and was faced with an annual deficit of more than one million francs.[141] The situation was further complicated when France, Britain, and Italy began negotiations to define their positions, interests, and responsibilities in Ethiopia. All work on the road ceased for several years until the financial and political problems could be solved.

When, by April 1905, no apparent progress had been made, the emperor called a meeting of the French, Italian, British, and Russian representatives and of various Ethiopian government officials and told them:

> For years now work [on the railway] has ceased and you know the reasons; time passes in sterile discussions . . . It is with great regret that I see the months and years slip away with our friends being unable to come to an accord on this question . . . It is to put an end to this state of affairs that I called you here today. I come to ask you to inform your governments [of] the decision that I desire to take relative to this question of the railway . . . I would be happy to see the guaranteed construction of the railway as soon as possible by an agreement between the several powers . . . Up to now, I have received no proposition on your part. If I receive[none] . . . nor any plan reconciling your . . . interests which puts an end to this conflict, I would see it necessary, to assure the construction of the railway, to undertake the construction myself, without asking nor accepting agreement from any part.[142]

About a year later on July 4, 1906, a tripartite treaty reconciling the differences between England, France, and Italy in Ethiopia was initialed, making it difficult for Menilek to take over the construction of the railway.[143] The treaty recognized the right of the French company to continue the railway from Dirre Dawa on condition that it practice no discrimination "in . . . matters of trade and transit." [144] But the treaty did not reconcile Menilek's differences with France, and so the emperor still would not permit the resumption of the company's opera-

141. Gouvernement de France, Tribunal Civil de la Seine, *La Concession du Chemin de Fer Franco-Ethiopien* (Paris, 1924), 1–2.

142. *Ibid.*, 3–6.

143. F.O. 401/9, Grey to Lister, July 4, 1906. For information on the tripartite treaty see H. G. Marcus, "A Preliminary History of the Tripartite Treaty of December 13, 1906," *Journal of Ethiopian Studies*, II, no. 2 (1964).

144. F.O. 401/9, Tripartite Agreement, Dec. 13, 1906.

tions. The series of negotiations to reconcile these differences were the last in which the emperor took a personal part. Even during the two years required for these talks he was seriously ill, but he showed the same determination to safeguard Ethiopia's integrity that he had displayed in his struggle with Italy. The emperor believed that the 1902 convention undermined the sovereignty of his country by impairing Ethiopia's control over the part of the line within her borders. The tripartite treaty only made matters worse for the emperor because it prevented Great Britain from giving him further diplomatic support.

In early 1907, when Menilek stubbornly continued to refuse to allow the railroad to proceed, the French government sent a special envoy to Ethiopia to negotiate a new railway agreement. On January 30, 1908, after months of hard bargaining, Menilek granted the French company a new concession in which Ethiopia's control over its section of the line was strengthened and its honor in no way damaged.[145] Unfortunately, Menilek never saw the completed railway; he became paralyzed shortly after the signature of the new concession, and further complications over construction delayed completion until 1917. Nonetheless, the existence of the railway, which opened up Ethiopia to the outside world, can be directly attributed to the persistence and foresight of the Emperor Menilek.

Probably his greatest achievement was the formation of a greater Ethiopia, a united entity whose creation he began as king of Shoa. As long as the emperor remained active and in full control of his capabilities, his empire was well-governed and prosperous. He administered and policed the outlying areas by establishing *ketemas*, or fortified garrison towns, in strategic high places. A system of communication between these posts made it possible for thousands of rifles to be rapidly concentrated at any point, thus efficiently controlling the population as well as presenting visible evidence of "effective occupation" to the adjacent European powers. Most European travelers in Ethiopia were convinced that Menilek "aims at, and for the most part succeeds in, governing with justice." One traveler found that "as rulers over conquered nations, so far as my observation went, the Abys-

145. Belambaras Mahteme-Sillase Wolde Meskal, *Zikre Neger* (Addis Ababa, 1950), 455–463.

sinians seemed just and not oppressive, and as long as the King's tithe was paid, and peace and order prevailed, there was very little interference with native customs and habits." Several Europeans further noted that the emperor's peace was general and well observed.[146]

One of the important results of these years of peace was the creation of a large economic unity. A British sportsman who visited Ethiopia in 1900 described this aspect of Menilek's empire:

> To the market place at Adis Ababa come grains and spices, pepper and condiments from every corner of the Kingdom, coffee from Harrar and Lake Tana, cotton from the Blue Nile, gold from Beni Shongul, and civet from the Galla country, while salt from the far north of Tigré is the current change for a dollar. Fine cotton shammas, heavy burrnouses of black, blanket-like cloth, jewelry and arms, saddlery and ploughs, all are here. In fact, here you can feel the commercial pulse of Abyssinia, gain some insight into the present state of her civilisation, and gather what she wants from the foreigner and what she has to offer in exchange.[147]

The Last Six Years

To administer his empire more efficiently and to protect it from possible anarchy should he die before naming a successor, Menilek instituted two very important reforms in 1907 and 1908. First, on October 25, 1907, he announced to the foreign powers that he was forming a nine-man ministry: "It is sometime since we thought of introducing a European system into our country. You have always . . . said it would be good if we adopt some of the European system. I have now started to appoint a Ministry, and, if it is the will of God, I will complete it." [148]

A building to hold cabinet meetings was erected in the Gibbi area, and at the first session, held in July 1908, several relatively minor decisions were taken by the new body. While many European observers felt that the ministers had only "the vaguest

146. Philip Maud, "Exploration in the Southern Borderland of Abyssinia," *The Geographical Journal*, XXIII:565 (May 1904); Pease, *Travel*, III, 16.

147. P. H. G. Powell-Cotton, *A Sporting Trip through Abyssinia* (London, 1902), 108.

148. F.O. 401/10, Hohler to Grey, Oct. 27, 1907; F.O. 401/10, Menilek to Hohler, Oct. 25, 1907.

ideas of their duties" and that the title of minister was meaning-
less, the diplomats believed that Menilek was "quite serious in
his scheme, and hopes to have achieved a piece of real progress
. . . [which will] tend to consolidate the Government and the
rule of his successor who will almost certainly be a minor." [149]
Menilek himself, however, made only perfunctory use of the
ministry as long as he was physically able to rule.

The second important reform was the strengthening of the
judicial branch of the government by dividing the country into
six districts; to each of these, two appellate judges and three court
recorders were assigned. It was hoped that this reform would de-
crease the considerable backlog of appeals pending as well as
diminish the number of disputes with which the emperor, as the
final appellate court, would have to deal.

Menilek's health first became a subject of concern in 1906; by
September of that year, the British minister reported that "it has
become a matter of common talk in the town that he will not
live many years longer." [150] At a meeting with the emperor, the
new British minister, Sir Thomas Hohler, asked him whether
he intended to be like King Solomon who had besmirched his
glorious reputation by failing to name an heir. Menilek replied:
"I have often thought of it . . . I must make a decision." He
said there were two possible choices — Lij Eyyasu,[151] his grandson,
and his daughter, Zauditu — and he promised that as soon as he
had decided he would announce his decision publicly, "for he
clearly saw the necessity of having someone firmly established
at the head of the country before he died." Some time later he
told Hohler that he had decided upon Lij Eyyasu, but he refrained from making a public proclamation to this effect.[152]

About a year later Hohler reported that Menilek had had an
attack of partial paralysis but had recovered within a week.[153]
In May 1908, after a more serious attack, the emperor called together his chiefs to discuss the matter of succession. The meeting
was stormy and factional, until the emperor ended the discussion

149. F.O. 401/10, Hohler to Grey, Oct. 28, 1907; Hohler to Grey, Oct. 30,
1907; San Giuliano to Grey, Nov. 6, 1907; Giuseppe Piazza, *Alla Corte di
Menelik* (Ancona, 1912), 102.
150. F.O. 401/9, Harrington to Grey, Sept. 11, 1906.
151. *Lij*, child, is an honorary title given to sons of certain noblemen.
152. Sir Thomas Hohler, *Diplomatic Petrel* (London, 1942), 135–137.
153. F.O. 401/16, Hohler to Hardinge, Aug. 20, 1907.

by declaring that Lij Eyyasu, the son of Ras Mikael, would be his heir. He still did not make a public proclamation, however, although he did officially transmit his decision to the foreign powers.

The emperor's health continued to deteriorate throughout 1908, until the empress and the *abun* insisted that he go to the monastery of Debra Libanos to take the holy waters and ask God for a miraculous healing. Dr. L'Herminier, Menilek's European physician, did not oppose this plan because he could give no further medical help. On December 1, 1908, Menilek and a small entourage moved to the holy town. Every morning Menilek bathed in the waters, which were so cold that his health deteriorated until he finally complained to L'Herminier: "It will kill me! Forbid the baths for me, because in two days, if you have not taken me out of their hands, it will be all over." [154]

To make matters worse, news of the pilgrimage and various rumors that the emperor had suffered a nervous breakdown threw the population of Addis Ababa into such an uproar that in order to calm affairs Menilek had to return to the city on February 13, 1909. He looked better, but his doctor told the Italian minister that "the improvement is more apparent than real, and . . . disquieting symptoms continue, although [they are] not of an immediate character." [155]

While Menilek had decided upon a successor and had created a ministry, he had failed to nominate a regent to lead the government as he became progressively less able to control public affairs. As no one was willing to take responsibility for major decisions, the central government's authority broke down in the border areas. At the same time the political vacuum brought on a power struggle in Addis Ababa. The Empress Taitu and her party of Tigre chiefs and relatives in the Yejju clan intrigued to block the public proclamation of Lij Eyyasu's succession. Taitu wished to replace the boy with her nephew's wife, Zauditu (Menilek's daughter). A group of Shoan and southern chiefs opposed this arrangement and appeared, in combination, strong enough to block the empress. In an attempt to end these intrigues, Lij

154. George Rémond, "L'Agonie de l'Empereur Ménélik," *Le Correspondant*, CCXLIV:339 (July 25, 1911).

155. F.O. 401/12, De Bosdari to Grey, Feb. 23, 1909.

Eyyasu was officially proclaimed heir to the throne on May 18, 1909, in the presence of Menilek, the *abun,* and all the great chiefs, who swore an oath of fealty to the new crown prince. As part of a political arrangement, Lij Eyyasu had, two days earlier, married Taitu's grandniece, the six-year-old daughter of the late Ras Mangasha of Tigre. It was hoped that this marriage would placate Tigre and prevent Taitu from again putting forward Zauditu's candidature. In the imperial proclamation delivered by Gebre Sellasie, Menilek repeatedly referred to Ethiopia's diversity prior to his accession, and asked his subjects "to live after me, as you have lived with me: in peace and in perfect union . . . You alone are capable of destroying yourselves . . . You are all brothers . . . Protect my son and with him defend the fatherland." [156] Probably because Menilek felt he retained sufficient control over his mental faculties, he still did not name a regent. He continued to appear in public until the middle of September 1909, when he presided over the New Year's feast at the Gibbi.

A few days later a series of paralytic attacks began which totally incapacitated the emperor by the end of October. A previously prepared proclamation was issued to the population confirming Lij Eyyasu as heir apparent and placing a curse upon all those who would not obey Menilek's wish in this matter. Ras Tesemma, a cousin, adviser, and close friend of Menilek, was named the successor's guardian.[157] Meanwhile, Taitu had made good use of the growing power vacuum created by the emperor's prolonged illness by concentrating more and more power into her own hands, thus becoming the *de facto* head of government. While the government and the new regent were adjusting to their new positions, she continued to strengthen her position by nominating her followers to important positions and constructing strategic alliances by marrying her relatives to important chiefs.

European observers regarded the empress' political group as quite weak in face of the armies of Ras Tesemma and other southern leaders and concluded that in the long run Menilek's supporters would undoubtedly gain final control of the country. Hoffman Philip, the American minister, reported that Taitu "maintains her supremacy at the Guebbi and I am credibly in-

---

156. As quoted in Mérab, *Impressions,* II, 65.
157. F.O. 401/13, Proclamation by Menilek, Oct. 20 (?), 1909.

formed that practically every decision now arrived at by the Government is at her instigation, or subject to her consent." Although Taitu was heartily disliked by the Shoan population and by the Amhara chiefs, as long as there was a possibility of a "word from him [Menilek] in support of the Queen," no "individual or party [was] sufficiently adventurous to jeopardize all personal interests and, perhaps life itself, by open opposition.[158] Ras Tesemma, already in the early stages of an illness which was to claim his life a year later, was apathetic and appeared powerless. As the regent's ineptitude grew and Menilek remained comatose, the southern chiefs decided to act independently. On March 21, in front of the *abun,* they pledged to limit Taitu's powers, allowing her henceforth to act only as Menilek's nurse.[159] To prevent her from resisting their decision, the chiefs seized the palace arsenal and artillery and surrounded the Gibbi, taking the empress completely by surprise. Her protests were in vain, and the United States consul, Love, concluded that "the hitherto strong power of the Empress Taitu would seem to be effectually broken . . . She . . . is to all practical purposes a prisoner in a portion of the palace." [160] Her supporters were too far away to offer immediate help, and were, over the next few years, gradually neutralized and removed from their positions of power.

With the power struggle thus settled, Lij Eyyasu, carrying the royal red parasol, for "the first time . . . acted in the capacity of the Emperor at a public reception" on April 14, 1910.[161] While Menilek lingered on until December 1913, his reign was effectively over by 1910. During his lifetime, he had grown from a crude princeling into the sophisticated monarch who created a polity strong enough to withstand the challenges of modern European imperialism and to cope with the stresses of technological innovation. There is no question that modern Ethiopia could not have been built without the foundations laid during the reign of Menilek II.

158. National Archives, Records of the Department of State Relating to Internal Affairs of Ethiopia, 1910–1929, Memo. on Current Affairs in Addis Ababa by Hoffman Philip to the Asst. Sec. of State, Jan. 15, 1910; see also Arnoldo Cipolla, *Nell'Impero die Menelik* (Milano, 1911 [?]), 15.

159. National Archives, Proclamation by Ras Tesemma, March 22, 1910.

160. National Archives, Love to the Asst. Sec. of State, March 24, 1910.

161. National Archives, Love to Asst. Sec. of State, April 26, 1910.

The Poor Man of God —
Muhammad Abdullah Hassan

---

by ROBERT L. HESS

Associate Professor of History
University of Illinois at Chicago Circle

From 1899 to 1920, a politico-religious leader who styled himself the Poor Man of God kept the Somali peninsula in turmoil. Europeans at first regarded Muhammad Abdullah Hassan only as a fanatic, a false mahdi, a savage ruler of *razzia*-bent barbarian Somalis. Even later, the Ethiopians and the Italians did not fully understand the nature of Muhammad Abdullah's movement, while the British, who called him the Mad Mullah, dismissed him and his dervish followers as so many religious fanatics and political opportunists. At best they thought him a nuisance. But the three powers soon discovered that the Poor Man of God threatened them with the loss of their recently acquired holdings in the Somaliland protectorate, the Ogaden, the Benadir (southern Somalia), and the two protectorates of Obbia and the Mijjertein. Few in those decades would have recognized Muhammad Abdullah Hassan for what he was — a proto-nationalist, a great poet, and a leader in tune with the political and religious developments of the Somali in more recent times.

The Muslim Revival in Somalia

In the late nineteenth century the Somali-inhabited area of northeast Africa was one of the least-known areas of the continent. Far removed from the main interests of the explorers, the Somali lands were not crossed by Europeans until long after light had been thrown on many other areas of the dark continent.[1] For the most part British and Italian explorers were more interested in the hunting than the commercial possibilities of the

1. Richard Burton, who was one of the first Europeans to explore Somaliland, wrote only about the coast and the caravan route from Zeila to Harar, the northwestern fringe of Somali territory. The major undertakings of Bòttego, Robecchi-Bricchetti, Swayne and A. Donaldson Smith took place only in the last decade of the century.

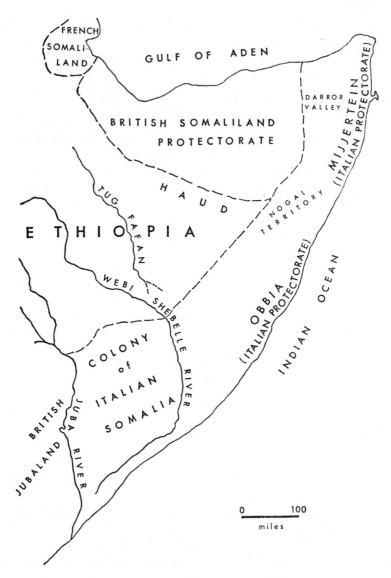

Physical and Political Map of Somalia

land, and their writings are less informative than the literature of exploration for other parts of Africa.[2]

Before the advent of the European and the Ethiopian, the Somali of the eastern horn of Africa lived the same life their ancestors had lived for at least the past five centuries. In northern Somalia most of the Darod, Dir, Ishaak, and Hawiya tribesmen were nomads whose wealth was measured in herds of camels and flocks of sheep and goats. Their main concern was water and pasturage for the survival of their herds and themselves, and rivalries between clans and tribes were strongest over watering and grazing rights. Before there were international boundaries in this arid part of Africa, the northern Somali set the pattern for their annual migration southward into the semi-desert Haud, where grazing was good after the beginning of the rainy season. To the Haud were also attracted the Ogaden Darod, whose way of life and whose needs were identical with those of their kinsmen north of the Haud. Between the northern Somali and the Ogaden lay the important, often-disputed permanent wells at Galkayu in the Mudug oasis, at Galadi, at Gerlogubi, and at Walwal. This pattern of nomadic wandering and intertribal raiding extended south and east as far as the Juba and Webi Shebelle rivers, the only permanent watercourses on the Somali peninsula.

But not all Somali were nomadic. In the northeast corner of the peninsula, the sultanate of the Mijjertein engaged in a steady stream of trade with southern Arabia, as did the coastal centers of Zeila, Bulhar, Berbera, and Las Khorai. These ports marked the northern terminus of caravan routes from Harar and the Ogaden and exported large numbers of livestock for the provisioning of Aden and the smaller coastal settlements of the south Arabian coast. Gums and incense woods from this area, which the ancients called *regio aromatifera,* also found their way into the export trade. Farther south, on the Indian Ocean coast, the Benadir ports of southern Somalia served the caravan trade of the Galla Boran and the southern Ogaden via the important inland center of Lugh. Somali and Arab coastal

2. The sole exception appears to be H. G. C. Swayne, *Seventeen Trips Through Somaliland: A Record of Exploration and Big Game Shooting, 1885 to 1893* (London, 1895), which he dedicated to his "brave and intelligent Somali followers."

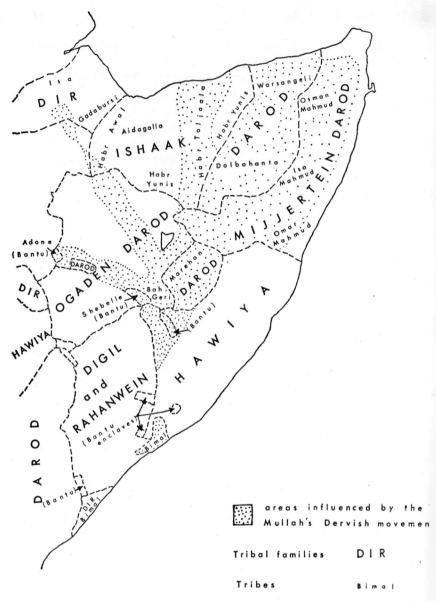

areas influenced by the Mullah's Dervish movemen

Tribal families   DIR

Tribes   Bimal

Tribal Map of Somalia

traders exported livestock, hides and dried meat to Zanzibar, Aden, and Bombay, and imported cereals, cheap cloth, hardware, slaves, and firearms.

In the interior of southern Somalia, along the two rivers, dwelt sedentary agricultural populations of Negroid and mixed Somali-Galla origins. Despised by the nomadic Somali, these agricultural peoples grew the grains which supplemented the milk and meat diet of the nomad and provisioned the coastal settlements.

The northern coastal settlements were generally pathetic little collections of mat huts and a few stone buildings. Berbera, the most important town on the northern coast, had a population of five thousand that swelled to five or six times that figure after the change in the monsoon winds opened the trading season. Las Khorai, the principal settlement of the Warsangeli Darod, contained at most sixty huts and a half dozen small stone forts, despite its important trade with the Dolbohanta Darod and the Mijjertein Darod of the interior. With the exceptions of Harar and Gildessa, which could not be called towns of Somali origin, there were no towns at all in the interior.

In the nineteenth century a religious revival swept the Somali country. The growth and spread of religious brotherhoods (*tariqa*) reinvigorated Islam in Somalia. Such movements, although not new to Islam, appear to have been a relatively recent development in Somalia. The earliest example of a *jama'a* (religious settlement) in Somalia is Bardera, which was established by a sheikh from Mogadishu in 1819. By 1840, his successor, Sheikh Ibrahim, was strong enough to declare a *jihad* against the lax Muslims of Brava. Elsewhere the *tariqa* were less fanatic, and their small agricultural settlements enjoyed immunity from the raids of their nomadic neighbors.

The oldest *tariq* in Islam, the Qadariya, may not have been introduced until the time of Sheikh Abdarrahman Zeilawi, who died in 1883. A second branch of the Qadariya flourished in southern Somalia under the leadership of Uways Muhammad al-Barawi, who died in 1909. At the time of Muhammad Abdullah Hassan, the Gadabursi, the Isa, most of the Ishaak, and the Ogaden were adherents of the Qadariya.[3]

The second important *tariq* to have an influence on events

3. I. M. Lewis, *A Pastoral Democracy: A Study of Pastoralism and Politics among the Northern Somali of the Horn of Africa* (London, 1961), 220.

in Somalia was the Ahmadiya, founded by Seyyid Ahmad ibn Idris al-Fasi (1760–1837). There are significant doctrinal and liturgical differences between the Ahmadiya and the Qadariya. By Islamic standards the Qadariya was much more lax and easy-going, while the Ahmadiya could certainly be called puritanical in its opposition to tobacco and *kat,* a mild narcotic chewed by the Somali and the Yemeni Arabs. But the greatest conflict between the adherents of the two groups was over the relative efficacy of the charismatic powers of the founders of each movement.

The Ahmadiya was not introduced directly into Somalia. Rather, two offshoots, the Salihiya and the Dandarawiya, were the agents for this movement. The Dandarawiya, the smaller of the two major subdivisions of the Ahmadiya in Somalia, was founded by Seyyid Muhammad al-Dandarawi in the mid-1880's. Among his followers were the Habr Awal, the Adan Isa, the Mahmud Isa, and some Habr Yunis. The Salihiya was founded by Muhammad Salih in Mecca in the late 1880's. Among Muhammad Salih's most important disciples were Sheikh Ismail, Sheikh Ishaak, and the Poor Man of God, Muhammad Abdullah Hassan. Both founders had Dolbohanta connections and maintained ties with Mecca. The Warsangeli and Dolbohanta, the Habr Toljaala, and some Habr Yunis supported the Salihiya.

At the end of the nineteenth century, the most important *tariq* settlement in northern Somalia was Hargeisa ("Little Harar"), whose founder, Sheikh Madar, hoped to make of his community of approximately one thousand inhabitants a city as renowned for learning as Harar. Hargeisa, inhabited mostly by Habr Awal followers of the sheikh, was well situated on the caravan routes from Milmil, Imi, Harar, and Gildessa to Zeila, Bulhar, and Berbera.

Farther east lay the settlements of Au Bakhadle, about twenty miles northeast of Hargeisa; Haji Nur's community at Sheikh, some forty miles south of Berbera; and Haji Musa's settlement at Hahe, to the south of Sheikh. In the Ogaden was the *jama'a* of Seyyid Muhammad al-Dandarawi on the *tug* (wadi) Fafan, a tributary of the Webi Shebelle. This community, which was as large as that at Hargeisa, had great influence on the Negroid Adone Muslims farther south in the Karanle region. Lastly, there was Faf, an important agricultural and trading center under

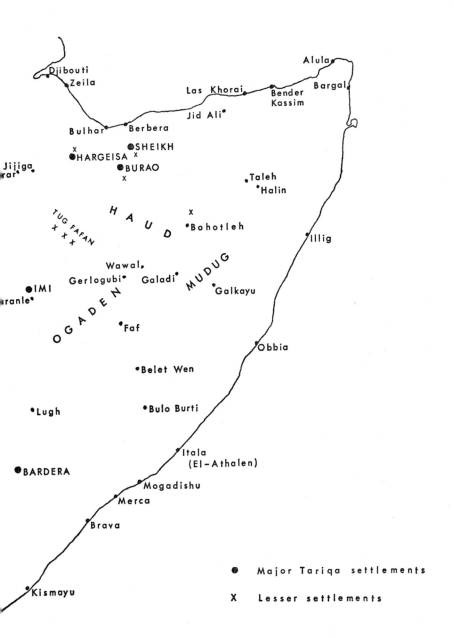

Tariqa Settlements of the Somali Peninsula

the direction of Haji Muhammad Nur. A number of lesser *jama'a*
were scattered throughout the area of the wadi Fafan, in the
valley of the Webi Shebelle, and in the alluvial plain of southern
Somalia. Most of the settlements maintained large areas under
cultivation and had large herds and flocks and a good water
supply.

The leaders of the *jama'a* played an important role in the life
of the Somali, who attributes supernatural powers to the sheikhs
and saints, the *au* and *wadad,* of his Islam.[4] The Somali *wadad*
enjoys not only great prestige among his fellowmen, but also
immunity from the usual intertribal struggles and raids. Ideally
no *wadad* would fight in temporal battles. If the *wadad* demonstrated competence in Arabic, even greater charisma was attached
to him and he was generally entitled to call himself *sheikh* and
enjoyed considerable influence and power over his followers.

These religious leaders are significant also in their opposition
to two of the basic elements of Somali life — tribalism and blood
money. As devout Muslims, the *wadad* preached the message of
the brotherhood of all who submitted to the will of God. The
brotherhood of Islam was thus first interpreted as the brotherhood
of all Somali, regardless of clan or tribal allegiance. For this
reason, too, the *dia* (blood money) was condemned as being against
the spirit of Islam. Needless to say, few Somali could act in
accordance with these Islamic ideals. The harshness of nature
seemed to blunt such idealism.

The power of the religious leader becomes even more important when one considers the weakness of Somali chiefs and
headmen. The clan head among the Somali, unlike his counterpart among the southern Bantu, has no real power inherent in
his office.[5] Thus the British, hoping to control the Somali through
a system of indirect rule such as they employed so successfully
elsewhere, found that the northern Somali did not easily lend
themselves to such administrative arrangements. The southern
Somali chiefs, on the other hand, had somewhat greater authority,
and the Italians made good use of them in their later policy of
"peaceful penetration" of the Benadir and its hinterland.[6]

4. *Ibid.,* 217.
5. I. M. Lewis, *Peoples of the Horn of Africa: Somali, Afar and Saho*
(London, 1955), 98–99.
6. R. L. Hess, "Italian Colonial Policy in Somalia, 1889–1935" (Uupubl.
diss., Yale University, 1959), 222–224.

Europeans did not generally understand the nature and circumstances of the Muslim revival in Somaliland. This is brought out by the reference that most later visitors constantly made to Burton's hasty judgment of 1854: "Much learning seems to make them mad; like the half-crazy Fakihs of the Sahara in northern Africa, the Widad, or priest, is generally unfitted for the affairs of this world, and the Hafiz or Koran-reciter, is almost idiotic." [7] It is unfortunate that this set of Victorian prejudices obscured a clearer vision of the Somali, for it was precisely his emotional appeal as a *wadad* that made the movement of Muhammad Abdullah Hassan so strong. In 1893, A. Donaldson Smith found that the *wadad* had made their mark in the Ogaden: "Most of the men understand Arabic; and you scarcely ever see a boy without his little flat board, on which are written verses from the Koran." [8]

Through the medium of the Muslim scholar the Somali of the Ogaden were apprised of developments in the Anglo-Egyptian Sudan in the mid-1880's. When F. L. James and his party attempted to enter the Ogaden in 1884, they discovered that the Somali tribesmen were hostile to them on religious grounds: "They had sent letters to the priests [*sic*] in Ogadayn, saying word had come from Mecca urging the people to stop us, as the English had lately killed a great many [Sudanese] Moslems." [9] As James penetrated south to the Webi Shebelle, he found that this feeling was shared by other tribes. The Somali communications network of letters sent from Berbera to the religious leaders of the various *tariqa* extended as far as Faf, "wherein dwelt that mighty host of priests we dreaded." At Faf, James met with the same religious hatred of foreigners encountered by so many Europeans in Somalia. The Somali camel drivers in the James expedition were berated by the holy men for accompanying infidels and were declared to be "no better than Kaffirs themselves." [10]

This trait of xenophobia, intensified by the religious revival,

7. Richard Burton, *First Footsteps in East Africa or, An Exploration of Harrar* (London, 1894), I, 78.
8. A. Donaldson Smith, *Through Unknown African Countries: The First Expedition from Somaliland to Lake Lamu* (London, 1897), 20.
9. F. L. James, *The Unknown Horn of Africa: An Exploration from Berbera to the Leopard River* (London, 1888), 129.
10. *Ibid.,* 142.

was marked among all elements of Somali. The German linguist, A. W. Schleicher, unintentionally gave a clear example of this hatred of foreigners in the text of a story told him by a Somali informant:

> An Englishman from Mombasa said to me: "Take this money and go by ship to Kismayu. When you get there buy for me ivory, spears, and leopardskins."

> I went there and bought what he told me to . . . Then I went to the mosque . . . One man said, "Who is this man? He's never been in Kismayu before." Another man said, "Where do you come from?" I said from Mombasa. Then he said, "What do you want in Kismayu?"

> I answered, "A European gave me money and told me to buy leopardskins, ivory, lances and shields for him."

> Then he said: "You infidel! get out of our mosque!"

> Then I said, "Don't you know I'm a Muslim?" They replied, "If you are a Muslim, then why do you work for a European?"

> I said, "Is it forbidden to work for a European?" They said, "It is forbidden." [11]

In contrast to these incidents of hostility, Swayne discovered on his first journey to the Webi Shebelle river that "the mullahs are the traveller's best friends in Ogaden; they are intelligent, have great social influence, and are particularly useful in giving introductions, passing a traveller on from tribe to tribe." [12] Swayne found Seyyid Muhammad al-Dandarawi at his settlement on the *tug* Fafan in 1893. The venerable religious leader was then old and feeble, but still had a lively mind. A Dolbohanta headman accompanying Swayne claimed that when the Ethiopians shot at Seyyid Muhammad their bullets melted.

Yet one wonders how Swayne would have written the following paragraph if he could have anticipated the rise of Muhammad Abdullah Hassan:

> If he were a fighting man the Seyyid would probably have developed into a first-class Mahdi, and long ere this he could have made a combined movement against Abyssinia; but his influence, like that of other Somali sheikhs and mullahs, is almost entirely social and re-

11. A. W. Schleicher, *Somali-Texte* (Vienna, 1900), 10–13.
12. Swayne, *Seventeen Trips Through Somaliland*, 202.

ligious . . . Among the nomad tribes the fighting elders abound, but they have not the wide influence of these cosmopolitan Mahomedan priests, and, moreover, there is no element of cohesion among them, each working for the good of his own clan and ignoring the general interests of the community.[13]

By the late nineteenth century these religious settlements found their very existence threatened as the Ethiopians extended their influence from Harar into the Somali lands. The Ethiopians pursued a deliberate policy of destroying the *tariqa* settlements as they expanded into the Ogaden. Thus Vittorio Bòttego reported in 1893 a meeting with Muslim religious leaders from the Ogaden, "where all of their belongings had been looted by the Amhara." [14] At Kulunkul, once a large *tariq* community, Bòttego found nothing but an abandoned site, sacked by the Ethiopians. For this reason, it may be hypothesized, many of the Ogaden Somali turned to the Salihiya. Nor did Muhammad Abdullah Hassan fail to capitalize on the fear that non-Somali had of the Ethiopians. His forces consisted not only of Somali dervishes, but also of Negroid Adone Muslims from the region of Karanle on the Webi Shebelle — directly in the path of the invading Ethiopian army.

Muhammad Abdullah's Early Successes

According to information given by one of his sons, Muhammad Abdullah Hassan was born on April 7, 1864, in the vicinity of Kob Faradod, between Widwid and Bohotleh in northern Somalia. All the older sources attribute to him a mixed background of Bah Geri and Dolbohanta antecedents. Drake-Brockman and others present only guesses about his upbringing, and later official and semi-official works quote these early speculations as if they were factual accounts.[15] Lewis and Andrzejewski claim that Muhammad Abdullah's grandfather, Sheikh Hassan Nur, a Bah Geri Ogaden Somali, settled among the Dolbohanta in 1826.

13. *Ibid.*, 260.
14. Vittorio Bòttego, *L'Esplorazione del Giuba: Viaggio di Scoperta nel Cuore dell'Africa* (Rome, 1900), 24.
15. B. W. Andrzejewski and I. M. Lewis, *Somali Poetry: An Introduction* (Oxford, 1964), 53; Ralph E. Drake-Brockman, *British Somaliland* (London, 1912), 175–177.

After marrying a Dolbohanta woman, he raised a family and evidently spent the rest of his life in northern Somalia, where he died in 1874.

At the age of fifteen, Muhammad Abdullah followed in his grandfather's footsteps and began to teach the fundamentals of Islam. Within four years his ability as a teacher won him a reputation for his learning, as well as the honorary title of sheikh. Apparently at this time, Muhammad Abdullah left the Dolbohanta country and traveled for some eight years. It is claimed that he visited Harar, which was highly respected by the Somali as a great seat of Muslim learning, and Mogadishu, the southern center of Islam in Somalia.[16] Whether or not he visited the Sudan and Nairobi, as his son asserts, is unverifiable. If he did visit the Sudan, however, he may very well have been impressed by the Mahdist movement there.

After a brief return to northern Somalia, in 1894 Muhammad Abdullah set out on his travels again. This time he visited Mecca and perhaps Palestine. It should be noted that he traveled in the company of thirteen other sheikhs, an indication of both the strong connection between Somalia and the center of Islam and of the high regard in which Muhammad Abdullah was held. It is also significant that he visited Hejaz, where the Wahhabiya had its puritanical impact in the early nineteenth century. At Mecca the young scholar studied under Muhammad Salih and joined his *tariq*.

Upon his return to Berbera in 1895, Muhammad Abdullah began to preach the Salihiya message of reform and immediately ran into the opposition of the Qadariya. At the same time the Muslim reformer became keenly aware of Christian penetration into northern Somalia, which had become a nominal British protectorate between 1884 and 1886. A French Roman Catholic mission had been established just outside Berbera, and he accused the Lazarist fathers of deliberately stealing Somali children by converting Somali orphans from Islam. Despite his outspoken sermons and because of the strength of the Qadariya, Muhammad Abdullah made no great impression on the towns-people and soon withdrew from Berbera. In 1897 he again returned to the Dolbohanta to establish his own *jama'a* around

16. Andrzejewski and Lewis, *Somali Poetry*, 53–54.

the mosque he constructed at Kob Faradod. There he continued to denounce the Christian missionaries and accused the skeleton staff of British administrators in the Somaliland protectorate of tacitly supporting the Roman Catholic mission.

Among the Dolbohanta, Muhammad Abdullah played the traditional role of the politico-religious leader of the Muslim faithful. He served as a mediator in clan disputes and won a reputation among both the Somali and the British for his successes among the Dolbohanta. It may very well be that he succeeded in healing the breach between the southern and northern branches of the Dolbohanta, who had fought against each other for years. Jardine, the author of the semi-official British account of his activities, estimates that between two and four thousand Dolbohanta rallied to his *tariq* at this time.[17]

Soon Muhammad Abdullah's distaste for the activities of Europeans in Somalia grew into an increasing dissatisfaction with the British. In 1897, the year he returned to the Dolbohanta, the British government recognized the transfer to Ethiopia of a large tract of the Haud, an act that had ominous implications for the future of the nomadic Dolbohanta. Then in 1898, the British Foreign Office took over the administration of the protectorate. Hitherto the Somaliland protectorate had been administered through Aden by the Indian government's political resident for the Somali coast, with three assistants at Zeila, Bulhar, and Berbera. Although the British presence prior to that time had been only nominal, the transfer to the Foreign Office meant that a British consul-general, Colonel Hayes-Sadler, would now reside at Berbera. All told, there were still only 10 British officials and 130 Indian troops in the protectorate when Muhammed Abdullah broke with the British.[18]

In 1899, the British accused the Poor Man of God of sanctioning the theft of a rifle. Although the evidence is far from conclusive, it appears that the thief did seek sanctuary in Muhammad Abdullah's *jama'a*. Muhammad Abdullah would not go against custom and turn the thief over to the British. It is this incident that is generally considered to have been the immediate cause of his rupture of relations with the British administration and

17. Douglas Jardine, *The Mad Mullah of Somaliland* (London, 1923), 48.
18. *Ibid.,* 49.

his subsequent declaration of a jihad on all infidels — Christian Europeans, Christian Ethiopians, and even Muslim Somali who refused to join the Salihiya.

It is interesting to note that Muhammad Abdullah's first acts of hostility were not against the British, whose strength he apparently did not want to test, nor against the Qadariya Somali, whom he at first hoped to win over to his *tariq*, but against the Ethiopians and against the tribal enemies of the Dolbohanta, to whom he was also related by marriage. In March 1900, the Poor Man of God struck; his dervishes, who must have had the aid of Ishaak allies, attacked the new Ethiopian fort at Jijiga. To judge from British accounts of the attack, the Ethiopians were greatly shaken by the daring of the dervishes.[19] What they feared most was that Muhammad Abdullah might attempt to rally all the Muslims of the eastern marches in a massive jihad against the eastward-expanding empire of Menilek. Historically, they had reason to fear this, for Muhammad Abdullah Hassan appeared to be a modern incarnation of the sixteenth-century hero of the Muslim Danakil and Somali, Muhammad Ahmad Grañ.

Muhammad Abdullah's strategy was dictated by the fact that dissatisfaction was strongest among the tribes of the Ogaden, whose support he could gain best by an anti-Ethiopian offensive. Secondly, he may have been hoping to gain a stronger position vis-à-vis the Somali of the western part of the protectorate, whose support he had never attracted. Thirdly, his religious motivation must have played an important part. If the Salihiya were to expand, then it had to do so in conjunction with the Ahmadiya *jama'a* in the Ogaden, especially in the *tug* Fafan. These religious settlements were especially fearful of the Ethiopian advance, and they alone could command a loyalty overriding tribal differences. Lastly, he knew that large supplies of arms and ammunition had poured into Ethiopia from French sources over the past decade. Raids against the Ethiopians might increase the number of weapons available to the Salihiya dervishes.

Rather than follow up this initial success with a suicidal assault on Harar, Muhammad Abdullah aimed at domination of the whole of the Ogaden. Flushed with victory, he then raided

19. Great Britain, War Office, General Staff, *Official History of the Operations in Somaliland, 1901–1904* (London, 1905), I, 50–52.

Qadariya tribes with impunity. His wealth in camels, provisions, and rifles grew with each raid, as did his reputation. Soon trade in the Ogaden and the British protectorate came to a standstill, and the pastoral economy of British Somaliland began to suffer. The British authorities, so few in number, were frankly worried that his dervish followers had occupied the summer grazing grounds upon which loyal British Somali relied for survival.[20] But the British government, distracted by the Boer War and uprisings among the Jubaland Somali, did not act until May 1901.

The Ethiopian government, which had been thoroughly alarmed by the presence of zealous Muslim invaders forty miles from Harar, suggested a joint Anglo-Ethiopian campaign to put down the dervish movement. A force of fifteen thousand Ethiopians, a thousand loyal Somali, and a few hundred Anglo-Indian troops was soon assembled.[21] While the vast stretches of waterless country impeded the eastward advance of the Ethiopians, Muhammad Abdullah withdrew into the region of the Mudug oasis after two indecisive encounters with British forces. But the Mudug region was not safe because it was claimed by Sultan Yusuf Ali of Obbia, whose sultanate was an Italian protectorate. Muhammad Abdullah then moved northward into the territory of the Italian-protected sultanate of the Mijjertein, where he could rely on the friendliness of Sultan Osman Mahmud, who looked to the dervish leader as a potential ally against his old enemy, Yusuf Ali, and supplied him with rifles imported from Djibouti. But Lieutenant-Colonel Eric Swayne, leader of the British column, deliberately ignored instructions from London and pursued the dervishes across the Italian border into the Mijjertein. Before his troops returned to the British protectorate, they burned villages as a punitive measure. By the end of July 1901, the British column returned to Burao, having failed to capture Muhammad Abdullah or to weaken his position in the interior; Ethiopian operations had accomplished little more than to block any westward movement by the dervishes.

Within six months the man whom the British now called

20. Great Britain, War Office, General Staff, Intelligence Division, *Military Report on Somaliland* (1907), I, 127–129.
21. Francesco S. Caroselli, *Ferro e Fuoco nella Somalia* (Rome, 1931), 20.

the Mad Mullah had regrouped his forces and again raided "infidel" Somali villages in the British protectorate. In February 1902, Swayne collected some 2,300 men for a second expedition. After marching around the interior in search of Muhammad Abdullah for several months, the British force was taken by surprise when the dervishes attacked fifty miles northwest of Galkayu. British losses from this encounter in the dry bush country were heavy, and they retreated to Bohotleh to await reinforcements.

Yet a third expedition was undertaken in January 1903, with important consequences for the spread of the dervish movement into Italian territory. After the failure of the first two expeditions, the British made their plans more carefully. London decided to initiate a three-pronged Anglo-Italo-Ethiopian attack against the dervishes, but the Italians refused to commit themselves to expensive military operations. Italian public and government opinion was still affected by the disaster at Adwa in 1896. The Italians could not, however, completely ignore the British request for cooperation and permitted General W. H. Manning to land a British force at Obbia and to proceed inland. Italian ships were to observe the operations at Obbia, and a small military mission was to act in coordination with the British.

The British plan of attack called for Manning to land some 1,900 Central African, Sudanese, and Indian troops in late December 1902, while a second British column of 2,000 English, Indians, Somali, and Boers was to advance southeast from Berbera. The Ethiopians, with 5,000 men under Fitawrari Gabre and two English officers, were to march down the Webi Valley from Harar. At the end of March 1903, the two British columns linked up, without having encountered a single dervish. The Ethiopians successfully repelled a dervish attack at Burhilli on the Webi, about thirty miles north of Belet Wen, on April 4. A month later the rainy season began, and Muhammad Abdullah ordered his forces to press hard on the British. By the end of June, suffering from fatigue and transportation difficulties, the British withdrew to the area between Bohotleh and Berbera. The dervishes then swept from the Dolbohanta country to the Indian Ocean coast and occupied the whole Nogal Valley from Halin in British Somaliland to Illig on the sea.

In July 1903, the British replaced Manning and made plans for yet another expedition against Muhammad Abdullah. General Egerton, the new commanding officer, raised a force of almost 8,000 men, including some 6,800 Somali. Once again joint action was planned with the Ethiopians, and once again the British agreed to cooperate with the Obbians, who were resentful of Manning's high-handed treatment of their sultan. The campaign got under way early in January 1904, when Obbian troops occupied the strategic wells at Galkayu. On January 10, the British for the first time gave the dervishes a sharp defeat in an encounter at Jidbali, northeast of Bohotleh. On March 19, the British attacked the dervishes at Jid Ali, in the country of the Warsangeli. But if the British had hopes of gaining on Muhammad Abdullah, they were disappointed by his rapid movement eastward again into the Mijjertein. This proved to be a tactical error, for Osman Mahmud, his erstwhile ally, became alarmed by what he thought to be a dervish invasion of his territory. In a brief battle in the Darror Valley, he cut off Muhammad Abdullah from his forces at Illig. Then on April 21, two British cruisers and a gunboat landed five hundred men, who quickly took Illig. This time the British thought that success was in the offing. Magnanimously, they offered the Poor Man of God safe conduct into permanent exile at Mecca. Haji Muhammad did not even bother to acknowledge the British offer.[22]

There is little doubt that the Mad Mullah's movement was greatly aided by British mismanagement of the Somali protectorate. To judge from the memoirs of officers who participated in the campaigns against the dervishes and from the official military reports, one could easily agree with one young captain who wrote: "It's all a very badly run show . . . the very worst run show you could possibly conceive . . . an awful bauchle." [23] Clearly Manning mishandled the landing at Obbia and unnecessarily alienated the shrewd old sultan, Yusuf Ali. But there was also constant friction between the troops brought in from

22. Caroselli, *Ferro e Fuoco*, 57; Jardine makes no mention of this offer.
23. Margaret Miller (ed.), *A Captain of the Gordons: Service Experiences, 1900–1909, Comprising the Letters of Captain David S. Miller, the Gordon Highlanders, while acting as A. D. C. Boer War, 1900–1902, and Special Service Officer Somaliland Campaign, 1903–1905* (London, n.d.), 158, 163, 165.

India and the Somali irregulars and African troops of the King's
African Rifles. Lastly, there was the condescending attitude of
the British officer, a factor in understanding why the British so
thoroughly misjudged the dervish movement among the Somali:

> I wish my regiment could see me
> Now, jogging along in the sun
> With a lot of smelly Somalis
> Behind, screaming just for fun.
>
> . . .
>
> That is what we are
> Known as — we are
> The Shots to blame.
> If holes are made
> In a ghee bag, and nothing
> Left of the same, —
> Any shortage of rations, —
> "Stealing again" they say;
> "Flog some —— Somalis,
>   The men that run away." [24]

The fact that the Italians had not participated in military
operations on a large scale intrigued Muhammad Abdullah, who
saw in them a way out of his troubles. The Italian government
did not relish the prospect of an expensive military campaign
in northern Somalia; British experience had already indicated
on more than one occasion that the outcome of any expedition
against the dervishes was highly doubtful. When the Italian
foreign ministry solicited the opinion of Italian officials in East
Africa about the difficulties of "cooperation" with the British,
Commander Eugenio Finzi of the *Caprera* reported that the
Italians had made an error in getting involved in the British
campaign. "I wish I were mistaken," he wrote, "but I fear that
the expedition will end in a fiasco; the Mad Mullah will become a myth for the British, who never will corner him, and
a serious worry for the Benadir and our sphere of influence." [25]
Governor Dulio of the Benadir proposed the radical solution of
waging war not only on the dervishes, but also on the two

24. *Ibid.*, 219.
25. Archivio Storico dell'ex-Ministero dell'Africa Italiana (hereafter
ASMAI), pos. 59/3, f. 43, report by Commander Finzi of the *Caprera* to the
Foreign Minister, Obbia, Mar. 14, 1903.

difficult northern sultans; in contrast, Giulio Pestalozza, Italian consul at Aden, advocated the appointment of a high commissioner for northern Italian Somalia with officials stationed at Bender Kassim and Alula, the preservation of the friendly sultanate of Obbia, and the creation of a third sultanate in the Nogal under Muhammad Abdullah.[26] This solution appealed to the Italian foreign ministry. The Poor Man of God had sensed correctly the Italians' desire to settle the problem. He dispatched an envoy to the Italians, who gave him a receptive audience.

It was Muhammad Abdullah's good fortune that the Italian foreign ministry sent Giulio Pestalozza to negotiate. On October 16 and 17, Pestalozza, the first European to lay eyes on Muhammad Abdullah Hassan, met with him at Illig and listened to him with a sympathetic and attentive ear. Muhammad Abdullah was highly resentful of the English and the Mijjertein Somali. He was willing to negotiate a general peace: "My people and I will be the Italian government's people, and we shall be dependent on it, if it will favor us and . . . permit us to build a town on the coast." [27]

With the basis for negotiations established, Pestalozza then sought the approval of the Obbians, the Mijjertein Somali, and the British. On March 3, 1905, Pestalozza returned to Illig for final negotiations. Two days later he and Muhammad Abdullah signed an agreement of peace and protection.[28] The Poor Man of God, regarded by the British as a madman and an outlaw, became the legitimate ruler of the territory of the Nogal between the sultanates of Obbia and the Mijjertein. Thus he became the ruler of a third Italian protectorate in northern Somalia. On March 24, the British authorities at Berbera expressed their approval of the agreement, which also permitted the dervishes to enter part of the British protectorate for pasturage in the dry season.

By the Illig agreement, the Italians increased the number of their protectorates in northern Somalia to three, but the quality

26. ASMAI, pos. 59/4 f. 59, report from Pestalozza to the Foreign Minister, Illig, Jan. 22, 1905.

27. ASMAI, pos. 59/4, f. 58, declaration by the mullah to Pestalozza, Illig, Oct. 17, 1904.

28. E. Hertslet, *The Map of Africa by Treaty* (London, 1909), III, 1120–1122.

of each remained unchanged. The territory of Nogal, it is true, acted as a buffer state between Obbia and the Mijjertein. Moreover, the threat of a dervish invasion of the Benadir was removed at a time when Italy was particularly concerned over the future of southern Somalia. It remained to be seen, however, whether the dervish leader would foment trouble between his new protector and the dissident elements of the hinterland of the Benadir. If anything, the Italians gained time while Muhammad Abdullah refrained in his own interest from committing any overt acts of hostility.

The Restless Years: Resistance and Compromise

For the Italians their new protégé posed a serious threat, since he was regarded not only as a rebel against the British, but also as a potential revolutionary threatening the tenuous peace between the Somali and their British, Italian, and Ethiopian rulers. After the establishment of the Nogal protectorate, the Italians were more vulnerable to such threats than Great Britain and Ethiopia. In southern Somalia they faced the complex colonial problems of substituting direct government administration for rule by chartered company, occupying the interior, putting down revolts by the Bimal and Wadan Somali, and suppressing slavery. Compared to these tasks, Britain's problems in the Somaliland protectorate were relatively simple.

As the dervish movement continued to grow in size, its reputation attracted followers from among Italian-protected Somali. These Somali regarded the *tariq* settlement as a sanctuary; here Muhammad Abdullah Hassan had tradition on his side. But his camp in the Nogal also attracted other elements, especially "outlaw" Somali who fled from *dia* payments or other responsibilities. As the movement began to take on the characteristics of a large-scale phenomenon, the new recruits undermined the original religious spirit of the *jama'a*.

Although Muhammad Abdullah and his dervish followers had become Italian-protected subjects, raiding continued back and forth between the Nogal and its neighbors. The dervishes, like all northern Somali, needed pasturage and water for their animals. Because the Nogal was inadequate to support them, they had no choice but to resort to the age old Somali custom of intertribal raiding. Muhammad Abdullah found that his dervishes delighted in raiding the Italian-protected Hawiya and Rahanwein Somali. Both of these groups were traditional enemies of the Darod, and religious animosity and economic pressures strengthened intertribal hostility.

Even more significantly, the dervish movement acted as an inspiration for general resistance to the Europeans, as well as a source of arms and ammunition. The Italian fears for the future of the Benadir were based on the very real threat posed by dervish agitators who urged the Bimal and the Wadan to rebel. The dervishes had little to lose by acting as revolutionaries, for the southern Somali were already disturbed by Italian attempts to abolish slavery and domestic servitude. From 1904 to 1907, the Bimal were almost continuously in revolt against the Italians, who were confined to feeble beachheads in the ports.[29]

It was for this reason that the Italians granted Muhammad Abdullah protectorate status in the Nogal Valley. The prospect of tribal uprisings in the Benadir meant not only that the Italians would continue to be confined to the coast and the interior Somali would be weakened by intertribal warfare, but also that the way would be wide open for Ethiopian penetration. Indeed, in March 1905, even as negotiations were being concluded, an Ethiopian column under Leul Sagad advanced to within forty miles of Mogadishu. The Italians hoped that by buying off Muhammad Abdullah they would cut off the Bimal from their arms supply, and they watched with trepidation as Bimal messengers appealed to him for arms in February 1907. Even after the final defeat of the Bimal in March 1908, the Italians felt that "the influence of the Mullah still kept in ferment certain groups which were either hostile to us to begin with or were fearful of retaliation."[30] For six more months the Italians dreaded Bah Geri dervish intervention as they contended with other rebels north of Mogadishu.

An uneasy truce prevailed from 1905 to 1908, and both Ethi-

29. R. L. Hess, *Italian Colonialism in Somalia* (Chicago, 1966), 87–92.

30. Giacomo de Martino, *La Somalia nei tre anni del mio Governo* (Rome, 1912), 43–44.

opia and Italy had reservations about the future. From time to time Ethiopian troops moved into the Ogaden to contain the dervishes. All too often the Italians learned that Ethiopian commanders, far removed from communication with Addis Ababa or Harar, had diverted their expeditions toward the more prosperous country behind the Benadir. In 1907, the Ethiopians actually attacked and defeated Italian forces near Lugh.

Thus, the Italians had good cause for concern over the future of their Benadir colony. The dervishes gave every indication that they would follow the secular pattern of the Somali nomad, moving to the south from the arid Mijjertein and Ogaden grazing lands to the comparatively greener lands of southern Somalia. While the Bimal revolt was at its peak, the Italians detected Muhammad Abdullah's influence on the rebels, for, the 1905 agreement notwithstanding, the Italian colonial government distrusted the Poor Man of God. Dervish activities in the Webi Valley were evidence enough that he would eventually cause trouble again.

The Italians, in fact, began to see the weakness of their own position. By recognizing Muhammad Abdullah Hassan as a political leader in the Nogal, they had inadvertently helped to increase the respect for him among Somali of all tribes. Although most of his followers were Darod Somali from the Dolbohanta and the Bah Geri Ogaden, his political influence extended even into non-Darod areas where he had been unsuccessful as a religious leader. It is clear that Muhammad Abdullah had become a symbol of revolt for all Somali, the living incarnation of their concept of freedom from all foreign influences. And for the Italians, "dervish" came to mean "rebel," and their Bimal and Wadan subjects — who cared not one whit for his religious message — understood the nature of his political triumph. Dervish messengers actively supplied the Bimal with guns sent by Muhammad Abdullah. On more than one occasion the Italians learned with dismay that his followers were spreading the word of revolt among the southern Somali.

If the dervishes were to be kept apart from the rebellious Bimal, then the Italians had to depend on the forces of Obbia and the Mijjertein to contain them in the north, while their small Benadir force "peacefully" occupied the middle Webi Shebelle to forestall the possibility of a Bimal–Bah Geri alliance.

But as the Obbians and the Mijjertein Somali tightened their circle about the Nogal, which both sultans had long coveted, Muhammad Abdullah strengthened his bonds with the Bah Geri and reached out to the Warsangeli for a useful alliance.

Italian officers with long experience in Somalia early sensed the futility of their policy. They could not suppress the illegal trade in arms and ammunition. Yusuf Ali and Osman Mahmud were not trustworthy; it was rumored that both sultans were playing an intricate game of duplicity with the Ethiopians and the British. The only real solution to the problem was one that the Italian government could not afford. Without an expensive military expedition, Italian officials could only lament: "From the political point of view our position could not be worse." "I have the impression that not only is our present position in Somalia false, but it is also beginning to be ridiculous." "Nobody takes the word *protectorate* seriously." [31]

Six months after the final defeat of the Bimal in March 1908, the dervishes made a major attack on Obbian territory. Their first move was to occupy the Mudug oases in search of badly needed water for their herds. From that new base they could then hope to renew contact with the Bah Geri. Their second move, in conjunction with the Warsangeli, was to invade the British protectorate again. Raid followed raid, and the uneasy truce of 1905–1908 came to an end.

When Gino Macchioro, the Italian consul at Aden, attempted to meet with Muhammad Abdullah Hassan, he was refused permission to land. The Poor Man of God was no longer convinced of the good intentions of the Italians, and Macchioro did not dare put ashore at Illig lest he be taken as a hostage. Bitterly disappointed, he recommended the renewal of warfare in alliance with the British, Ethiopians, and loyal Somali. At the same time, after the dervishes had again invaded their protectorate, the British made plans to take the field. Three British warships were sent to the Somali coast, a force of four thousand men was amassed, and orders given for the military occupation of the interior.[32]

31. ASMAI, pos. 59/4, f. 59, Cappello to the Foreign Minister, Aden, Mar. 20, 1906; *ibid.*, Aug. 15, 1906; T. Carletti, *I Problemi del Benadir* (Viterbo, 1912), 324.

32. ASMAI, pos. 59/5, f. 80, Relazione Macchioro sulla sua missione nelle coste della Somalia Settentrionale, 1908.

Before the Italians engaged in military operations against the dervishes, they made one last attempt to undercut Muhammad Abdullah's power. One of his close advisers, Abdullah Shahari, had recently defected after a dispute over his marriage to a Mijjertein woman. Apparently on his own, Abdullah Shahari went to Mecca and obtained from Muhammad Salih, Muhammad Abdullah's venerable teacher, a letter tantamount to excommunication of the dervish leader: "From this moment on I wish to have nothing to do with you and your people. I will not write to you again, and I do not want you to write to me. Those who follow the path of God have his protection, but those who do evil shall surely be punished." [33] After consulting with Italian and British authorities at Aden, Abdullah Shahari sailed to Illig to deliver Muhammad Salih's message.

The reaction in Muhammad Abdullah's camp was electrifying. When the *Qadi* of Illig and eight other men sided with Muhammad Salih, Muhammad Abdullah angrily ordered their execution on the spot. Confusion reigned. Despite the protestations of loyal dervishes that the letter of excommunication was a forgery, more than four hundred dervishes quit the movement and departed for their tribal areas. Only in southern Somalia, where the Italians had suppressed Somali uprisings, were the charges against Muhammad Abdullah accepted. In the north, he suffered only a temporary loss of prestige, quickly recovered after the British sent Sir Reginald Wingate and Rudolf Slatin Pasha on a vain mission to negotiate peace with the dervishes. Was war to be the only alternative open to his enemies?

A campaign to end the threat of Muhammad Abdullah and his dervishes once and for all was destined never to materialize. The British and Italian parliaments were unwilling to approve the large investment that such an undertaking required, and the Ethiopian government was paralyzed by Menilek's illness. On November 12, 1909, a disastrous new policy was implemented. When the policy was in full effect by March 1910, the British had completely evacuated the interior, concentrated their mea-

---

33. An Italian translation of the Arabic letter appears in Caroselli, *Ferro e Fuoco*, 129–131, and an English translation in Jardine, *Mad Mullah*, 184–185. The English text is not entirely accurate.

ger forces on the coast, and armed friendly tribes against the impending onslaught of almost ten thousand dervishes.[34]

The immediate effect of the policy of withdrawal was large-scale resumption of intertribal raiding. Habr Toljaala clans fought among themselves, while the Habr Yunis raided Ogaden tribes across the border in Ethiopia. Soon civil war broke out among the Aidagalla and between the two main divisions of the Habr Yunis; the Dolbohanta raided the Habr Toljaala, and the Mijjertein Somali made frequent incursions into the territory of their neighbors, unmindful of the concern of their Ethiopian, British, or Italian rulers, who were soon compelled to return to the policies in effect before 1905.

By July 1910, the pressures of Mijjertein raiding and of a prolonged drought led Muhammad Abdullah Hassan to move westward in search of food and ammunition. Gradually the dervish pressure on the Warsangeli and other tribes of the British protectorate was stepped up, and by March 1912, the dervishes had retaken Bohotleh and had occupied much of the eastern half of British Somaliland. Although the British felt that Muhammad Abdullah was acting out of desperation and that his successes were attributable to surprise attacks and to the terror inspired by atrocities and mutilations, they grudgingly admitted that the friendly Somali were generally demoralized and that "the old dread of the dervish name has reappeared." [35] After a restless period as ruler of an Italian protectorate followed by two years of operations limited by a shortage of ammunition, Muhammad Abdullah Hassan again had raised high the banner of revolt.

"A Force in the Land to Be Reckoned With"

The second decade of Muhammad Abdullah's struggle against foreign domination differed in several significant aspects from earlier phases of resistance, compromise, and nomadism. Before 1911, Muhammad Abdullah was an international problem. After his withdrawal from the Nogal Valley territory, the Italians

34. Memorandum by Commissioner Byatt, Berbera, April 30, 1912, in Great Britain, Cmd. 5000, *Correspondence Relating to Affairs in Somaliland* (London, 1910), 1–3.

35. *Ibid.*, 4.

tended to regard him purely as a British problem; they had
achieved their limited "negative purpose of preventing the expansion [of the mullah southward]." [36] There is also some evidence that his health had deteriorated, and this may help to
account for his increasing cruelty in his last years. Whereas
Muhammad Abdullah had been in the prime of life in 1900
and was then described as "dark-coloured, tall and thin, with
a small goatee beard," he seems to have changed greatly by 1912,
when informants told the British that he had become so heavy
that he could mount his steed only with great effort.[37]

After his return to British Somaliland, Muhammad Abdullah
began to reach much further afield for allies. In June 1912, he
made overtures to the Ethiopians at Harar; two years later he
followed this up with protracted negotiations for a marriage
alliance with the Muslim-leaning Ethiopian Emperor Lij Eyyasu.
Some modus vivendi with the Ethiopians was essential, for he
could no longer count on the Warsangeli and the Mijjertein
Somali for a steady flow of arms and ammunition smuggled in
from French Djibouti or from southern Arabia. To procure
arms, Muhammad Abdullah sent his uncle, Amir, to the country of the faithful Bah Geri, who dispatched a caravan from
Wardair (near Walwal) with food, clothing, and ammunition
procured from Ethiopian sources.[38]

Once reestablished in the British protectorate, Muhammad
Abdullah actively courted those tribes which had remained
loyal to the British and hostile to his movement. With the
evacuation of the interior, the protectorate experienced a fluid
political situation approaching anarchy. The British had all but
abandoned the friendly Somali to the advancing dervishes. At
one time even Muhammad Abdullah found the situation too
difficult to handle. In December 1912, he wrote to the British
commissioner in Berbera that "most of the dervishes have got
beyond my control, and frequently raid the people without my
orders." [39] In his frequent letters to his Somali opponents, his
arguments were designed to gain new adherents:

36. Martino, *La Somalia nei tre anni del mio Governo*, 44.
37. Letter from Commissioner Byatt to Secretary of State, Berbera, Feb. 5,
1913, in *Correspondence . . . Somaliland*, 26.
38. *Ibid.*, Nov. 14, 1912, 12–13.
39. The text of this letter appears in Jardine, *Mad Mullah*, 209.

It is no offence in you to fight the infidels and hypocrites, for fighting them is the duty of every Moslem. You are Moslems, and they are infidels, and it is not good to repent of annoying the infidels.

I am a pilgrim and a holy fighter, and have no wish to gain power and greatness in this world, neither am I of the Dolbahanta, the Warsangeli, the Mijjertein, nor the Ogadein. And I am not of the hypocrites. I am a dervish, hoping for God's mercy and consent and forgiveness and guidance, and I desire that all the country and the Moslems may be victorious by God's grace.

This is a time in which corruption and adultery spread, this is a time in which the infidels defeat the Moslems . . . It is a time in which the learned men do serve the Christians. This is the end of all things. May God guide us.

Regret not what you have lost, for God will compensate you fully in this world or in the Resurrection, or both.[40]

But the Poor Man of God was constantly troubled by defectors and unreliable allies, as he had been in earlier years. For this reason, it is impossible to know how many followers he could command at any given moment. The number of his followers increased or decreased in accordance with the rise or fall of his prestige. Their numbers must have greatly risen after forty mounted dervishes daringly raided Berbera on March 13, 1914, and threw the town into considerable confusion.

Meanwhile, Muhammad Abdullah depended less and less on the shifting *harun,* or military camp. As he gained effective control over the Dolbohanta-Warsangeli-Habr Yunis-Habr Toljaala lands, he constructed a number of fortified towns. The strongest of these was at Taleh, thirty miles west of Halin, commanding the head of the Nogal Valley and the north-south route in that part of Somaliland. Because the Somali dervishes had little or no building skills, Muhammad Abdullah imported Arab masons from southern Arabia. At Taleh, a number of forts were built, with walls as much as fourteen feet thick at the base and towers rising to a height of more than sixty feet. Each fortification of the main enclosure and each of thirteen subsidiary structures had its own wells and granaries. From 1913 to 1920 Taleh served as the semi-permanent capital of the

40. Translation of an Arabic letter from Muhammad Abdullah to the Gadwein tribe, n.d., received in Berbera, Jan. 20, 1913, in *Correspondence . . . Somaliland,* 24–25.

dervish theocracy. Lesser forts, equally impressive in their massive strength, were constructed at Jid Ali and Madisha to the northwest of Taleh.

To protect the friendly tribes, the British organized a small mobile striking force based at Berbera. Its main purpose was to keep the roads to Berbera clear. In 1912, the Somaliland Camel Corps under Richard Corfield became the weak symbol of British sovereignty in Somaliland. Hopefully, the British commissioner wrote, "As the friendly dreads the dervish, so the dervish dreads camelry." [41] Yet the Camel Corps could do little more than engage in punitive measures against intertribal raiders near Berbera. At best the British could claim that the Camel Corps' presence assured the security of caravan routes by July 1913. They seemed to have had little awareness that the caravan trade was essential not only for the coastal Somalis, but also for the Ogaden in the interior and for the dervishes, all of whom benefited from trade in food, cloth, and guns. The weakness of the British position became apparent on August 9, 1913, when a force of dervishes led by Au Yusuf Abdullah Hassan, Muhammad Abdullah's brother, utterly defeated the Camel Corps at Dul Madoba. Corfield, having overstepped the boundaries of his very limited orders, paid for his daring with his life. The death of Corfield, immortalized in Somali poetry, placed the dervishes within twelve miles of Burao, at the crossroads of central British Somaliland.[42] Dervish scouts seemed to be everywhere. Regretfully, Acting Commissioner Archer wrote: "There can be no doubt at all, then, in the light of present knowledge, that the dervishes, so far from being a negligible quantity, are a force in the land to be reckoned with . . . As fighters they are still possessed of extraordinary courage, and . . . they are fully imbued with the old fanatical spirit." [43] If Dul Madoba had not been fought, the British might have salvaged their prestige among the Somali.

41. Memorandum by Byatt on the political situation in Somaliland in April 1912, in *Correspondence . . . Somaliland*, 5.

42. Andrzejewski and Lewis, *Somali Poetry*, 70–74, "You have died, Corfield, and are no longer in this world,/ A merciless journey was your portion."

43. Acting Commissioner Archer's memorandum on present situation, Aug. 27, 1913, in Great Britain, Cmd. 7566, *Further Correspondence Relating to Affairs in Somaliland* (London, 1914), 3.

If, on the eve of World War I, the British felt that Muhammad Abdullah could drive them into the sea if he chose to, the Italians found themselves for the first time relatively secure in their hold over their Somali subjects. As the peaceful penetration of the Benadir continued, Italian troops undercut the influence of the Bah Geri in the middle Webi Shebelle Valley. The occupation of Bulo Burti in May 1914 gave them an advance post against the Bah Geri, who were then led by another brother of Muhammad Abdullah, Khalifa. Although the Bah-Geri continued to harass the Bantu tribes along the river and to preach religious revival and political revolt among the Italian-protected Hawiya Somali, they felt the pressure of the Italian advance. When the Obbians, under Italian leadership, occupied the Mudug oases in 1915 the Bas Geri were cut off from contact with the main body of the dervishes. From the Italian point of view, the dervish movement had been contained.

Like the sixteenth-century Muslim leader, Muhammad Ahmad Grañ, Muhammad Abdullah Hassan represented the Muslim threat to Christian Ethiopia. After the death of Menilek in 1913 and the accession of Lij Eyyasu, the dervish movement became a cause of grave preoccupation for the Amhara. The young Lij Eyyasu was playing a dangerous game in a land where rivalry between Christianity and Islam had been rife for more than five centuries. Pressed on by his German and Turkish advisers, the emperor became more and more identified with the cause of Islam. Rumors reached Mogadishu of Ethiopian Muslim leaders in the camp of Muhammad Abdullah and of the expected conversion of Lij Eyyasu to Islam. The British and the Italians soon realized that an alliance between the Muslims of Ethiopia and Muhammad Abdullah's dervishes almost certainly would aim at "liberating" their lands from the Christian Europeans and the Amhara.[44] When Lij Eyyasu announced his conversion to Islam in April 1916, their fears appeared to materialize. But Lij Eyyasu's Islamic tendencies had already unleashed a storm of opposition within Ethiopia, and on September 27 he was deposed and forced to flee into the Danakil country.

European fears of a Muslim alliance were not baseless, for

44. ASMAI, pos. 59/8, f. 118 passim, "Situazione politica, 1915–1916."

Lij Eyyasu *had* contacted the Poor Man of God and arranged a marriage with one of Muhammad Abdullah's daughters. Six weeks before his fall, Lij Eyyasu had sent his agents from Harar to Taleh to return with his Somali bride, and only his precipitous flight prevented the celebration of the marriage. The emperor had already given indication of a willingness to come to terms with the Somali by installing a completely Muslim administration at Harar, and for a time he had a strong attraction for the Ogaden Somali. The chances for a Muslim coup in Ethiopia in combination with the Salihiya, however, disappeared with the suppression of Lij Eyyasu's Muslim supporters in the aftermath of his fall. Although a successful Muslim axis between Harar and Taleh was most unlikely, European fears were kept alive by the sporadic contacts that continued between the deposed emperor and Ethiopian and Somali Muslims.

The British and Italians became fully aware of the implications of the Muslim alignment when they intercepted a dervish messenger.[45] Curiously, Muhammad Abdullah denied any contact with the Ethiopian Muslims. Whether or not he was acting rationally is unclear, for by this time he was applying the term "infidel" indiscriminately to all his personal and political enemies. In March 1917, the British received a lengthy letter from him refuting their charges:

> It was suggested that we were in communication with Lijj Iasu and had dealings with the Germans and the Sultan of Turkey; that feeling weak we required assistance . . . It is you who have joined with all the peoples of the world, with harlots, with wastrels, and with slaves, just because you are so weak. But if you were strong, you would have stood by yourself as we do, independent and free. It is a sign of your weakness, this alliance of yours with Somalis, Yibir [an outcaste tribe living among the Darod], and Perverts, and Arabs, and Nubis, and Indians and Baluchis, and French and Russians, and Americans, and Italians, and Serbians, and Portuguese, and Japanese, and Greeks and Cannibals [*sic*], and Sikhs and Banias, and Moors and Afghans and Egyptians. They are strong and it is because of your weakness that you have had to solicit as does a prostitute. So much my answer to you.[46]

45. The Italian consul in Harar informed the governor of Eritrea of Lij Eyyasu's relations with Muhammad Abdullah on Aug. 14, 1916. See Caroselli, *Ferro e Fuoco*, 219.

46. The full text of this letter appears in Jardine, *Mad Mullah*, 249.

The haughty Muhammad Abdullah, however, was not above exploring the possibilities of any alliance offered him. Italian authorities in the Mijjertein sultanate discovered correspondence between him and the Turkish commander in southern Arabia in the summer of 1917. The captured documents clearly indicated that Muhammad Abdullah had solicited foreign aid and was willing to place himself under Turkish protection.[47]

Only after World War I ended could the British do more than barely hold on to their protectorate. The Ishaak Somali had continuously opposed the dervishes and helped to confine the activities of the Salihiya to southeastern British Somaliland, where the dervishes gradually decreased in number as warriors drifted back to their clans rather than stagnate in the unfamiliar environment of Taleh, Madisha, or Jid Ali. Ignored by the Qadariya Somali, by the British, by the Italians, and by the Ethiopians, the dervish movement lost its strength. Muhammad Abdullah, unable to lead a jihad, found that peace was his worst enemy, and he too passed his peak strength. The British governor of the protectorate was now confident that limited military operations could achieve the final defeat of the dervishes.

In October 1919, the British cabinet approved a plan of operations against the dervishes. The Somaliland Camel Corps, which had been reorganized after Corfield's disaster, was comprised of eighteen British officers and five hundred Somalis. In addition to this colonial military force, there were on hand the four hundred men of the Somaliland Indian contingent and a temporary garrison of four hundred men of the Indian infantry.[48] Augmenting these forces were an additional fifteen hundred tribesmen and "Z" unit of the Royal Air Force. Pleased with the performance of the air force in the European war, the Colonial Office was confident that aerial bombardment would thoroughly disrupt the dervishes and prepare the way for the land forces, which would then destroy the dervishes once and for all. There was every reason to believe that the time to strike had arrived. Muhammad Abdullah had alienated a large segment of the Dolbohanta, and the defection of the Khayr, a clan

47. The Arabic original and the Italian translation of the related correspondence appear in Caroselli, *Ferro e Fuoco*, 222–225.
48. Jardine, *Mad Mullah*, 239.

of *wadads* who collectively had a religious prestige almost equal to that of the Poor Man of God, was a blow from which he could not easily recover.

The new British tactics were successful. Although "Z" squadron was not able to destroy the fortresses at Madisha, Jid Ali, or Taleh with its relatively feeble twenty-pound bombs, it did spread terror among the dervishes beginning January 25, 1920. Uncertain of this new turn of events, Muhammad Abdullah retreated from Madisha to the southeast. Early in February, the Camel Corps captured a group of dervishes that included his wives and sons, but the Mad Mullah's whereabouts were unknown. The elusive Muhammad Abdullah again had escaped capture. When Taleh fell on February 12, the British found within its walls more than six hundred captured rifles. There they also discovered the dervish leader's Turkish adviser Muhammad Ali, as well as a group of Arab masons who, after building the fortress, had been held as prisoners and perhaps slaves.

It was commonly feared that Muhammad Abdullah was heading for the Ogaden. There he would be safely in Ethiopian territory and could make for the Bah Geri lands. Dervishism among the Somali again seemed dead, but as long as Muhammad Abdullah Hassan was at large, there remained the danger that the movement could again come to life. Once more the British hoped to negotiate. Acting Commissioner Archer hoped to get him "to settle down in his own *tarika* in the Protectorate, where he would be under control." [49] Accordingly, a deputation of three influential sheikhs and seven loyal Somali clan leaders were sent, against their will, to meet with the dreaded Mad Mullah. Included in the groups were Abdullahi Madar, son and successor of Sheikh Madar of Hargeisa, and Ismail Ishaak, one of Muhammad Salih's most important disciples in Somaliland.

The fearful Somali leaders were given safe conduct to the dervish encampment at Shinileh. According to one British account, the man they met there, corpulent and about six feet tall, seemed to be insane and threatened them: "None of you are Muslims; you are all infidels. No one can read the Koran as I do, and it is written there that all the followers of the English, the

49. Geoffrey Archer, *Personal and Historical Memoirs of an East African Administrator* (Edinburgh, 1963), 108.

Italians, and the Ethiopians are infidels. The Salihiya, too, are infidels. Muhammad Salih himself was a pauper from the Sudan, a petition writer. I made him what he was." [50] There was no coming to terms with him, and the deputation returned to Burao on May 26. The possibility remained that Muhammad Abdullah might regroup his dervishes in the Ogaden for a new invasion.

It was important that Muhammad Abdullah not be permitted to reenter the British protectorate, and a tribal levy of three thousand loyal Somali was hastily assembled at Bohotleh, crossed the unmarked Ethiopian border, and moved in the direction of the Fafan, where Muhammad Abdullah's camp had been set up. At the end of July they attacked the camp, and more than seven hundred dervishes, weakened by a smallpox epidemic which had already claimed the lives of Muhammad Abdullah's eldest son Mahdi and his brother Khalifa, died in battle. The dervish threat had been real enough, for the tribal levy captured some sixty thousand head of stock, a rough indication of the gathering strength of the Dervish-Ogaden concentration in eastern Ethiopia. The Poor Man of God, however, was not to be found among the dead.

Shortly after the dawn attack, Muhammad Abdullah and a handful of his closest followers fled the camp. After wandering about for several months, attracting several hundred followers, he established his camp at Imi on the Webi Shebelle. But if the British and their Somali tribal levy could not take him, death could. He died at the age of fifty-six, a victim of either pneumonia, influenza, or malaria. His date of death has been variously fixed at November 23, December 21, or early January 1921.[51]

How Mad Was the "Mad Mullah"?

To analyze the character of Muhammad Abdullah Hassan would require access to materials that do not exist. Few Euro-

---

50. *Ibid.*, 110–111.
51. The November date is given by Jardine, *Mad Mullah*, 307. Italian sources are consistent in the January date: see Caroselli, *Ferro e Fuoco*, 299. Andrzejewski and Lewis, *Somali Poetry*, 55, give the December date on the basis of information from Muhammad Abdullah's son, Sheikh Abdurrahman Muhammad, and his brother Sheikh Hassan Abdullah.

peans ever saw the elusive Poor Man of God. Until an oral-history project can fully exploit Somali memories of the twenty eventful years of his revolt, he must be judged by what may be found in European accounts and in his own writings.

Muhammad Abdullah Hassan cast himself in the role of religious reformer. Circumstances permitted him to become a political leader, while European and Ethiopian opposition helped him to develop as a successful military commander. His poetry, preserved in its Arabic written form and still sung in its Somali oral form and transmitted from one generation to the next, reveals yet another facet of his character. Taken together, these activities made him the most important Somali of his generation. Small wonder that the contemporary Somali regard him as the father of Somali nationalism. His movement was, in the words of I. M. Lewis, "the main event in the modern history of Northern Somaliland" before the advent of an independent Somali Republic in 1960.[52]

As a religious leader, Muhammad Abdullah Hassan was in keeping with the spirit of reform that swept Islam from the time of the Wahhabiya in the early nineteenth century. His condemnation of worldly pleasures, tobacco, kat, and adultery clearly identifies him with puritanical Islam and the religious revival evidenced in the *tariqa* movement among the Somali. Moreover, he shared the disquiet of Arab Muslims when confronted with the apparent superiority of the Christian West. The beginning of Muhammad Abdullah's revolt against the West may be traced to his first contact with Christians, in this case the Lazarist fathers in Berbera in 1899.

Although Muhammad Abdullah was aware of the revolt against the British in the Sudan, he did not cast himself in the same role as the Sudanese *mahdi*. The British and the Italians later assumed that he styled himself *mahdi*, but this was not so. His correspondence indicates that he preferred to call himself *seyyid*, the honorific employed by learned men. Nor did he apparently think of his movement initially as a political movement. His followers, who were urged to drop their clan and tribal affiliations, were called *Darāwīsh*, and the dervish uniform of white robe and turban called attention to their religious purity and dedication.

52. Lewis, *Pastoral Democracy*, 25.

Nonetheless, Muhammad Abdullah's followers evidently did regard him as both their religious and their political leader. This was in keeping with both the Somali *tariqa* system and with Islamic tradition. Their loyalty to the Poor Man of God went beyond the rational to the emotional and even the fanatic, permitting him to assume absolute power. His exceptional military prowess, his successful use of cavalry and guerrilla tactics, won him a reputation as a warrior and further enhanced his religious charisma. His military successes explain in part why the attempt to excommunicate him in 1909 failed.

As a religious movement, Seyyid Muhammad's *tariq* strongly opposed the waywardness and laxity of the Qadariya Somali, many of whom resented the puritanical doctrines of the Salihiya. For this reason, as well as for reasons of tribal loyalty, most Qadariya Somali remained pro-British throughout the revolt. That the conflict had a religious motivation is also demonstrated by Muhammad Abdullah Hassan's bitter condemnation of the Qadariya in his sermons and poetry. Indeed, he went so far as to sanction the assassination of Qadariya Sheikh Uways by his Bah Geri followers. Even now, so deep is this religious cleavage in Somali society that adherents of the two *tariqa* clashed head on in a bloody exchange in the Haud as recently as 1955. During Muhammad Abdullah's revolt, religious divisions served to sharpen traditional tribal antagonisms, and the success of the *tariq* in furthering its proclaimed goal of religious solidarity was therefore limited by divisions between tribes and clans. Nevertheless, until the modern establishment of Somalia as a nation-state, the *tariq* was the sole means of unifying Somali of different genealogical loyalties.

Muhammad Abdullah did not organize his movement into a strict political system; in traditional Somali fashion, he kept administration to a minimum. But although no bureaucratic or administrative apparatus developed, he and his lieutenants maintained their political power through the strict discipline of the Salihiya and the war camp. Thus the two criteria by which he measured his followers were strict observance of Muslim law and loyalty to him and his lieutenants. Loyalty and devotion to the Poor Man of God were intended to be stronger than the attraction of the clan, and for this reason he deliberately distinguished between his followers, whom he never called anything but dervishes, and his tribal enemies, whom he always referred to disparagingly as "the Somali."

Because the movement could not always overcome Somali clannishness, Seyyid Muhammad often found it to his advantage to use kinship ties as bases for his political alliance system. It is no coincidence that his movement was strongest first among the Dolbohanta of his mother and second among the Bah Geri of his father. Nor did he refrain from two other traditional means of winning allies. As a religious man, he was often called upon to mediate intertribal or interclan disputes; it was as a successful mediator that he first came to the notice of the British. Success in mediating a dispute gained him respect and additional followers. A shrewd political leader, he used marriage ties as a means of cementing alliances with tribes and clans with whom his relations were poor. Lewis points out that Muhammad Abdullah contracted more than twelve politically useful marriages.[53] His marriage contracts built a web of traditional relationships with as varied individuals as Sultan Osman Mahmud of the Mijjertein and Emperor Lij Eyyasu of Ethiopia.

As a military leader, Muhammad Abdullah Hassan demonstrated great skill and resourcefulness. Although the British troops were considerably better armed than his own dervishes, they were never able to meet the dervishes in open battle. They could not force the Mullah to fight when he or his lieutenants were unwilling. Whenever a large force entered the area dominated by Muhammad Abdullah, the dervishes withdrew before them. If the British commander unwisely chose to divide his men, the smaller groups would be outnumbered and overwhelmed by the dervishes who had been waiting for this opportunity. Like Napoleon, he rarely fought unless he was assured of numerical superiority. If the British commander chose to advance with his whole force, he found that nature was a staunch ally of the dervishes. Lack of water invariably plagued the British forces.

British irregulars and Somali tribesmen could not effectively counter Muhammad Abdullah's series of skirmishes, raids, and surprise attacks. Like other Somali, the dervishes generally attacked at dawn or in the afternoon, when the men of a tribe were

53. Andrzejewski and Lewis, *Somali Poetry,* 55.

off raiding other tribes. First Muhammad Abdullah would send in his scouts, then raiders in groups of from twenty to two hundred would move in. The raiders, traveling quickly on their ponies, carried only a small water bottle and some dried meat. Unencumbered by equipment, they could rapidly cover as much as seventy miles in a half day. On their return, they moved as scattered parties protected by a strong rearguard.

In battle, the dervish spearmen formed the first line in single rank at a one-pace interval. On the flanks were the cavalry — usually the tribal elders — the slingers, and the riflemen. In the second line were Midgan archers, and more spearman. The horsemen, slingers, and riflemen came into action first, after which the dervishes threw their short spears. Then the warriors rushed the enemy, shouting their war cry in the name of Muhammad Salih and wielding their long spears, swords, and clubs. The tactics were no different than those of most Darod Somali. Only the religious enthusiasm of the dervishes set them apart.[54]

After battle the enemy dying and dead were often mutilated. The poetry of Muhammad Abdullah Hassan has more then one reference to the emasculation of enemies. In all fairness to Seyyid Muhammad, it must be recognized that mutilation was not unusual in Somali warfare. In 1854, Speke noted that the Dolbohanta, who later became the most ardent followers of Muhammad Abdullah, "observe the Galla practice of murdering pregnant women in hopes of mutilating a male fetus." [55] The Ogaden tribes too customarily mutilated enemy dead. In the eyes of the British such behavior only confirmed their predisposition to regard the Somali as barbaric and the Mad Mullah as bloodthirsty. Yet the Ethiopians, to whom the practice was not completely alien, and the Italians, who to their misfortune had learned of the custom at Adwa, make no mention of it. If the practice became more widespread during Muhammad Abdullah's lifetime, one can only assume that increased warfare offered increased opportunities. It may also be suggested that Muhammad Abdullah Hassan, who owed so much to Arab Muslim influence, might have encouraged the practice, which was sanctioned by Arab custom. At any rate, the British, after meeting the dervishes on the battlefield, were

54. *Military Report on Somaliland*, I, 164.
55. Burton, *First Footsteps*, II, 133.

horrified to discover the mutilated bodies of those who had fallen. Muhammad Abdullah knew how to instill fear in his enemies.

Intertribal warfare was an integral part of the nomadic Somali's life, and intertribal raiding was an accepted means of increasing the size of one's herds. By far the vast majority of the dervishes depended on their herds for their livelihoods, although their leader encouraged them to engage in agriculture or trade. By 1904, when the dervishes moved in the direction of the Nogal, the traditional pattern of raiding had reasserted itself. In that year, the Omar Mahmud, a tribe occupying the area just south of the Nogal Valley, raided a great number of camels belonging to Muhammad Abdullah's followers. The dervishes naturally sought revenge and restitution, and in the following raiding season surprised the Omar Mahmud throughout the length and breadth of their tribal territory. When the Omar Mahmud were taken by surprise again in 1906, they sent 370 warriors after their lost herds. So bloody was the ensuing battle, that only ninety Omar Mahmud returned from the encounter. But if intertribal raiding accounted for most of the warfare between the dervishes and the other Somali, Muhammad Abdullah also had a political reason for nearly annihilating a group of the Omar Mahmud — they were allies of Sultan Yusuf Ali of Obbia.

Razzia and vendetta were commonplace in Somalia, but by 1912 the Omar Mahmud were so weakened that they sided with the dervishes against their old ally in Obbia. But they were no longer able to defend themselves against any attacker, and many of their women were captured. One suspects that in this fashion the dervish wars contributed to the extinction of many lineage groups. Moreover, the raids were multilateral. In 1917, Sultan Yusuf Ali of Obbia sent a large expedition to raid the southern dervishes' flocks near the Webi Shebelle; and for the first time in their history the Mijjertein Somali penetrated through Hawiya lands as far as the river.

Politics, raiding, and tribalism went hand in hand. In 1919, the sultan gave refuge to the Khayr, a Dolbohanta clan of *wadads* known for their great number of learned religious men. Their defection was a great loss for Muhammad Abdullah, and many of them enlisted in the sultan's service. The wrath of the Poor Man of God was soon unleashed on Obbia, for the refugee Khayr had fled with large numbers of his own camels. For two years, raiding went on back and forth between the Obbians and the dervishes, who were now based in the Ogaden. It is significant that tribalism undermined these new alliances; the Obbian troops refused to obey the orders of another defector, Muhammad Aden, a Wabenaya Mijjertein. They mutinied, put their own fellow tribesman in command, and then went off to raid the dervishes.[56]

Muhammad Abdullah Hassan, of course, did not rule alone. To help him in his religious, political, and military decisions, he drew upon a small group of lieutenants who were often closely related to him. One of his chief advisers was Sultan Nur, formerly a chief of the Habr Yunis, who had fled to the dervish camp to avoid paying blood money after slaying a rival. Another was Ahmad Warsama, known as Haji Sudi, who had served as a guide to English hunters in 1895. Haji Sudi was a member of the Adan Madoba Habr Toljaala, which had almost been wiped out in intertribal raiding by the Dolbohanta. When Muhammad Abdullah intervened to mediate the dispute, he deliberately sought to enlist Haji Sudi on his side; he proved to be an invaluable adviser, for he knew the British very well. Haji Sudi had spent some time as an interpreter on an English warship in the Red Sea and could speak English, Hindi, Arabic, and Swahili. At one time Haji Sudi visited Suakin, where he learned much about the Mahdist movement.[57] He remained loyal to his master until his death near Taleh in February 1920.

Muhammad Abdullah also drew on a small group of foreign advisers and craftsmen. During World War I, Turkish advisers from among the Ottoman forces in southern Arabia were to be found in his camp. In 1916, Lij Eyyasu sent him an unwitting gift in the person of Emil Kirsch, a German mechanic who was forced to repair firearms for the dervishes at Taleh and Madisha.[58] Lastly, he imported Yemeni Arab masons, who constructed impressive fortifications for him: the nine-foot-thick walls of the

---

56. Enrico Cerulli, *Somalia: Scritti vari editi ed inediti* (Rome, 1957), I, 106.
57. Malcolm McNeill, *In Pursuit of the "Mad" Mullah: Service and Sport in the Somali Protectorate* (London, 1902), 112–114.
58. H. Rayne, *Sun, Sand and Somals: Leaves from the Note-Book of a District Commissioner in British Somaliland* (London, 1921), 215.

fort at Jid Ali, the strong forts at Madisha, and the almost impregnable complex of fortresses at Taleh. All this shows Muhammad Abdullah to have been a man of great energy and broad imagination.

Until recent years outside of Somalia little was known about Muhammad Abdullah Hassan as a poet. Indeed, next to nothing was known about Somali poetry in general. Yet Somali poetry enjoys immense prestige among the illiterate Somali, who have learned to employ that art form not only as a means of preserving the past, but also as an effective means of communicating political ideas. Although the British were aware that the Somali applauded skillful versifiers, so little was known about the importance of poetry to the Somali that they did not recognize one of Muhammad Abdullah's messages to them as poetry rather than as the disjointed Arabic prose of an allegedly mad mullah.

Andrzejewski and Lewis demonstrate the power of Somali poetry in their recent anthology. They record how a poem by Salan Arabey, a contemporary of the dervish leader, is even now employed for nationalist purposes in Somalia:

> Death is better than a life of shame.
> Sometimes prosperity and repletion
>   are degrading and vile.[59]

This sentiment also characterizes the poetry of Muhammad Abdullah Hassan.

That Muhammad Abdullah recognized the use of poetry as a political device is evidenced by his appointment of men who were entrusted with memorizing his poetry. In his Arabic written poetry and in his Somali oral poetry, he provides an insight into the nature of his power.[60] He deliberately cultivated an aura of charisma. And to the Somali such formalized traditional rendering of events was also understood to reflect the personality of the charismatic leader. Through poetry he sought to identify himself with the Prophet Muhammad:

59. Andrzejewski and Lewis, *Somali Poetry*, 58. See also R. L. Hess, "The 'Mad Mullah' and Northern Somalia," *Journal of African History*, V:415–416 (1964).

60. Following quotations in Andrzejewski and Lewis, *Somali Poetry*, 66, 74, 80–110 *passim*.

> A djinn set them against me,
>> otherwise they would not have harmed me . . .
> They would not have rejected my preaching
>> insulting and flaying the Prophet.

In a message to the Ogaden tribes, he made more than one direct reference to his divine assistant:

> God does not refuse my prayers for grace.
> When I curse a person God cuts his tendon.

In his sermons he emphasized his holy mission:

> My portion is to walk in the company of the
>> Sura Watīn and the blessings of Divine Praise.

Nor could a devout Muslim not think twice about his accusation of the British:

> You are against both worship and the Divine Law.
> You are building a . . . partition between [the
>> Warsangeli] and the streams of Paradise and Heaven.
> You are casting them into the raging fury and fumes of
>> Hell.

Through the invective and scorn of his poetry, the Poor Man of God gives insights into his tactics, his goals, his personality:

> And friendship and openheartedness was my wont
>> until the hateful envy of the infidels
>> was unleashed upon me.

The dervish movement was meant to be characterized by a bond of brotherhood that cut across tribal lines:

> He who does not favour those to whom he is close in
>> genealogical descent . . . Is he not worthy of respect?
> . . .
> Who welcomes you like a kinsman in your day of need
> And who at the height of the drought does not bar his
>> gate against you,
> Is not he who never fails you in your weakness one of
>> the brethren?

Yet Muhammad Abdullah could not ignore the tribal and clan lines which divided the Somali nation, and as the offspring of

Ogaden and Dolbohanta parents, he shared the distaste of the
Darod for the Ishaak:

> And since the day of Adam, it is their lot to trot
> in terror behind the infidels,
> They are fated to understand nothing and condemned
> to madness.

When he appealed to the Ibrahim Ogaden, he claimed their
support on the basis of blood relationship. When they refused
to support him, he berated them in traditionalist terms:

> Tell everyone that it is shameful to shirk duty.
> Proclaim the message to the women, to the children,
> and to grown men.
> Ibrahim, whose clan I am, gives me no support.
> They are near kinsmen, of the same flesh and blood
> and maternal ancestor.

When another Darod group of clans deserted the movement, he
wrote:

> Having gone into hiding, [they] would not have
> fired at me;
> They would not have married the stupid women of the
> Habar Magaadle [Ishaak] clans
> [Unless a djinn set them against me].

For those who supported him, Muhammad Abdullah promised
a reward in this world as well as in the next:

> But I can guarantee to give you whatever you want.
> A thousand that run, thousands of those that are swift
> and raise their tails,
> A thousand that raise their necks and vie with the
> birds of prey,
> Thousands of saddled ones and thousands without saddles . . .
> You will drink your fill of the milk of milch-camels
> that have given birth,
> You will fall upon the vessels of sour milk as camels
> fall upon water . . .
> Weapons, possessions, property, livestock, and gifts
> without end,
> Whatever you expect from me, you will receive.
> Come to me! You will be drenched in God's munificence.

For those who did not, there was another threat:

> I meant to cut off the testicles of the menstruating
> infidels . . .
> The Dervishes are like the advancing thunderbolts
> of a storm, rumbling and roaring.

Somali poetry also provides an evaluation of Muhammad Abdullah by one of his lieutenants, Ismail Mire, in whose work there is a strong element of Muslim predestination: "Everyone will receive what has been prescribed for him." A trusted follower of Seyyid Muhammad, Ismail Mire was nonetheless aware of his leader's great weakness:

> O men, pride brings disaster: let that be remembered.
> Again and again the Seyyid made war and people helped him;
> Thousand upon thousand, all with white turbans,
> he brought to the battle of Beerdiga,
> But what brought his downfall was the day when he
> destroyed the Khayr people.
> O men, pride brings disaster; let that be remembered.

Was Muhammad Abdullah Hassan mad? The evidence presented above indicates that he had something of a genius for political, religious, and military organization and that he must have exerted a powerful charismatic attraction upon his followers. Moreover, his skill in composing poetry in both Somali and Arabic — although completely misunderstood by the British, who mistook his verses for incoherent messages and his particular kind of religious fervor for fanaticism — enhanced his role as politico-religious leader. Until more evidence about this alleged insanity can be produced, no objective judgment can be made. Muhammad Abdullah Hassan apparently never lost sight of his goals nor did he ever mismanage his military forces in a way that would indicate a lack of contact with objective reality. Yet his later writings and statements, particularly those attributed to him by Abdullahi Madar and Ismail Ishaak in their interview with Muhammad Abdullah at Shinileh in May 1920, indicate some instability. This may be explained either by the nature of the sources or by an alternative hypothesis that the Poor Man of God deliberately belittled his enemies by magnifying his own virtues — a technique not unknown in most human societies. Or again, his actions would be interpreted in differing ways by the European and the Somali. Lastly, examples of his cruelty fall within the context of Somali culture; they can outrage only the European who wishes to be outraged. Until new evidence becomes available, the question of Muhammad Abdullah Hassan's madness will continue to intrigue the European reader and will probably exasperate the Somali. The only judgment can be a Scotch verdict: not proven.

There is little doubt now, however, that the so-called Mad Mullah was a great man. With the three greatest powers in the Horn as enemies and with little access to European munitions or to coastal towns, for more than two decades not only did he harass the British, the Ethiopians, and the Italians, but he also regularly won military, political, and even diplomatic victories over them. The Muslim revival which produced Muhammad Abdullah's dervish movement has continued as an influence in the Islamic Somali Republic, where nationalism has been closely tied to religion. The traits of xenophobia visible in the nineteenth century and in the twenty-year period of the Poor Man of God's rebellion may still be detected on the Somali scene. In retrospect, he represents the one quasi-nationalistic force in the Somali lands which were then being divided among the three Christian powers. For this reason Somali nationalists attach to Muhammad Abdullah Hassan a patriotic aura and claim him not just as a symbol of a supratribal unity based on Islam but also as the very embodiment of the Somali's love of independence and — rightly or wrongly — as the first modern Somali nationalist.

Sheikh Mbaruk bin Rashid
bin Salim el Mazrui

by T. H. R. CASHMORE

Sir John Gray has recorded in detail the collapse of the Mazrui power at Mombasa. In 1837, Seyyid Said bin Sultan's son Khalid enticed twenty-five of the leading Mazrui into Fort Jesus; there they were seized and later put on board a corvette lying in Mombasa harbor. The prisoners sailed by way of Zanzibar to a long imprisonment and eventual death in the dungeons of Bunder Abas.[1]

The disaster of 1837 was not, however, the end of the Mazrui as a force in the politics of the east coast. When Rashid bin Salim, the last Mazrui governor of Mombasa, was seized in Fort Jesus, many of his clan, hearing of his fate, fled from the city with their families. To the north fled Hamis bin Rashid, head of the Zaherite branch of the clan. He settled at Takaungu, and other refugees gathered around him. Abdullah bin Hamis, the late governor's cousin and heir by custom, fled to the south, taking with him Rashid bin Salim's sons, among whom was a seven-year-old boy called Mbaruk.[2]

Abdullah settled at Gazi, and around him gathered the malcontents, embittered by the events of 1837 and ready to seize any opportunity to strike at the power of the sultan. Both groups of Mazrui settled in lands formerly ruled by their clan and drew strength from the proximity of the Nyika, their traditional allies in the struggles of the eighteenth and early nineteenth centuries. But neither at Takaungu nor at Gazi were the Mazrui strong enough to challenge Said's hold on the coast; the memory of their leaders' fate was still too fresh in their minds. Said for his

---

1. Sir John Gray, *The British in Mombasa, 1824–1826* (London, 1957), *passim.*
2. "Maisha ya Sheikh Mbaruk bin Rashid Al Mazrui," *Proceedings of the East Africa Swahili Committee,* 31:156 (1960). This source suggests that Mbaruk was taken by his mother to her people in Takaungu, and only later went to Gazi. See note 4.

part was content to leave them unharmed and divided. He held Mombasa and was well satisfied.[3]

In the years 1846 to 1848, Captain Guillain of the French navy visited the coast of East Africa, and he has left us an account of the Mazrui at Takaungu and Gazi. Takaungu was at peace with the sultan, although the events of 1837 were by no means forgotten.[4] About seven hundred people lived in the town and on the surrounding plantations the Mazrui had as many slaves. They owned ships and used the ports of Kilifi and Takaungu for the export of millet, cattle, sheep, ivory, and other local produce, which they obtained from the Galla and Nyika of the neighborhood. In exchange they imported cotton goods and iron implements. Their chief at this time was Rashid bin Hamis.[5]

The situation at Gazi was very different. The treachery of Seyyid Said had engendered such bitterness there that within a decade of their collapse at Mombasa the Gazi Mazrui were in conflict with the sultan. The moving force in this community of three hundred free persons and five hundred slaves was a woman, Khoca binti Ahmed. The chief of the settlement was Abdullah bin Hamis.[6] The Mazrui had interrupted the land

3. Gray, *British in Mombasa*, 191. After the seizure of the twenty-five leading Mazrui, Said's representatives declared themselves content and assured all others to trust in the sultan's clemency.

4. Ludwig Krapf visited Takaungu in 1843, where he received a friendly welcome but found the elders bitter at Said's treachery and saying that "the English had left the Masrue of Mombasa in the lurch." J. Ludwig Krapf, *Travels, Researches, and Missionary Labours, during an Eighteen Years' Residence in Eastern Africa* (London, 1860), 115. Krapf visited Takaungu again in 1846 when he referred to a meeting with the lady of the former governor of Mombasa. Unfortunately he does not give her name, so it is impossible to say for certain whether she was a widow of Rashid bin Salim, Mbaruk of Gazi's mother (see note 1). *Church Missionary Record* [hereafter *CMR*], XVIII:3 (1847).

5. M. Guillain, *Documents sur l'Histoire, la Géographie et le Commerce de l'Afrique Orientale* (Paris, 1856), II, 263 ff., calls the chief of Takaungu Rashid bin Salim bin Abdullah. Hardinge, in *Parliamentary Papers, Africa* [hereafter *PPA*], VI (1896), item 26 and enclosures, asserts that Rashid bin Hamis succeeded the first chief of Takaungu; the genealogical table attached to his memorandum, however, suggests that Hamis bin Rashid was succeeded in 1846 by his brother Said, who died in 1850, and was then succeeded by Rashid bin Hamis, whom Mbaruk of Gazi tried to depose. See the genealogical table in "Maisha ya Sheikh Mbaruk," 176–177.

6. Guillain, *Documents*, II, 263–265. A visitor to Gazi in 1857 stated that

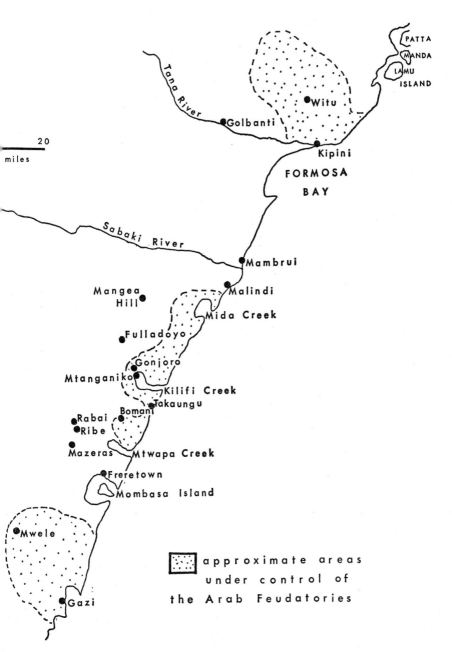

The Kenya Coast, 1895

113

communications between Mombasa and Tanga, compelling Said
to dispatch a number of expeditions against them. They had
also allied themselves with the Digo and supported them in their
struggle against the Segua.[7] Even more serious, the settlement
at Gazi was a refuge for growing numbers of runaway slaves, who
settled at Mouacniombe, a village in the interior not far from
Gazi. The Mazrui of Gazi also pillaged the stores of the Banyan
traders in their locality. Even so, the chief of Gazi was compelled
to acknowledge the overlordship of the sultan.

Sometime between the years 1846 and 1850 the chief of Takaungu died and was succeeded by Rashid bin Hamis. There
was now played out a further chapter in that fratricidal feuding
within the Mazrui clan which had enabled Said to gain possession
of Mombasa in the first instance and which was later to play a
part in the final downfall of the Mazrui in 1896. The son of the
last Mazrui governor of Mombasa, Mbaruk bin Rashid of Gazi,
was now a man. Through his mother, who was a Zaherite, he
had pretensions to the chieftainship of Takaungu, and his claims
were encouraged by other Mazrui. Drawing on the armed retainers of his "uncle" Abdullah, he attacked Takaungu and drove
out Rashid bin Hamis. Sultan Said, delighted to encourage divisions among his enemies and loath to see the Mazrui lands reunited, went to the aid of Rashid. Mbaruk was driven out of
Takaungu, and fled south to Gazi where Said was content to leave
him unmolested.[8]

In 1856, Seyyid Said died and was succeeded at Zanzibar by
his son Majid. During the latter's reign, probably about the
year 1865, Abdullah, chief of the Gazi, died. Majid recognized
Mbaruk bin Rashid as Abdullah's successor, and, in the hopes of
securing Mbaruk's loyalty more surely, granted him a subsidy.
Unfortunately, Mbaruk, though a man of great character and
considerable charm, was not fated to be a man of peace. During

---

the town was under the rule of Sheikh Abdullah bin Hamis and that a sister
of Sheikh Mbaruk of Mombasa lived there who displayed particular energy.
Richard F. Burton, *Zanzibar* (London, 1872), II, 165.

7. Guillain spells the name of the tribe as "Oua-Céguéyo," which I have
taken to be the Segua and not the Segeju.

8. *PPA*, VI (1896), item 26. This document, a memorandum written by
Hardinge for the Foreign Office, gives a brief history of the Mazrui. "Maisha
ya Sheikh Mbaruk," 156, suggests that Mbaruk was engaged in three attacks
on Takaungu in the 1850's and 1860's attempting to gain the sheikhdom.

the 1860's he was at war with the tribes of the interior, with his relative Rashid of Takaungu, and finally with the sultan himself. Once during the course of these conflicts, Mbaruk visited the Methodist mission at Ribe with two or three hundred men. The *liwali* (governor) of Mombasa feared that the Mazrui might kidnap the missionaries. On his advice, the missionaries Wakefield and New retired to the safety of Mombasa. At about this time, during his struggle with the sultan, Mbaruk established a fortress on the forested hill of Mwele as an inland refuge. Eventually he was forced to come to terms, but when he made his peace Majid refused to renew the subsidy.

In 1870, Majid died and was succeeded by his brother Barghash. Mbaruk began the new reign well, and Barghash restored the subsidy to him. But Mbaruk could not keep out of trouble; by 1872 he was at loggerheads with the powerful *akida* of Fort Jesus, Muhammad bin Abdullah, and once again at war with the sultan. At first he was successful, threatening Mombasa after defeating the sultan's forces. At this time he went so far as to offer his territory and services to the British (a frequent practice of the Mazrui).[9] But with reinforcements, the *akida* counterattacked and took Mbaruk's forest fortress of Mwele, whereupon Mbaruk sued for peace, which was granted.

In 1873, however, Mbaruk was once more on the warpath. He was defeated by the sultan's forces drawn from Mombasa; one of his brothers was wounded and taken prisoner to die in Mombasa. Mbaruk fled north to the hinterland of Malindi, and Barghash decided that an all-out effort must be made to finish the rebellion. He bought off two of Mbaruk's brothers by making one, Khutam, chief of Gazi and another chief of Onyambo (near Mida Creek). Barghash then sent the *liwali* of Lamu to Malindi with four hundred reinforcements, bringing his total force up to two thousand. At the same time, Barghash sent a message to Mbaruk through Rashid bin Hamis of Takaungu, that he should either quietly occupy some port on the coast or come and render submission at Zanzibar, or finally settle the quarrel by force of arms. Mbaruk, recalling his father's fate, placed little faith in the promises of the sultan. Still, he sent word that he would

9. See Gray, *British in Mombasa*, 16, 20, 30, for the early offers. For the 1885 incident, see below.

settle at Kilifi, near Takaungu. In view of Mbaruk's previous attempts to seize Takaungu, Barghash refused to agree to this proposal. Mbaruk's camp was attacked, and though he himself escaped, his following was dispersed; Mbaruk fled south. What followed is uncertain, but Mbaruk appears to have made peace with the sultan again.

In the latter part of 1874, Barghash was fully occupied with troubles in Mombasa, a feud between his *liwali* and the *akida* of the fort, Muhammad bin Abdullah. In January of 1875, the *akida*, with 350 armed men of the garrison, opened fire on the *liwali's* house. For a time it seemed as though the *akida* would gain possession of the town. Fortunately for the sultan, two hundred armed men came from Takaungu to the aid of the *liwali*, most of them retainers of the Mazrui chief of Takaungu.[10] The *akida* was brought to heel after the fort was bombarded for three hours by H.M.S. *Nassau* and H.M.S. *Rifleman*, which intervened on behalf of the Zanzibar government on the instructions of the British consul. The *akida* and his followers (in addition to the 350 fighting men, there were some 650 camp followers) were removed to Pemba, and from thence to Hadhramaut.

Mbaruk had considered the troubles in Mombasa a golden opportunity to reestablish his power and to revenge himself on the *akida*. He declared himself on the side of the sultan, and offered his services to put down the revolt. The sultan told him not to interfere.[11] In early January of 1875, a party of Mbaruk's men under Abdullah, one of Mbaruk's lieutenants, visited the Rabai mission station, ostensibly seeking to break away from Mbaruk. J. Rebmann, the Church Missionary Society missionary, who was about to depart from the Kenya coast, expressed his fears to his companion, the Reverend Salter Price, that Mbaruk was planning to seize the two missionaries and to hold them as hos-

---

10. These troops arrived on January 15, 1875. A British report of 1874 put the sultan's troops at Kilifi and Takaungu at ten men; thus it is likely that the majority of these reinforcements were Mazrui supporters from Takaungu. Prideaux to Foreign Office, Feb. 2, 1875, Zanzibar Archives. The then Chief of Takaungu, Rashid bin Hamis el Mazrui, was nicknamed *Vitwavinanne*, "The Eight-headed," due to a physical deformity.

11. *Parliamentary Papers, Slave Trade* [hereafter *PPST*], IV (1876), item 2. Mbaruk must have returned to Gazi as a British official reported him there in July 1875. *Ibid.*, item 84.

Emperor Menilek II of Ethiopia

Sheikh Mbaruk bin Rashid bin Salim el Mazrui

Lobengula, King of the Matabele, 1889

Gungunhana (left) in exile at Angra do Heroismo, on Terceira in the Azores. This photograph was probably taken in 1899 the day of his baptism as "Reinaldo Frederico Gungunhana."

Chief Gungunhana with two of his wives shortly after his capture at Chaimite in 1895.

tages. These fears proved groundless.[12] There were fears that Mbaruk, rebuffed by the sultan, might ally himself with his erstwhile enemy, the *akida*. Mbaruk, however, let the opportunity pass, and from 1875 onwards he contented himself with making war on the neighboring tribes of the interior.[13] By June of 1875, the coast was sufficiently pacified for Barghash to hand over his sultanate to a regent while he proceeded to England on a state visit.

The uneasy truce lasted for several years, but in 1882 Mbaruk once more revolted against the sultan. The causes of this new uprising are obscure. Some suggest that it began because Barghash had imprisoned some of Mbaruk's relatives; others said it was caused by the refusal of the town of Vanga to provide Mbaruk with a wife. In any case, in February 1882, Mbaruk attacked and sacked the port of Vanga. He had a force estimated at two thousand men, some of them Masai. Seventeen were killed in the town, and the Banyan traders placed their losses at twelve thousand dollars. Barghash immediately took steps to uphold his authority and to reinforce the port of Tanga, which was thought to be threatened by the rebels. He sent General Lloyd Mathews, commander of his army, to Tanga with three hundred men on the S.S. *Akola*. He also offered a reward of a thousand dollars for Mbaruk's head. Mathews counterattacked and Mbaruk's forces melted away. Mbaruk himself was driven back to his refuge at Mwele (also called El Hazam) where he was besieged. Attempts to bombard the fortress proved unsuccessful because the "rotten carriages of the Sultan's field pieces broke down on the first discharge." [14] Thirteen war rockets and a tube for firing them were borrowed from the British naval squadron at Zanzibar and sent to Mathews. On March 29, 1882, after a siege of almost three weeks, Mwele was stormed and the armed rebels in it put to the sword. Mathews intervened to stop the slaughter and to save the surviving men, women, and children — 390 people in all. He also recovered the store of gunpowder and Mbaruk's papers;

12. *Church Missionary Intelligencer* [hereafter *CMI*], XI:153 ff. (1875). Abdullah may very well have been sincere, since Price records he helped dig a missionary's grave.

13. In January 1877, there were rumors that Mbaruk was about to attack the Freretown mission, but they were unfounded. *PPST*, III (1878), item 273.

14. *PPA*, I (1882–1883), item 48.

everything else was taken by the Zanzibari *askaris* during the sack. Mbaruk, however, succeeded in cutting his way through the besiegers and escaped, accompanied by one of his wives. They were pursued and some three miles from Mwele the woman was shot in the back and killed. Mathews then returned to Zanzibar, having destroyed the fortress. Barghash increased the reward on Mbaruk's head to two thousand dollars.[15]

Mbaruk, once more an outlaw, sought refuge in the bush. He gathered around him a band of desperadoes, many of them Nyika. In May 1882, while the Reverend Salter Price was on safari in the Duruma country with the Reverend A. D. Shaw, they were met by a group of Mbaruk's followers. These men told Price that Mbaruk was coming to see him, and they then departed. Salter Price, fearing that Mbaruk wanted to take both himself and Shaw as hostages, decamped at once. (The *liwali* of Mombasa, however, was convinced that Salter Price was in league with the rebels.)[16] By July of 1882, Mbaruk had grown sufficiently strong to threaten Mombasa and Freretown. That month, Mbaruk visited the mission station at Rabai, then in the charge of an African catechist, Fundi Jones. Though Mbaruk stated that his visit was a friendly one, Jones maintained a strict neutrality, which was to prove fortunate for the station. Barghash, hearing of the threat to Mombasa, had on July 19–20 sent reinforcements of six hundred men to the town on the S.S. *Star* and the S.S. *Sultani*. At the close of the month of Ramathan and after the feast of *Id El Fitr,* the *liwali* of Mombasa led some fifteen hundred men against the rebels. Rabai's neutrality was respected by both sides. But in late July the *liwali* proceeded to wreak vengeance on all the surrounding tribes who had aided Mbaruk. On July 23 he destroyed Kaya Ribe. Mbaruk kept out of his way.

Failing in his attempts to defeat the rebels decisively, Barghash sought to end the rebellion by offering terms: Mbaruk might take up residence either at Pemba or at Takaungu (among relatives who had little reason to love him). Barghash hoped to trap

15. *Ibid.*, items 132, 148, 149.
16. *CMI*, VII:572 (1882); *PPA*, I (1882–1883), item 62 and enclosures. The anti-slavery views of the mission were the root of the trouble. See Norman R. Bennett, "The Church Missionary Society at Mombasa, 1873–1894," *Boston University Papers in African History*, I (Boston, 1964), 157–194.

Mbaruk if he agreed to the terms, after allowing sufficient time to lapse to lull his suspicions. Mbaruk refused these peace overtures and remained an outlaw in the bush. But in November 1882, Lloyd Mathews negotiated a peace; Mbaruk was not allowed to return to Gazi for the time being and surrendered his sword as a token of submission. In 1883, however, he was once again an outlaw in the bush.

It was during the 1880's that the problem of runaway slaves began to cause increasing concern and unrest. The mission stations on the coast had on a number of occasions offered refuge to the runaways. In addition, the runaway slaves had in time set up their own settlements in the interior. One such settlement was at Fulladoyo, south of Mangea Hill and near the Sabaki River, originally an outpost founded by Giryama converts of the Church Missionary Society. As early as 1881, Fulladoyo was so important as a center for escaped slaves that Salim of Takaungu, who had succeeded to the chieftainship unopposed in 1876, bribed the Giryama with gifts of cloth to attack it. When they delayed he sent them by way of a reminder a measure of corn and an arrow, gifts of peace or war.[17]

In October of 1883, while Mbaruk was still an outlaw, three thousand Swahili and Arabs banded together to attack Fulladoyo. The settlement was burnt to the ground, and six of its inhabitants were killed; but a majority of the former slaves escaped. Sir John Kirk, British representative at Zanzibar, reporting the incident to the Foreign Office, commented that about 250 of the runaway slaves had joined Mbaruk, thus strengthening his hand.[18] Kirk shortly afterward visited Mombasa and the coast to the north. He called at Takaungu and found Salim, its chief, "excessive in his cordial welcome," but bitter at the Church Missionary Society over a plot of disputed land in Mombasa, a matter which Kirk settled on behalf of the society by a cash payment. No mention was made of the whereabouts of the rebel Mbaruk, nor did Kirk hint that Salim showed any sympathy toward his rebel kinsman.[19]

17. *CMI*, VI:45 (1881).
18. *PPST*, I (1884), item 159; *Proceedings of the Church Missionary Society* [hereafter *PCMS*], (1882–1883), 40–43.
19. This was Kirk's second visit to Takaungu. During a previous visit in 1874, he had found three thousand inhabitants, fourteen of them Indians. It was during this visit that the current chief, Rashid bin Hamis, had

For the next eighteen months Mbaruk continued to live obscurely in the bush. Toward the end of this period, Barghash, using Sir John Kirk as an intermediary, offered fresh terms: a *shamba* in Zanzibar and four hundred dollars per annum if Mbaruk would make peace. Mbaruk refused the offer. This was the state of affairs when Bishop Hannington of the C.M.S. visited the rebuilt Fulladoyo settlement, on May 1, 1885. Hannington at first received a hostile reception from Mbaruk's retainers, who were in the vicinity. He succeeded, however, in contacting Mbaruk, and the two men met. Eager to get Mbaruk out of Fulladoyo so that the C.M.S. could resume its work there, Hannington decided to intervene in matters not strictly within the realm of the spiritual. When Mbaruk told him that he was tired of his lawless life and desired peace, Hannington persuaded him to write to Sir John Kirk and promised to forward the letter. Not only did Hannington send the letter to the vice-consul at Mombasa, but he himself wrote to Kirk, putting in a friendly word. Mbaruk's letter to Sir John asked for British protection for himself and his people, a phrase that Hannington took to mean that he placed himself under the directions of Sir John. Be that as it may, Kirk wired the Foreign Office on June 7, 1885, that, "the rebel Mbaruk asks for British Protection. If refused says that he has other friends." The Foreign Office replied, "Act with great care. You should not permit any communications of a hostile tone to be addressed to German agents or representatives by Zanzibar authorities." [20] The point of the last signal was that Zanzibar was being subjected to intense German pressure as a preliminary to German demands for a stake in East Africa. Mbaruk did not hesitate to fish in troubled waters.

No doubt because of this preoccupation with German threats, Barghash appears to have made peace with Mbaruk and allowed him to return to Gazi. In November of 1885, Mbaruk wrote to

---

shown him the 146-year-old deed appointing a Mazrui governor of Mombasa. *PPST*, VIII (1874), item 68.

20. E. C. Dawson, *James Hannington* (London, 1887), 326–327; Sir John Milner Gray, "Correspondence Relating to the Death of Bishop Hannington," *Uganda Journal*, XIII:3–4 (1949). (I am indebted to Sir John Gray for drawing my attention to Hannington's letter to Kirk, May 4, 1885.) Sir R. Coupland, *The Exploitation of East Africa* (London, 1939), 418.

the sultan concerning his subsidy: "Please my master allow me my monthly salary as before." [21] But in January of 1886, Herr Lucas visited Gazi on behalf of the Gesellschaft für Deutsche Kolonisation. He persuaded Mbaruk to hoist the German mercantile flag and the German company's flag. Retribution was swift; Gazi was attacked by troops from the sultan's garrison at Mombasa, and Mbaruk was forced to flee again.[22] As a footnote to this little diplomatic episode, it should be added that when the three commissioners visited the east coast in 1886 to delimit the possessions of the sultan, Schmidt, the German commissioner, insisted that Gazi be excluded from the territories of the sultan. This exclusion was entered in the report of the three commissioners. In the final settlement between Great Britain and Germany in which the boundaries of the Sultan's coastal territories were laid down, the German claim was dropped and Gazi was included with the ten-mile strip of land awarded to the sultan.[23]

Once more, Mbaruk "was on his travels." The Reverend W. E. Taylor of the C.M.S., in a letter written in mid-1886, recounted the events of the preceding months. He reported that Mbaruk had been harrying the Swahili settlements on the coast, and had destroyed one village to the north of Takaungu. The Swahili of

21. *Ibid.*, 457.

22. Lieutenant C. Smith, British vice-consul at Mombasa, had written to Mbaruk on May 16, 1885:

> Recently in a previous letter I have shown you that without doubt some Christians — Germans — will come to you. Their intention is to enter into an agreement with you. They will tell you many pleasant things and will assure you that they alone will come to you in time of necessity.
> I hope that God will show you only that which is good for you. The Germans are coming not for your advantage but for theirs, let this be understood by you.
> Furthermore I tell you, "Be careful, Be careful!" If they say to you "Take paper and write" sign nothing by way of confirmation. If you do sign, do not write "I agree to this," but write "I do not understand these proposals." Be careful! Be careful! We write this as a friendly warning. It is best if you never write, "I agree." That is best of all. Be careful! Be careful! And yet again Be careful! Be careful! God commends this to you.

Translated by Sir John Gray from the German version in Fritz Ferdinand Müller, *Deutschland-Zanzibar-Ostafrika* (Berlin, 1959), 528.

23. Coupland, *Exploitation of East Africa*, 473 ff.; *PPA*, III (1887), item 73.

Jomvu, near Mombasa, so Taylor informed the society, devised an ingenious means of revenge. Banding together, they visited Kaya Ribe (rebuilt since the sack of 1882) and produced a forged authority purporting to come from the *liwali* of Mombasa. They then demanded of the elders a sum of thirty dollars as a fine for having allowed Mbaruk to pass. The elders plaintively asked how they could have prevented him, but they paid the fine. The Jomvu, emboldened by their success, proceeded to try similar tactics with the Rabai. Here, however, the mission intervened, and on the advice of Fundi Jones payment was refused. The Jomvu withdrew.

Mbaruk's fortunes took a turn for the better in 1887 with the negotiations which led to the Imperial British East Africa Company concessions. George Mackenzie, the company's administrator, in his efforts to make treaties with the inland chiefs through his namesake E. N. Mackenzie, found Mbaruk's friendship invaluable.[24] Mackenzie told Mbaruk in a private interview that he intended to recommend "that he should be given under the Administrator in Chief, the entire control of the territory from our boundary at Wanga up to Kilifi."[25] Mackenzie also agreed to persuade Barghash to allow Mbaruk to settle once more at Gazi and to obtain the release of his followers who were still prisoners. Barghash refused. But Barghash had not long to live and on his death in early 1888, his successor Khalifa proved more amenable. On Khalifa's accession, Mbaruk dispatched one of his sons, together with some of his adherents, to Zanzibar where the sultan received them well, giving them handsome presents and a thousand dollars in cash. He then gave Mbaruk leave to return to Gazi and permitted Mbaruk's retainers and slaves taken prisoner in 1882 to return to their lord. In July of the same year, Lloyd Mathews was sent to Mombasa to escort Mbaruk to Zanzibar for an audience with the new sultan. Either at this inter-

24. See E. Hertslet, *The Map of Africa by Treaty* (London, 1909), I, 374–375, for a treaty between the IBEA and Mbaruk dated June 9, 1887, in which Mbaruk placed the "Gienjou Country" in Duruma under IBEA protection. See also *PPA*, VII (1888), items 16, 23; Euan Smith to Salisbury, Feb. 9, 1890, enclosing Mackenzie to IBEA Directors, Jan. 12, 1888, Zanzibar Archives.

25. Mackenzie to IBEA Directors, Jan. 12, 1888, in Euan Smith to Salisbury, Feb. 9, 1890, Zanzibar Archives.

view or shortly thereafter, the subsidy was restored to Mbaruk, a subsidy now fixed at a thousand rupees a month.[26]

Mbaruk was now to enjoy a period of seven years of comparative peace and prosperity. He was a man of great influence with the new Imperial British East Africa Company, which had taken over the administration of the mainland from the Umba River in the south to the Tana River in the north. The company had also taken on itself the payment of his subsidy. In return he proved his loyalty to his new masters by providing them with troops when needed. He sent men to Mombasa to check an incipient revolt; and again, when trouble was likely, he sent a force to Teita. He continued, however, to engage secretly in the slave trade, shipping slaves captured up-country to the island of Pemba. In 1888, when trouble once more arose over the runaway slaves harbored at the Rabai and Ribe mission stations, the company intervened to preserve the peace by paying compensation to the Arab (though not the Nyika) owners and freeing the slaves. In all, a sum of £3,500 was paid out.[27] Mbaruk was determined to have a share of the profits; accordingly he visited Rabai with three hundred armed followers to establish his claim. It was during this visit that he met the Reverend Robson, who has left us an account of the man. He found that Mbaruk commanded absolute obedience among his wild retainers: "he thinks nothing of shooting down an unwilling follower with his own hands." Robson added: "He is fairly well educated and rather interesting in conversation." (Another Englishman was equally impressed by Mbaruk. In 1893, when C. W. Hobley visited Gazi, he commented that Mbaruk was, "a fine figure of a man with courtly manners," although he terrorized the Digo.)[28]

26. *PPA*, VII (1888), items 16, 23, 31. There is some confusion about the size of the subsidy paid to Mbaruk. I quote Euan Smith's figure. But compare Euan Smith to Salisbury, Oct. 2, 1890, to which is attached George Mackenzie's letter of Jan. 1, 1888, Zanzibar Archives. This gives the total subsidy as 1,940 rupees a month.

27. P. L. McDermott, *British East Africa or IBEA* (London, 1893 edition), 26 ff. See also F. D. Lugard, *The Rise of Our East African Empire* (London, 1893), I, 225.

28. *Anti-Slavery Reporter*, IX:30 (Jan.–Feb. 1889), letter of Jan. 12, 1888; C. W. Hobley, *From Chartered Company to Crown Colony* (London, 1929), 64. See also W. Salter Price, *My Third Campaign in East Africa* (London, 1890), 230, where Mbaruk is described as having "an aristocratic face and

Neither Mbaruk of Gazi nor Salim of Takaungu attempted to take advantage of the Witu troubles which arose in 1890–1893 after the surrender of the German protectorate there to the British in 1890; the consul general at Zanzibar fully expected them to do so. The furthest that either of them went was the marked, and somewhat humorous, discourtesy with which Salim treated Colonel Euan Smith during the latter's visit to Takaungu after the first Witu expedition.[29]

As the years passed, the Imperial British East Africa Company ran into financial difficulties; by early 1895 it was apparent that it would have to surrender its concession and withdraw from the coast. That it would hand over the administration of the coastal strip to the sultan appeared certain, but as Zanzibar had become a British protectorate in 1890 this was tantamount to saying that the administration of the coast would fall to agents of the British Crown.[30] Such niceties, however, were lost on the Arabs of the coast, who assumed that they would return to the easy and often ineffectual rule of the sultan himself. Furthermore the company had done little to crush the power of the semi-independent feudatories who in practice ruled large stretches of the Kenya coast. In the year 1895 there were five feudal lords, each with a band of armed retainers. Mzee bin Seif of Faza held sway over the Bajun to the north of Lamu (but he was to be deported to Zanzibar early in 1895). The sultanate of Witu, in spite of two punitive expeditions, was still in existence, though without a sultan since the last heir of the ancient house of Nabhan, former rulers of Pate, had been deposed. To the south

---

fine physique, although possessing a worn out and battered look." Compare also Sir A. Hardinge, *A Diplomatist in the East* (London, 1928), 171.

29. Sir Frederick Jackson, *Early Days in East Africa* (London, 1930), 351. Salim's greeting to Euan Smith, who was anchored off shore, was to send a messenger to the jetty where he turned round, lifted his *kanzu*, exposing a bare posterior, and patted his buttocks.

30. For the account of the Foreign Office discussions concerning the future administration of the Kenya coast, see Foreign Office Prints 6489, 6693, 6717 and 6761 (Seely Library, Cambridge University). Hardinge advocated a union of much of the area with Zanzibar but failed to get his way. The sultan as a result was considerably upset, and the treaty with Zanzibar concerning the sultan's mainland dominions was not signed until December 1895. The sultan's Civil List was increased to sweeten the blow, but even then Hardinge had to address him "in somewhat plain and emphatic terms." F. O. Prints, 6693, item 283; 6827, item 26.

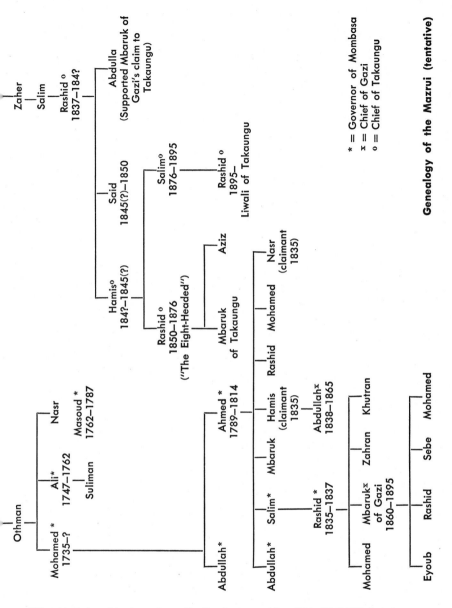

Genealogy of the Mazrui (tentative)

* = Governor of Mombasa
x = Chief of Gazi
o = Chief of Takaungu

This table is based in the main on Hardinge's memorandum (*PPA*, VI (1896), item 26). There are, however, a number of discrepancies between Hardinge and others. See Richard Reusch, *History of East Africa* (Stuttgart, 1954), 274–275; A. E. Robinson, "The Shirazi Colonisations of East Africa," *Tanganyika Notes and Records*, 3:79 (1937); "Maisha ya Sheikh Mbaruk," 176–177.

Sir John Gray, *British in Mombasa*, 189, makes the last Mazrui governor of Mombasa Rashid bin Salim bin *Abdulla* el Mazrui. He is called Rashid bin Salim bin *Ahmed* by Coupland, *East Africa and its Invaders*, 292; "Maisha ya Sheikh Mbaruk"; and Hardinge's memorandum.

of Witu lay the chieftainship of Takaungu, ruled by Salim bin Hamis, who had a band of twelve hundred armed slaves at his disposal. Farther to the south lay the Swahili chieftainship of Mtwapa, ruled by Hamis bin Kombo, descendant of the old princes of Malindi. He had a force of some three hundred armed slaves.[31] Finally, there was Mbaruk of Gazi, many times a rebel against the sultan, still chief after thirty-five years of struggle. He had at his disposal eleven hundred fighting men. Such was the political structure of the coast in February of 1895, when the company was faced with a new crisis as it prepared to wind up its affairs.

In early February, Salim, the chief of Takaungu, died. A successor had to be found. By custom, his heir was his nephew Mbaruk bin Rashid bin Hamis of Takaungu (to avoid confusion, he will be referred to as Mbaruk the younger or Mbaruk of Takaungu). Young Mbaruk, however, was considered a troublemaker by company officials, and his brother Aziz, a firebrand, had a considerable influence over him. McDougall, the company's representative at Malindi, accordingly intervened to decide the succession. He called a *baraza* of elders at Takaungu, and after all had agreed to abide by the decision of the company, he nominated Rashid, the twenty-eight-year-old son of the deceased chief, as *liwali* of Takaungu.[32] For a while all remained calm. The new *liwali*, in an attempt to win over his disgruntled kinsmen, gave Mbaruk of Takaungu all his late father's fighting slaves. By May of 1895, however, quarrels had broken out between the new *liwali* and the younger Mbaruk. The latter with-

31. I am obliged to Sir John Gray for pointing this out. Thomas Boteler, *Narrative of a Voyage of Discovery to Africa and Arabia* (London, 1835), II, 8, tells that the chief of the Swahili of Mombasa was "the hereditary Prince of Malinda." Hardinge in an 1896 dispatch describes Hamis bin Kombo as a Swahili representing the aboriginal rulers of Mombasa, who had governed its five towns; Hardinge states that he was regarded by the Swahili of Mombasa as their chief.

32. Hardinge to Kimberley, May 1, 1895, *PPA*, VI (1896), item 2. Hardinge commented that the title of *liwali* was new at Takaungu and that "Salim himself never used [it] considering it inconsistent with the independent position claimed by him." Similarly Salim had never received a subsidy from the sultan of Zanzibar, though he had frequently visited the sultan's court or sent a representative to collect an annual present. On the whole Salim remained on good terms with the sultan, although he was once imprisoned for a period of six months, probably by Barghash.

drew to Gonjoro with his brother Aziz, where he seized the guns and ammunition stored there and concentrated his armed force, threatening Takaungu. The situation became so grave that on May 23, 1895, Hardinge, the consul general at Zanzibar, informed the Foreign Office that the company had requested the dispatch of a gunboat to Takaungu to forestall a threatened attack. A gunboat was sent. Hardinge was to admit later that the company's decision over the Takaungu succession might well be considered unwise, but as heir apparent to the company he was determined to uphold the decision to establish a strong administration — if necessary by using force to bring the overmighty Arab chiefs to heel. After sending a subordinate to see Mbaruk of Takaungu to try to persuade the latter to keep the peace, he visited Takaungu.[33] On June 14, at a *baraza* in Takaungu he confirmed the company's decision that Rashid should be *liwali*. On June 15 a notice in the *London Gazette* proclaimed a British protectorate in East Africa, although the formal handing over of power did not take place until July 1.[34]

Hardinge then attempted to bring the malcontents to terms by sending four elders to interview them and to persuade them to come to Takaungu to make their submission. When they failed to come in, Hardinge proclaimed them rebels on June 15, 1895. The following day he led an expedition of over five hundred men from the naval squadron and the Zanzibar Regulars against the rebel stronghold at Gonjoro which was believed to be fortified. The force proceeded up Kilifi Creek by boat and landed near

33. Mbaruk of Takaungu's reaction was not hostile. He wrote to Mathews: "In the Name of the Most Merciful God. To the Honourable the Adviser General, Sir Lloyd Mathews. The Wakil of the Zanzibar Government — may God always befriend him. After greetings, Your friend is quite well and I hope you are the same. Mr. Wilson came to us and we interviewed him. He knows all our affairs because we do not hate the commands of Government but are always prepared to execute them. All that you order us on behalf of Government we will submit to and salaams. Written by Mbaruk bin Rashid bin Khamis with his own hand on this day of 6th Dhull Hajj 1312 [May 31, 1895]." In the margin is a note, "The rest of the news take from him (Wilson). He is sufficient." Translation of "Squid Ink" letter in the Peace Museum, Zanzibar, by Sir John Gray.

34. *PPA*, VII (1897), 1; *British and Foreign State Papers*, LXXVII (1894–1895), 1036. In certain areas, however, officials of the IBEA continued to administer due to the government's preoccupation with the coast rebellion until as late as October of 1895.

Gonjoro. Though the banks of the creek were swarming with armed rebels, no opposition was made to the landing. In fact no hostilities occurred at all until a party of Hardinge's men tried to seize an armed rebel who passed close to them. A gun went off accidentally; then firing became general. The rebels were pursued and fled from Gonjoro, which, contrary to reports, was unfortified. But on the following day, a rebel force under Aziz attacked and sacked Mtanganiko and then retired into the bush. In retaliation, huts and crops in the neighborhood were destroyed. On June 24 Hardinge proceeded to Malindi, following a report that the rebels were massing in the bush nearby. They had in fact cut the Mombasa–Malindi telegraph line and burnt four small coastal villages. Government forces then moved on Arabuco where Aziz had his forces; the village was stormed and taken with the loss of one Nubian soldier. The rebels again fled, this time towards Fulladoyo, once again cutting the telegraph line as they passed.

In the meantime, Mbaruk of Gazi had remained quiet. The fire of his youth had passed, and Hardinge, in a dispatch of June 25, 1895, commented: "his attitude has been cautious and at least externally loyal." [35] But by early July, many of the rebels, including the younger Mbaruk, had sought shelter in Gazi.[36] Hardinge proceeded to Mombasa to contact Mbaruk of Gazi and demand the surrender of the rebels. Hardly had Hardinge left for Mombasa than the rebels, led by Aziz, attacked Takaungu at 4:30 A.M. on the morning of July 8. The place was garrisoned by 138 men drawn chiefly from the Zanzibar forces under Cap-

35. In a dispatch of May 1, 1895, Hardinge stated that he believed Mbaruk of Gazi was supporting Mbaruk of Takaungu. *PPA*, VI (1896), item 2. But in mid-June, Hardinge was corresponding with the chief of Gazi concerning the rebels. "I am in friendly communication with [the chief of Gazi] and hope shortly to be able to secure the rebel leaders." Hardinge's attitude to Mbaruk of Gazi is rather confusing: on occasions he appears convinced of his duplicity; at other times he considers him a useful ally. Contrast the Likoni meeting of July 5 with Hardinge's remark in his report on the protectorate of July 1897, in *PPA*, VII (1897), 66, where he speaks of Mbaruk being in communication with the Germans at Tanga as early as 1894 to ask if they would support him if he rebelled against the IBEA. Probably the fairest summary of Mbaruk's motives for joining the rebellion is given in Hardinge's dispatch of April 12, 1896, in *PPA*, VI (1896), item 72.

36. It was Mbaruk himself who reported the arrival of the rebels to the acting administrator at Mombasa. *Ibid.*, item 14.

tain Raikes. The attack was beaten off, the rebels suffering between thirty and fifty casualties. The garrison lost three men and eight were wounded; Captain Raikes was among the latter.

On July 5 Hardinge, together with Lloyd Mathews, met Mbaruk of Gazi at Likoni, to the south of Mombasa. At first Mbaruk proposed that he should be allowed to put down the rebellion. On this point Hardinge overruled Lloyd Mathews' favorable opinion, considering that such action would reflect adversely on the prestige of the new administration. Mbaruk then suggested that Hardinge should pardon the rebels, and when they had disbanded and grown careless, seize the ringleaders. Finally and reluctantly, Mbaruk agreed to seize his own kinsmen while they sheltered at Gazi and to hand them over to Hardinge, who presumably would come to Gazi to support Mbaruk if necessary and take delivery of the rebel leaders. Hardinge, in reporting the results of the meeting to the Marquis of Salisbury, commented that should Mbaruk keep his side of the bargain, well and good, but if he failed to do so he would treat the chief of Gazi as a rebel. "The absolute supremacy of Government must be established beyond a doubt and the tribal Chiefs taught to respect and obey it." [37] To soften the blow Hardinge sent Mbaruk a parting gift of a quantity of gunpowder — under the circumstances an overgenerous gift! [38] Hardinge then returned to Takaungu and the north where he remained until July 18.

On July 22, Hardinge moved by land from Mombasa with a force of more than three hundred men, drawn from the Navy, the Sudanese force at Witu, and the Zanzibar Regulars. His objective was Gazi and the apprehension of the Takaungu rebel leaders. At the same time, ships were to approach Gazi from the sea. But on July 24 Hardinge received information that the town was deserted and that the rebels had fled, Mbaruk of Gazi with them. Examination of the town proved that Mbaruk had left in a hurry: lamps were found still burning in his house.

37. Hardinge to Salisbury, July 6, 1895, *ibid.*, item 14.
38. Hardinge was not the only one who gave gifts of gunpowder. In October 1895, McDougall complained that all the gunpowder Piggott had given Hamis bin Kombo had found its way into Mbaruk's hands. Shelf 72, file 46, Malindi, In 1895–1898, letter of October 7, 1895, *Mombasa Provincial Archives* [hereafter *MPA*].

Among other items, a Koran belonging to Mbaruk was found in his house; this, as a gesture of good will, Hardinge returned to Mbaruk by a messenger. Hardinge was still in some doubt as to whether or not the old fox of Gazi had joined the rebels. No sooner had he left Mombasa for Gazi than a series of letters had arrived from Mbaruk. The first confirmed the promises Mbaruk had made and made tactful inquiries as to what sort of subsidy he would receive after his good deed. The second letter stated that the rebels were too strong for him to overcome by himself; he asked Hardinge to come by sea to aid him. The third letter informed Hardinge that the rebels had fled, and in it Mbaruk accused Hardinge with breaking his promise by coming with troops by land. If, Mbaruk said, Hardinge meant peace, let him leave his troops behind; he would await his arrival and keep his promise.[39] Hardinge, however, had continued the approach with his force by land and Mbaruk had fled. (It must be remembered that the letters were all delayed in reaching Hardinge since they were taken first to Mombasa and forwarded from there.) Hardinge was in something of a quandary. He therefore sent another letter to Mbaruk charging him with duplicity and giving him a fortnight in which to prove that he was really on the side of government. With the letter he sent the Koran, mentioned earlier.

On July 26, two days after Hardinge reached Gazi to find that the birds had flown, armed followers of Mbaruk of Gazi clashed at Vanga with *askaris* formerly employed by the old company. The reasons for the attack were obscure; one report suggested that the company *askaris* had stolen goats from Mbaruk's men. But the net result was that Vanga was again sacked — Mbaruk's opening move in an earlier rebellion.[40] Hardinge delayed awhile, but by early August he accepted the sacking of Vanga as a declaration of war and made his preparations to deal with the rebels of Takaungu and Gazi, most of whom were concentrated at the forest stronghold of Mwele.

On August 12, 1895, a two-week period of grace having expired,

39. *PPA*, VI (1896), item 23(6).
40. Hardinge at first considered the attack accidental; later he believed Mbaruk had planned it beforehand as the opening move in his rebellion. *Ibid.*, items 17, 23, 25. See also the Collector of Vanga's opinion in Vanga 1895–1897, letter of July 24, 1895, *MPA*.

Hardinge and Lloyd Mathews, with a force of four hundred naval ratings, Zanzibar Regulars, and Sudanese troops, accompanied by seven hundred porters, left Gazi for Mwele. On August 16, approaching Mwele, they ran into an ambush laid by Mbaruk's son Eyoub but managed to drive off the rebels; Lloyd Mathews was slightly wounded in the skirmish. By August 17 the expedition was in position for an attack on the fortress from two directions. By early afternoon the assault had succeeded with but light losses. Most of the rebels fled. Mbaruk himself had narrowly missed being killed by a war rocket. His brother Zahran stayed and was killed fighting to the last. The whole village and its fortifications were then destroyed, massive trees being blown down with gun cotton charges, and the area around Mwele cleared of all forest. In the fortress Mbaruk's gunpowder magazine was captured intact with its contents of two thousand pounds of gunpowder. Hardinge had good reason to hope that he had delivered a knockout blow and that the rebels would submit; his hopes were raised by reports that Mbaruk of Gazi had already sent in a messenger suing for peace but that the latter had either been killed or had been too frightened to approach. Hardinge at once dispatched a message by one of the slaves captured at Mwele proclaiming an amnesty for any rebel who surrendered.[41] Meanwhile, the work of destruction at Mwele continued; Hardinge recorded the fatalistic reply of one of the locals, to his neighbor's complaint about the destruction of his possessions: "Do you complain of injury suffered by yourself? Alas my friend when two elephants meet in conflict what becomes of the grass beneath their feet?" [42]

The capture of Mwele did not, however, prove as decisive as Hardinge had hoped. Mbaruk was still at large with a considerable force and did not come in to make submission. Now that he was cut off from his base, he was forced to take to the bush and to fight a guerrilla war for which all his past experience of rebellion and survival in the wild proved invaluable. It was a type of warfare that Hardinge, with his limited forces, was to find frustrating and indecisive. The initiative in the struggle

41. Hardinge to Salisbury, August 26, 1895, *PPA*, VI (1896), item 25; Robert Nunez Lyne, *An Apostle of Empire* (London, 1936), 137–138.
42. *PPA*, VI (1896), item 25.

gradually passed to the rebels. Many of Hardinge's men were drawn from the naval squadron and were not suited to flying column work or to bush warfare of long duration. In addition, the rebels had no base to defend, and were free to move and attack where they willed, provided always that they could live off the country. They had, in fact, for the greater part of the rebellion, the sympathy and passive aid of the Nyika tribes of the hinterland. More and more, Hardinge found his forces tied up defending vulnerable points — ports, missions, and similar places. He had garrisons at Gazi, Wassin, Mombasa, Takaungu, Malindi, Freretown, Ribe, Rabai, Mtanganiko, Jomvu, Sokoke, Jilore, and Jimba. By October 1895, the situation had deteriorated to such an extent that Hamis bin Kombo, an old man of eighty years, refused to answer a summons to report to Mombasa and went over to the rebels with his supporters at Mtwapa. By November of 1895, Hardinge had committed 745 men to a defensive role as garrisons for the towns and stations and was unable to undertake any but local operations. Inevitably he was forced to ask for more troops and to possess himself in patience until they arrived. From the fall of Mwele until the end of 1895, there occurred a series of skirmishes, none of them large or decisive. Most were rebel-inspired. In one, on October 16 near Gazi, a British officer, Captain Lawrence, was killed. His men broke and fled. In this same action, the acting *liwali* of Gazi, Ali bin Salim, showed considerable coolness and courage. One odd incident occurred after this action. Lawrence had been riding a horse at the time of his death; the horse fell into rebel hands, and Mbaruk of Gazi had it sent into Mombasa where it was handed over to Mr. Piggott, the acting administrator. When Hardinge heard of this, he had Piggott send Mbaruk a note of thanks. In many ways this was a very gentlemanly rebellion.[43]

On November 2 the rebels struck at three different points while the government forces were preparing to attack Mtwapa and Bomani. The attacks were on Rabai mission station, Ma-

43. Hardinge, in addition to returning Mbaruk's Koran, demonstrated *his* disposition by placing the women he captured in the care of a loyal Mazrui, the secretary to the *liwali* of Mombasa. See also the curious draft of a letter to Mbaruk, perhaps from Hardinge in Zanzibar In 1895, *MPA*. The date is unclear but appears to be Sept. 21, 1895.

zeras village, and on a Smith Mackenzie caravan traveling into the interior. The attack on Rabai was beaten off, but the other two were successful. At Rabai, where there was a garrison of forty men, the rebels lost thirty-five men, but twelve Wa-Rabai were killed and wounded and ten huts were destroyed. At Mazeras, the Mazrui destroyed sixty huts. After the attack on the Smith Mackenzie caravan, it became necessary to send caravans up-country once a month under military escort. By December, Mbaruk was reported in the north, living with the Giryama. On December 29 Hardinge's reinforcements arrived: three hundred Indian troops (Pathans) under Captain Barrett. Eight days earlier, Hardinge was cheered by the surrender of 150 rebels.

Not all the Mazrui were in rebellion. A number of them sided with the government. In addition to the young *liwali* of Takaungu, there was Muhammad bin Said, who reoccupied and garrisoned Roka after it was sacked by Aziz. There was also Muhammad bin Abdallah, who was with Captain Harrison and the *liwali* of Takaungu during the successful action at Gabina. The son of another Mazrui, Abdullah bin Rashid, held the stockade at Mtandia with thirty armed followers.

The new year came, and with it, disappointments. On January 21, 1896, the rebels felt strong enough to attack the C.M.S. mission station at Freretown which was garrisoned and had a Nordenfelt gun mounted on the mission roof. The attack was beaten off, but such attacks forced Hardinge to maintain his garrisons, a heavy drain on his meagre forces. He complained to Salisbury that in February of 1896, he had no more than two hundred men to spare for active operations, as opposed to garrison duties. Nevertheless, such men as he had after the arrival of the reinforcements were organized into two flying columns. One operated to the north and one to the south of Mombasa, and both proved invaluable in the following weeks. For hardly had the flying columns started operations than the rebels attacked Malindi on the night of February 12. Though the attack was beaten off, the African quarter was almost destroyed and four hundred huts were burned to the ground. The Giryama wavered and were only checked from going over to the rebels by the work of the northern column, whose efforts enabled McDougall to persuade the tribal elders in early March to swear

their loyalty to government on "the hyena" oath, and break
with the rebels (the hyena was the sacred totem of the tribe).
A firepower demonstration at which war rockets were exploded
suitably impressed the elders. More effective still was a successful
action at Gabina on March 5, in which Mbaruk of Takaungu
and his brother Aziz with four hundred men were defeated and
driven into the bush. But even in defeat, the Giryama feared
Mbaruk of Gazi, and warned the government of his power to
bewitch them all.

If the Giryama were impressed by the attack on Malindi, so
was Hardinge; he signalled urgently for more troops, this time
a whole Indian regiment.[44] Before further reinforcements could
arrive, the rebels were engaged in a series of sharp clashes that
went far to break their strength. The actions were centered
around Changoni and Shimba to the north and south of Mombasa, where the two flying columns had left behind strongly
manned posts. In the period between February 25 and March 8
the rebels lost sixty-nine men around these two posts. Perhaps
the fiercest attack was that delivered on the Shimba post on
March 8. The post was held by Lieutenant Scott with twenty-
five rifles. The attackers were under Sebe, a son of Mbaruk of
Gazi. He had been told by his father not to return unless he
had driven out the English from Shimba post. He failed and
in the attempt left twenty-four dead behind.

By early March, therefore, the rebels had received a series of
unpleasant setbacks, and then Hardinge had sufficient forces to
finish the fight. On March 15, the 24th Baluchistan Regiment
under the command of Colonel Pearson arrived from India. It
consisted of 721 officers and men. Hardinge had also succeeded
in recruiting some Sudanese in Egypt: a hundred of these troops
arrived and were dispatched to Malindi at once under Captain
Raikes on the S.S. *Kilwa*. Operations were now intensified. A
campaign of food denial was undertaken, and a chain of posts
was established along the Umba River and along the Uganda
road. Flying columns were turned loose in the area between
the two chains. By April 10 one column under Major Tulloch

44. *PPA*, VI (1896), items 49, 50, 53. Salisbury believed the situation to be
very serious and had to be reassured by Hardinge that the British position
was only temporarily insecure.

was in contact with Mbaruk (the rebels were now splitting up). It succeeded in capturing Mbaruk's "Office Box," a gold-hilted dagger, and forty-eight kerosene tins filled with gunpowder. By April 15 Mbaruk had crossed over to German East Africa. The Germans at once delivered an ultimatum to him to surrender or suffer the consequences. Meanwhile British forces lined the frontier to prevent his return. Mbaruk was in no position to argue, yet he spun out negotiations for six days longer. At first he proposed to the Germans that they should join with him in a combined attack on British East Africa. When he saw that his old game of playing the ends against the middle no longer brought success, he tried new tactics. What rank and pay would he get, was the question he asked, if he should agree to surrender and settle in Tanganyika. Finally he could delay no more; but when it came to the surrender on April 21, 1896, his following had shrunk from the three thousand originally reported as having crossed the frontier to a mere eleven hundred followers. Of these, six hundred were fighting men, two-thirds of them armed with guns.[45] Hardinge attended the surrender and once more met Mbaruk of Gazi, finding him ill at ease and shivering from an attack of fever.

With the surrender of Mbaruk the rebellion was over. Hardinge proclaimed an amnesty, from which only ten persons were excluded.[46] Those rebels still at large in the British East Africa protectorate came forward to surrender, particularly in the area of Takaungu where the rebellion had started. Only a very few irreconcilables remained hidden in the bush, among them Muhammad, son of Hamis bin Kombo, and Akida Bakari, a lieutenant of Mbaruk of Gazi; they do not appear to have caused much trouble. The crushing of the rebellion had cost the protectorate £20,927.[47] The new protectorate rapidly settled down

45. *Ibid.*, item 73. Of the four hundred guns surrendered, only eighteen were breechloaders. This at first caused some concern since the British were believed to have given Mbaruk 136 breechloaders shortly before the rebellion. However, four hundred more firearms were later handed in from the area to the south of Mombasa. *Ibid.*, items 74, 76, 77. The rebels at the time of surrender were very short of bullets, using melted telegraph wire or baked clay to make them.

46. *Ibid.*, item 73; proclamation of amnesty in Zanzibar In 1895, folio 93, letter of April 27, 1896, *MPA*.

47. *PPA*, VI (1896), item 78.

after a rebellion that had broken the power of the coastal chiefs. So satisfied was Hardinge with the condition of the protectorate that he allowed two of Mbaruk's sons who had not been personally engaged in the rebellion to return to the Kenya coast so that they might establish their claim to their father's property in the event of his death. And of course, Rashid bin Salim of the Mazrui remained *liwali* of Takaungu. The failure of this uprising brought an end to the power of the Mazrui on the coast. It is ironic that their own feuds were instrumental in bringing about their final destruction. The history of the Mazrui is indeed a tale of fratricide requited.

As for Mbaruk of Gazi, he settled down in German East Africa near Dar es Salaam. He appears to have won the respect of the German government as they paid him a subsidy of one hundred rupees a month. This action caused the British administration some embarrassment, and in 1907 it was proposed to pardon Mbaruk of Gazi. In December 1907, the governor of the East Africa protectorate wrote to the Colonial Office proposing that Mbaruk be pardoned and granted a subsidy of one hundred rupees a month. He spoke of Mbaruk as an unwilling rebel who had been forced to war by the demand that he surrender his cousin of Takaungu, "a demand which he felt it against his honour to comply and that he made a pathetic appeal for peace, before he was obliged to become an outlaw." [48] The governor, Hayes Sadler, added that since Mbaruk was over seventy years of age "it will not be necessary to pay him a salary for many years." The object of the British in getting Mbaruk to return was to check the drift of the Mazrui to German East Africa, which was apparently impoverishing the British East Africa coast. The Colonial Office approved and a pardon was granted.[49]

Mbaruk was profuse in his thanks, but although some of his clan returned, the old man was content to remain in Dar es

48. Governor's dispatch of Dec. 2, 1907, shelf 63, file 76, *MPA*.

49. Shelf 63, file 76, especially the governor's dispatch of Dec. 2, 1907, *MPA*. The Colonial Office documents concerning these negotiations are in C.O. 533/33, Public Record Office, London. The only comment of the Colonial Office was a minute to the effect that it seemed a curious thing to give an ex-rebel a pension.

Salaam, where he died in 1910.[50] So ended the career of a remarkable professional rebel whose life of adventure equalled all
the tales of his gallant ancestors that were sung in the ballads.

50. Shelf 13, file 1/1, letter of March 18, 1915, *MPA*. The Takaungu District Records put his death in 1910. When war broke out in 1914, Mbaruk's
sons allied themselves with the Germans. Sebe was taken prisoner and deported for spying after the sultan of Zanzibar had proclaimed him a rebel.
Ayoub and Salim, two other sons, were also captured and deported. Sebe was
a political prisoner held in the Seychelles as late as 1923. Of the original rebel
leaders, Mbaruk bin Rashid of Takaungu died in 1898 and Hamis bin Kombo
died in 1903. Her Majesty's Commissioner In 1898, letter of August 22, 1898,
Her Majesty's Commissioner Out 1903, letter of Feb. 26, 1903, *MPA*.

Mwinyi Kheri

by NORMAN R. BENNETT

Associate Professor of History
Boston University

When Germany and Britain began their partition of east central Africa, the sultan of Zanzibar's claims to territory in the African interior were quickly brushed aside. German diplomats asserted that the inland authority of Zanzibar was merely commercial and did not extend to the political rule of any African peoples.[1] The British representatives in Zanzibar, for their own reasons, supported an inland authority for the sultan, although their superiors in London did not choose to uphold these assertions.[2] The basis for the abortive British support for Zanzibar came from the statement, common at the time, that the dominions of the sultan of Zanzibar extended to the Lake Tanganyika port town of Ujiji. There, Mwinyi Kheri had lived for several decades as a merchant and head of the resident Arab community and was usually recognized by visitors, both Arab and European, as representing the authority of the distant rulers of Zanzibar.[3] But as elsewhere in African centers with ties to Zanzibar, an analysis of the character of the leader and members of the Arab residents, plus the political and economic organization of the African people in direct relationship with the Arabs, is necessary to understand the exact nature of the commercial and political system that developed between the sultan in Zanzibar and his subjects in inland Africa.[4] The study of Mwinyi Kheri's life in Ujiji hopefully will illustrate the Arab-African relationship in the area of Lake Tanganyika.

1. Hatzfeld to Plessen, June 19, 1885, F.O. 84/1718, Public Record Office, London [Hereafter P.R.O.].
2. Kirk to Granville, May 9, 1885, F.O. 84/1725; Holmwood, "East Africa — the hill district of Kilimanjaro," F.O. 84/1680, *ibid.*
3. The designation "Arab" in this study is a cultural one; it includes the issue of Arab and African ancestors who had been incorporated into Muslim communities of the East African coast.
4. See for example the study of Mwinyi Mtwana of Mduburu in Norman R. Bennett, *Studies in East African History* (Boston, 1963), 76–80.

Mwinyi Kheri and the other Arab residents of Ujiji settled among the Ha inhabitants of the lake town when the network of trade routes leading from Zanzibar reached Lake Tanganyika during the first third of the nineteenth century. In this period, Arab traders from Zanzibar and the opposite coast began moving inland, following routes opened for them by African trading groups visiting the Indian Ocean littoral.[5] The main reason for this long-delayed penetration from the old coastal Islamic centers appears to be the relatively late formation of the stable African political entities necessary to ensure the safety of visiting traders and to provide markets of sufficient size for profitable commerce.[6]

The impetus came from the growing commercial center of Zanzibar where Said bin Sultan, ruler of Zanzibar and Masqat from 1804 to 1856, gave intelligent stimulation to the economic development of his African dominions. Said's interest coincided with a search for new markets in the western reaches of the Indian Ocean by Indian, American and European traders. The Americans in particular, visiting Zanzibar from at least 1818, created a steady and increasing demand for ivory, the one com-modity — apart from slaves — that could withstand the high cost of human porterage from the interior to the East African coast.[7] Indian traders had preceded the Americans to Zanzibar; new arrivals from India served as middlemen between African and foreign traders and reaped the benefits flowing from Zanzi-bar's new prosperity.[8] British, French, and German competitors added their demands to the market in the years before mid-century.[9]

The earlier trade with the interior probably centered in Afri-

5. See Sir John Gray, "Trading Expeditions from the Coast to Lakes Tan-ganyika and Victoria before 1857," *Tanganyika Notes and Records*, 49:226 ff. (1957); Oscar Baumann, *Durch Masailand zur Nilquelle* (Berlin, 1894), 234.

6. Roland Oliver and Gervaise Mathew, eds., *History of East Africa* (Ox-ford, 1963), I, 169 ff., 253 ff.

7. Broquant to Ministère des Affairs Etrangères, March 10, 1845, Archives de l'Ancien Ministère de la France d'Outre Mer, Paris.

8. The course of American trade and relations with Zanzibar's Indian merchants can be followed in Norman R. Bennett, "Americans in Zanzibar: 1825–1845," Essex Institute *Historical Collections*, XCV:239–262 (1959); "Ameri-cans in Zanzibar: 1845–1856," *ibid.*, XCVIII:36–61 (1962).

9. Gray, *Zanzibar*, 239 ff.; Paul Masson, *Marseille et la Colonisation Fran-çaise* (Marseille, 1906), 412 ff.; Ernst Hieke, *Zur Geschichte des Deutschen Handels mit Ostafrika* (Hamburg, 1939), *passim*.

can hands, with representatives of the fiercely competitive Indian firms of Zanzibar crossing over to the mainland to induce the ivory-carrying Africans to their particular centers. Intensive and protracted bargaining would follow until sales were completed.[10] This complicated system, subject to so many factors beyond the control of the merchants of Zanzibar, was uncertain, especially in the face of increasing world demand for ivory.[11] Thus, Arab-led trading expeditions were sent inland by Said bin Sultan and other interested individuals to protect and expand their sources of supply. The resulting search for ivory took the exploring merchants ever deeper into the continent: by 1839 trading journeys of a year and a half in duration were reported; by 1848 and 1849, of three to three and a half years.[12] The success of these searches can be judged from the report of one American trader that three times as much cotton cloth — a staple of the East African trade — was required for the trade in 1850 as was necessary in 1847.[13]

Long expeditions into the interior required the establishment there of centers for provisioning and protecting the Arab traders. Minor centers such as Zungomero were used until the most important center developed in the territory of the Nyamwezi people of central Tanganyika, which was probably reached by the Arabs around 1825. Later a permanent Arab settlement was formed at the town of Tabora in the 1850's.[14] Meanwhile, Arab

10. Richard F. Burton, "The Lake Regions of Central Equatorial Africa . . . ," *The Journal of the Royal Geographical Society*, XXIX:57 (1859); R. P. Waters to J. Waters, April 8, 1843, Waters Notebooks, Peabody Museum, Salem, Mass.; "Dr. A. Roscher's Tagebuch über seine Reise nach dem Lufidji, 6. Februar bis 24. März 1859," *Mittheilungen . . . von Dr. A. Petermann*, VIII:2 (1862).

11. See for example, McMullan to Shepard, Feb. 5, 1851, Shepard Papers, Peabody Museum, Salem, Mass.; Fabens to Shepard, May 4, 1846, Ward to Shepard, Feb. 2, 1848, Fabens Papers, Peabody Museum; Erhardt to Venn, April 9, 1853, F.O. 54/15, P.R.O.; Richard Gray, *A History of the Southern Sudan, 1839–1889* (Oxford, 1961), 28; Bennett, *Studies in East African History*, 89.

12. R. P. Waters, "Journal," entries of March 23, 1839, June 24, 1839, Peabody Museum; Ward to Shepard, May 2, 1849, Fabens Papers; Jelly and Masury to West, July 28, 1849, West Papers, Peabody Museum.

13. Ward to Shepard, March 28, 1850, Shepard Papers.

14. Burton, "Lake Regions," 16, 78–80, 180 ff.; R. H. Gower, "Ukutu in the Nineteenth Century," *Tanganyika Notes and Records*, 51:208 (1958); Baumann, *Durch Masailand*, 242–243.

traders had pushed westward to Lake Tanganyika, reaching its shores before 1830. At Ujiji an important secondary center for trade to Zanzibar developed in close association with Tabora.[15]

The port town of Ujiji was located in Bujiji, one of the six independent chiefdoms of the Bantu-speaking Ha people who now inhabit the area roughly bordered by the Moyowosi River to the east, by Burundi and Lake Tanganyika to the north and

15. Mr. Macqueen, "Notes on African Geography . . . Visit of Lief Bin Saeid to the Great African Lake," *Journal of the Royal Geographical Society,* XV:371 ff. (1845). Reports of Ujiji began to reach the coast in the 1840's. William Desborough Cooley, *Inner Africa Laid Open* (London, 1852), 60; Charles Pickering, *The Races of Man* (London, 1863), 203.

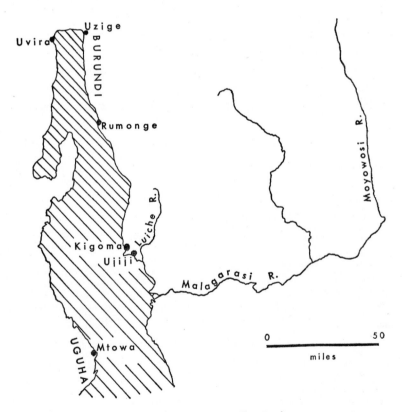

Northern Lake Tanganyika Region

west, and by the Malagarasi River valley to the south.[16] The Bujiji chiefdom extended along Lake Tanganyika from the Luiche River in the south to Burundi in the north; its inland extent was estimated at twenty miles.[17] Only those Ha living around Ujiji, usually called the Jiji, would have commercial relations with the Arabs.[18] The remainder, inhabiting the tsetse-fly-free highlands to the west, lived an isolated life, drawing harsh words from visitors because of their unfriendly nature. To Stanley they were "the most extortionate tribute-takers in Africa." [19]

The Jiji shared this reputation. According to Richard F. Burton, the first European, along with J. H. Speke, to visit them, they were "considered by the Arabs . . . the most troublesome race upon this line of road" and were "rude, insolent, and extortionate." [20] Nevertheless, the Ujiji region, strategically located on Lake Tanganyika's shores, was a vital one to the Arabs. Although the harbor of Ujiji was not fully satisfactory, the fertility of the area, with its regular rains and famine-free harvests, provided the Arabs with the necessities for an inland station.[21] And, in spite of their reputation, the Jiji proved willing to receive and to live in peace with visiting merchants.

The rulers of the Ha states were usually Tusi immigrants, but by the middle of the nineteenth century both noble and commoner possessed the same language and culture. The ruler of a

16. The author's thanks go to Beverly Bolser for helpful information on the Ha. See J. H. Scherer, "The Ha of Tanganyika," *Anthropos,* LIV:841–904 (1959); M. d'Hertefelt, A. Trouwborst and J. Scherer, *Les Anciens Royaumes de la Zone Interlacustrine Meridionale* (London, 1962), 177 ff.

17. Henry M. Stanley, *Through the Dark Continent* (New York, 1878), II, 5; Edward Coode Hore, *Tanganyika* (London, 1892), 67–68.

18. A recent survey described the Jiji as "more Ha than anything else, although the inhabitants of the large African town of Ujiji are a curiously mixed lot and contain representatives of no less than fifty different tribes in Tanganyika and the Congo." J. P. Moffett, ed., *Handbook of Tanganyika* (2nd ed.; Dar es Salaam, 1958), 271.

19. Stanley, *Dark Continent,* I, 508.

20. Burton, "Lake Regions," 223.

21. Herman Wissmann, *Unter deutscher Flagge quer durch Afrika von West nach Ost* (Berlin, 1889), 235; Scherer, "The Ha," 844, 853; E. A. Leakey and N. V. Rounce, "The Human Geography of the Kasulu District, Tanganyika," *Geography,* XVIII:300 (1933); C. H. B. Grant, "Uha in Tanganyika Territory," *The Geographical Journal,* LXVI: 417–418 (1925).

chiefdom such as Bujiji was the *abami* (plural, *umwami*) who
ruled over subordinate chiefs, the *abatware banini* (singular
umutware munini); they in turn controlled districts for the
abami in a kind of feudal relationship. The *abatware banini*
divided *their* territories into sections under the control of local
officials called the *abatware batoyi*.[22] The port of Ujiji was included in the territory of the two districts of Ugoy and Kawele,
each ruled by a separate *umutware munini*.[23] The *abami* did
not possess great military strength and usually left the routine
duties of administration to the *abatware banini* who were often
the hereditary rulers of their districts. They collected the revenues, taking their share and passing the remainder on to the
abami. The system was a loose one, and the *abami's* strength
was based on his power to appoint or confirm the *abatware
banini* in their positions.[24] In practice, as far as Ujiji was concerned, this administrative structure functioned satisfactorily and
gave the stability a community of Arab merchants needed.

To the Arab merchants, ever in search of ivory, Ujiji was a
necessary jumping off place for their penetration of the Lake
Tanganyika region and the territory to the west and southwest
of the lake. The crossing of Lake Tanganyika occurred in the
1840's when Arab traders, including Said bin Habib, perhaps
the greatest of all Arab travelers from Zanzibar (he eventually
crossed the African continent), began to seek new ivory- and
slave-producing regions.[25] The success of these ventures is indicated by an 1863 report from Zanzibar stating that the great
bulk of the ivory arriving on that island came from the interior
route passing through Tabora and Ujiji.[26] The slaves taken in
these regions, fewer in numbers than on the more southern
Arab routes into the interior, usually did not reach the East

22. D'Hertefelt *et al., Les Anciens Royaumes,* 172, 208–211.
23. Stanley, *Dark Continent,* II, 1–2; Edward C. Hore, "On the Twelve
Tribes of Tanganyika," *The Journal of the Anthropological Institute of
Great Britain and Ireland:* XII:8 (1882–1883).
24. Audrey I. Richards, ed., *East African Chiefs* (London, 1960), 217.
25. Said bin Habeeb, "Narrative . . . of an Arab Inhabitant of Zanzibar,"
Transactions of the Bombay Geographical Society, XV:146–148 (1860). See R.
F. Burton's comments in the *Proceedings of the Royal Geographical Society,*
III:363 (1858–1859); J. H. Speke, "On the Commerce of Central Africa,"
Transactions of the Bombay Geographical Society, XV:141 (1860).
26. Playfair to Bombay Government, June 15, 1863, F.O. 54/20, P.R.O.

African coast. Many were sold in Ujiji or along the route to the coast as Arab caravans proceeded homewards.[27]

Mwinyi Kheri probably arrived in Ujiji in the early period of Arab settlement — in the mid-1870's he reported he had been thirty years in the area.[28] We can assume that Mwinyi Kheri and other Arabs, financed by the Indian merchants of Zanzibar, either independently or in the entourage of more prosperous Arabs, entered the Ujiji region to make their fortune. Most Zanzibar Arabs returned home once their future was assured, but Mwinyi Kheri and his compatriots at Ujiji were among those who decided to take up permanent residence in the interior.[29]

The first direct information concerning Ujiji dates from 1858, when the explorers Burton and Speke reached Lake Tanganyika. They described Ujiji as a small and unhealthy town without, as yet, a major Arab settlement. At that time it was chiefly used as a trading depot for "flying caravans" from Tabora; these secured the desired goods as quickly as possible and then returned to the healthier base in central Tanganyika.[30] Both Kawele and Ugoy were visited by Arabs, with Kawele having one Arab *tembe* (residence). Rusimba was *abami* of Bujiji; his *umutware munini*, Kannena, had a very unfavorable reputation due to his exactions from visitors. Mwinyi Kheri was not mentioned by Burton or Speke; perhaps at the time he was absent from Ujiji, or equally likely, perhaps he was not yet important enough to notice. No one Arab appeared to control Ujiji, the community there probably being too new and insignificant to require a leader. The *abami* had a powerful position and through his subordinates received presents and revenues from visiting caravans.[31]

27. Rigby to Wood, May 1, 1860, F.O. 54/17, *ibid.;* Burton, "Lake Regions," 162; Hore to L.M.S., April 16, 1879, London Missionary Society Archives, London [hereafter L.M.S.].

28. Stanley, *Dark Continent,* I, 44; *ibid.,* II, 12.

29. Abushiri bin Salim, one of the leaders of the 1888–1890 uprising against the Germans in Tanganyika, was a good example of the Arab fortune seeker. See Fritz Ferdinand Müller, *Deutschland-Zanzibar-Ostafrika* (Berlin, 1959), 385.

30. Burton, "Lake Regions," 215, 218.

31. *Ibid.,* 216, 224–226.

In 1858, it did not appear that Arab activity had extended significantly from Ujiji to the west and southwest. A few enterprising individuals had made the beginnings of this expansion, however — Said bin Habib being a notable example — and the path to Ujiji's future prosperity was indicated.[32]

Because of this expansion of activity around Lake Tanganyika's shores, a resident Arab community began to grow at Ujiji. The precise nature of the early community and its leadership remains unclear until the late 1860's. In 1869, Livingstone arrived at Ujiji to find a "headman," Mwinyi Mokaia, also called Katomba; he was the brother of Mwinyi Kheri.[33] Other information of 1869, from a British missionary in Zanzibar, referred to a "Governor" in Ujiji who might have been Mwinyi Mokaia.[34] One other souce of coastal authority was a representative of the powerful customs master of Zanzibar, Ladha Damji. Since most Arabs of the interior were deeply in debt to the Ladha Damji or to other Indians, this official could have played a most influential role, even if the great distances involved made actual control difficult.[35]

Mwinyi Mokaia was a Swahili or coastal Arab and therefore was probably included in Livingstone's well-known blasts against those he considered — he labeled one a "Moslem Nigger" — not "pure" Arabs. He said: "They are nearly all miserable Suaheli at Ujiji, and have neither the manners nor the sense of Arabs." These invectives had little meaning since Livingstone freely acknowledged the services of such individuals as Muhammad bin Gharib and Tippu Tip who were both of mixed Arab-African ancestry. As for Mwinyi Mokaia, Livingstone recognized him as a pioneer of the Arab movement to the west of Lake Tanganyika,

32. See Richard F. Burton, *The Lake Regions of Central Africa* (London, 1860), II, 61, 116, 120–121, 147–152; James Hanning Speke, *What Led to the Discovery of the Sources of the Nile* (London, 1864), 199; Richard F. Burton, *Zanzibar* (London, 1872), II, 300–302.

33. Horace Waller, ed., *The Last Journals of David Livingstone* (London, 1874), II, 7, 11, 25, 95. Mwinyi Kheri is given as "Moneghera" in this account.

34. R. M. Heanley, *A Memoir of Bishop Steere* (London, 1888), 75.

35. Waller, *Livingstone's Last Journals*, II, 8. See the amusing comment of an Arab, Juma bin Sinti, on the problem of debts to Indians, in C. Waldemar Werther, *Der mittleren Hochländer des nördlichen Deutsch-Ost-Afrika* (Berlin, 1898), 42.

saying "he knows more than anyone else about the country."
After meeting Mwinyi Mokaia in Manyema, Livingstone met
him again at Tabora, while the Arab was returning to Zanzibar.
Mwinyi Mokaia became seriously ill at Tabora, and despite
efforts by Livingstone to succor him, he died there in March
1873.[36]

The successor to the leadership of the Arabs of Ujiji was Muhammad bin Sali el Nabhani.[37] This Arab merchant had spent
long years in the interior. Livingstone had encountered him at
the court of the Lunda ruler, the *Kazembe,* where Muhammad
bin Sali had been detained since around 1842, either a prisoner
of the *Kazembe* or because he had lost all his trade goods in
a local war and feared to return to his creditors. Muhammad
bin Sali left the *Kazembe's* court and arrived at Ujiji shortly
after Livingstone; the latter described him as "a fine portly black
Arab with a pleasant smile, and pure white beard," and also as
"well advanced in years"; he arrived at Ujiji in 1869.[38]

When the British explorer Cameron reached Ujiji in 1874, he
considered Muhammad bin Sali the "practical head" of the local
Arabs, although he had no official appointment from the sultan
of Zanzibar. Mwinyi Kheri was described as "next in importance"
to Muhammad bin Sali. During Cameron's visit Mwinyi Kheri
married "the daughter of the chief of Ujiji." [39] Thus, although
Mwinyi Kheri was then only one of a company of Arabs that
included Muhammad bin Gharib and others, his marriage clearly
put him in the path for future advancement.

Meanwhile, during the period of the late 1860's and early
1870's, Ujiji was changing in character; it was no longer just an
outstation of Tabora. A significant penetration of the territory
west of Lake Tanganyika had occurred in the late 1860's, led
by such men as Mwinyi Mokaia from Ujiji and Tippu Tip,

36. Waller, *Livingstone's Last Journals,* II, 12, 25, 87, 95, 143, 172–173.
37. Also called Muhammad bin Saleh, or Muhammed bin Salib. See Ian
Cunnison, "The Reigns of the Kazembes," *The Northern Rhodesia Journal,*
III:135 (1956).
38. Burton, "Lake Regions," 257–259; Waller, *Livingstone's Last Journals,*
I, 248, II, 9; *Maisha ya Hamed bin Muhammed el Murjebi yaani Tippu Tip*
(Supplement to the East African Swahili Committee Journals, No. 28/2, July
1958 and No. 29/1, Jan. 1959), 55.
39. Verney Lovett Cameron, *Across Africa* (London, 1885), 177–181.

who traveled around the lower end of the lake.[40] The resulting discovery of the rich ivory lands of Manyema and Urua led to "a sort of California gold-fever" which caused increasing numbers of Arabs to seek their fortunes in the newly known regions.[41] What sold for $120 in Zanzibar could now be gained for twenty-five cents worth of copper in Manyema or Urua.[42] Caravans were soon reported returning to Zanzibar with from eighteen to thirty-five thousand pounds of ivory; the rush to secure a share of these profits soon became general.[43]

With this movement to the west, Ujiji became a vital center with a dual role — to exploit the Lake Tanganyika region and to provide supplies for caravans going westwards. One group of Arabs remained resident at Ujiji; the others — including many of the most famous Arabs of central Africa — merely visited Ujiji on their passages to and from the coast, or sold their merchandise and received new trade goods there. These visitors included Tippu Tip, Juma Merikani, and Said bin Habib. Such men, however, played no prominent role at Ujiji until around 1884.[44]

Thus, control of Ujiji in the 1870's and 1880's, with its estimated population of from three to eight thousand Africans and about two dozen Arabs, was left to those Arab traders who were content to trade and raid in the less wealthy areas around Lake Tanganyika.[45] This group hardly ever returned to Zanzibar

40. The two routes remained essentially separate, the Ujiji Arabs not visiting the southern Lake Tanganyika regions. Hore to L.M.S., April 12, 1880, L.M.S. Archives; V. L. Cameron, "Examination of the Southern Half of Lake Tanganyika," *Journal of the Royal Geographical Society*, XLV:206 (1875).

41. Livingstone to Murchison, April–July 1870, *Proceedings of the Royal Geographical Society*, XVIII:276 (1873–1874).

42. Kirk to Murchison, Nov. 10, 1871, *New York Herald*, Dec. 11, 1871.

43. Livingstone to Maclear, Nov. 17, 1871, *Proceedings of the Royal Geographical Society*, XVII:70 (1872–1873). The resulting commerce was so considerable that the coastal center of Bagamoyo trebled in size from 1867 to 1871. Kirk to F.O., Feb. 18, 1871, P.R.O. See also L. A. Ricklin, *La Mission Catholique du Zanguebar* (Paris, 1880), 4.

44. For the story of the Arabs who passed west to the Congo regions, P. Ceulemans, *La Question arabe et le Congo (1883–1892)* (Bruxelles, 1959).

45. François Coulbois, *Dix Années au Tanganyka* (Limoges, 1901), 68; *A l'Assaut des Pays Nègres. Journal des Missionnaires d'Alger dans l'Afrique Equatoriale* (Paris, 1884), 300. Stanley in 1876 estimated Ujiji had a population of three thousand while the Bujiji chiefdom as a whole included thirty-

once in the interior, and they were very little known to the authorities of that island.[46]

Muhammad bin Sali remained leader until his death. Then Mwinyi Kheri bin Mwinyi Mkuu el Ghasani[47] took first position. Information concerning his person is meager. Mwinyi Kheri was born on the African coast opposite Zanzibar; in 1876 he was described as "of vast girth"; in 1883 as being about sixty years in age, with "gray hair, regular features, but of an extremely dark complexion." He was unable to read, although this did not hamper him greatly since some of his subordinates could.[48] Most of these subordinates were his relatives; Mwinyi Hassani served as secretary to Mwinyi Kheri in Ujiji and was usually left in command during his absences.[49] Mwinyi Kheri's sons were active, while another relative of importance was Bwana Mkombe, a nephew, who was reported at times in Zanzibar preparing to lead caravans to Ujiji.[50]

Mwinyi Kheri drew his power from his standing as senior member of the Arab community and from his personal fortune. In 1876 his wealth, in Ujiji values, was estimated at $18,000; it included 120 slaves, 80 guns and 9 canoes.[51] The guns were a vital factor, since it would later be asserted that the Arabs were able to prevent the Jiji from obtaining firearms.[52] Possession of firearms alone does not, of course, explain Mwinyi Kheri's dominance in Ujiji until his death in 1885. Mwinyi Kheri's real source of strength came from the relations he worked out with the Ha power structure of Bujiji. The *abami*

six thousand inhabitants. Stanley, *Dark Continent*, II, 5. Stanley is considered a very reliable observer. See the comments on his Baganda statistics in L. A. Fallers, ed., *The King's Men* (London, 1964), 83.

46. See, for example, Kirk to Bombay Government, Feb. 9, 1872, E-62, Zanzibar Archives.

47. So named by Tippu Tip in *Maisha ya Hamed bin Muhammed,* 121.

48. Cameron, *Across Africa,* 181; Stanley, *Dark Continent,* II, 6; Coulbois, *Tanganyka,* 63–64.

49. *A l'Assaut des Pays Nègres,* 298. Mwinyi Hassani made a rather unfavorable impression on Europeans. See Hore to L.M.S., April 16, 1879, L.M.S. Archives; Stanley, *Dark Continent,* II, 8.

50. *A l'Assaut des Pays Nègres,* 298, for his son Suliman. *Missieleven in Africa. Uit de Brieven van des West-Vlaamschen Missionaris Ameet Vincke der Witte Paters* (Leuven, 1927), 78.

51. Tippu Tip in 1881 called him the senior Arab. *Maisha ya Hamed bin Muhammed,* 121; Stanley, *Dark Continent,* II, 7.

52. Hore, "Twelve Tribes of Tanganyika," 10.

lived inland and seldom visited Ujiji and was content to recognize the Arab presence in Ujiji because it drew trade.[53] He supplied Mwinyi Kheri with provisions and in return received revenues from visiting caravans.[54] Thus left alone, Mwinyi Kheri could easily control the *abatware banini* of Kawele and Ugoy. To a British missionary the subchiefs seemed mere "puppets" under Arab control, accepting their lot because of the undoubted benefits brought by Arab trade.[55]

Thus the Arabs and Africans of Ujiji came to terms in a manner which brought them the greatest mutual profit. The strength of the relationship was based on Mwinyi Kheri's having assimilated himself, by marriage and other means, into the local political structure. The Arabs received a safe base for their commercial operations and were amply provisioned; the Jiji received duties on these operations and were left in control of most aspects of their daily life.[56] Their acceptance of the Arab presence showed in the absence of serious friction between Arab and African, friction that was common at the Arab center among the Nyamwezi at Tabora.[57]

In this dual authority structure, the normal course of events left each group to settle its own problems. Stanley reported that an aggrieved individual could go either to the *umutware munini* or Mwinyi Kheri for justice, but that in all important cases the Arabs and Jiji elders met jointly to reach a settlement "because it is perfectly understood by both parties that many monied interests would be injured if open hostilities were commenced." [58] Such an arrangement was essential in a port town with a busy market, drawing Africans from most of the tribal groups represented on Lake Tanganyika's shores and putting them in contact with the usually well-armed and boisterous retainers of the

53. Several sources give a ritual significance to this — it was asserted that the *abami* would die if he saw Lake Tanganyika. Stanley, *Dark Continent,* II, 5; *A l'Assaut des Pays Nègres,* 294. See also Pater Capus, "Eine Missionsreise nach Uha und Urundi," *Dr. A. Petermanns Mitteilungen,* XLIV: 124 (1898).

54. Stanley, *Dark Continent,* II, 2.

55. Hore, *Tanganyika,* 70.

56. For examples of the benefits received by the *abami* and others, Stanley, *Dark Continent,* II, 6; Cameron, *Across Africa,* 185; Hore to L.M.S., April 16, 1879, L.M.S. Archives.

57. See Bennett, *Studies in East African History,* 1–7.

58. Stanley, *Dark Continent,* II, 6.

Arabs.[59] Crises could and did occur, but good sense always prevailed. For example, in 1880, Arab slaves got out of hand in the market. When the responsibility for the fracas could not be settled at a joint meeting, the Jiji affirmed that the affair was so serious that all the Arabs except Mwinyi Kheri, Mwinyi Hassani, and Mwinyi Akida, an old Arab resident at nearby Kigoma, would have to leave Ujiji.[60] Taking the Jiji at their word, all the Arabs, including the exempted three, packed their belongings and left town. The ruse worked; before the Arabs had gone far the Jiji recalled them and all was settled in peace. Clearly the disorder of a busy market was preferable to the economic loss that would follow removal of the Arab community.[61]

Other examples of Mwinyi Kheri's secure position can be cited. Once, previous to 1880, Abdullah bin Suliman, an Arab resident of Kasimbu, a nearby settlement, decided to punish Mwinyi Kheri for difficulties stemming from the conduct of the latter's followers. Mwinyi Kheri, faced with an invasion, called on the Jiji authorities for support. A general rallying of the men of Ujiji resulted, causing Abdullah bin Suliman to let his grievances drop without settlement.[62] The secure position of Mwinyi Kheri and his Arab community was effectively demonstrated when a new *abami* of Bujiji had to be chosen. The elders, probably wishing to avoid any civil disorder, called on Mwinyi Akida — Mwinyi Kheri was absent from Ujiji — to supervise the election. He presided over the ceremonies effectively, and a son of the former *abami* was elected and installed as new ruler.[63]

Thus, in visitors' eyes, Mwinyi Kheri was "to all intents and purposes the King of the country." [64] By a skillful policy, he had utilized his position as head of the Arab community to secure his own interests, but he had done so in a fashion that did not

59. There are many descriptions of the Ujiji market. See, for example, Hore, "Twelve Tribes of Tanganyika," 8–9; Hutley to L.M.S., Oct. 19, 1879, L.M.S. Archives.

60. Mwinyi Akida held a position at Kigoma similar to Mwinyi Kheri's at Ujiji. Both had arrived on Lake Tanganyika's shores at about the same time, but Mwinyi Akida was not as successful as Mwinyi Kheri. Hore to Kirk, Feb. 9, 1880, N-7, Zanzibar Archives.

61. Hutley to Mullens, Nov. 7, 1880, L.M.S. Archives.

62. Stanley, *Dark Continent*, II, 8–9.

63. Hore to L.M.S., Feb. 9, 1880, L.M.S. Archives.

64. Hore to L.M.S., May 27, 1879, *ibid.*

attempt to force Arab domination on the Jiji, who thus could cooperate with the visitors to their mutual benefit and that of the busy commercial center they both occupied.

Mwinyi Kheri was so secure in his position at Ujiji that he could spend long intervals away from the town, leaving his relatives, usually Mwinyi Hassani, to act in his stead. Mwinyi Kheri's particular area of endeavor was in opening up to trade the territories around the northern end of Lake Tanganyika. There had been a long Arab interest to the north; in 1858 Burton listed slaves for sale at Ujiji from Burundi and Uvira and mentioned an Arab depot at Uvira where ivory, slaves, and iron were all plentiful and cheap.[65] Mwinyi Kheri is usually considered one of the pioneer Arab visitors to the northern regions; he may have gone there as early as the mid–1840's.[66] The northern shores were a difficult area for Arab traders. The state of Burundi was a powerful African entity, little disposed to allow Arab visitors within its territorial limits. This "boisterous, barbarous tribe called Warundi" remained in control of the situation and the Arabs in general were reconciled, if not content, to confine their operations to port towns such as Uzige.[67] Mwinyi Kheri apparently had a good position there; Livingstone reported in 1869 that the chief of Uzige had sent an ivory tusk to "his friend" Mwinyi Kheri, even though there had previously been hostilities between the two. Livingstone also mentioned, however, that the Arab trader had tried to go inland by force, a venture that had been checked since the Barundi did not wish foreign visitors.[68] Mwinyi Kheri nevertheless continued to hold a commercial center in Uvira, and a profitable one, until his death.[69]

65. Burton, "Lake Regions," 221, 229, 240, 250–251.

66. J. M. M. van den Burgt, *Un Grand Peuple de l'Afrique Equatoriale* (Bois-le-Duc, 1903), 24, 64. Some rather unclear oral accounts of Mwinyi Kheri in that region appear in Armand Abel, *Les Musulmans noirs du Maniema* (Bruxelles, 1960), 83.

67. J. H. Speke, "Journal of a Cruise on the Tanganyika Lake, Central Africa," *Blackwood's Edinburgh Magazine*, LXXXVI:352 (1859). For the Barundi trade, Hans Meyer, *Die Barundi* (Leipzig, 1916), 96.

68. Waller, *Livingstone's Last Journals*, II, 14–16. Burton reported an earlier Arab failure against the Barundi. Burton, "Lake Regions," 249.

69. See Hore, "Twelve Tribes of Tanganyika," 11–13. Arabs tried to force their way north in 1884 and later with similar lack of success. See Meyer, *Die Barundi*, 165; Van den Burgt, *Grand Peuple*, 65.

The first serious threat to the position of Mwinyi Kheri among the Jiji came from increasing European penetration of the Lake Tanganyika regions in the late 1870's. Permanent European residents now replaced the earlier harmless European explorers who were generally well-treated by the Arabs and Africans of Ujiji. Following Livingstone's death in central Africa in 1873, increased financial support allowed the British London Missionary Society to continue what they considered the explorer's unfinished work. The society decided to establish a mission at Ujiji, the location made famous by the meeting of Stanley and Livingstone in 1871.[70] Arriving in Zanzibar in 1877, the L.M.S. party set out for the interior and after many difficulties, two of its members, E. C. Hore and J. B. Thomson, attained Ujiji in August 1878.[71]

Mwinyi Kheri, aware that the group was coming, welcomed the potentially troublesome visitors at first. He offered them their choice of a location for a station; the missionaries favored the area of Kigoma Bay, about three miles from Ujiji. But then, perhaps because of murmurings from his fellow Arabs, Mwinyi Kheri informed Hore and Thomson that they should not move from their temporary camp until their reasons for coming to Ujiji were made public.[72] At a meeting of the assembled Arabs, about fifteen in all, Thomson eloquently said:

> We had come to help open up the country, to instruct the people, to improve their social and moral state as well as to teach them all sorts of handicraft and to better their domestic position. Further I told them we wished to examine the lake and make ourselves acquainted with the people on its shores. In short, I told them that we had not come to trade but wished to encourage trade and to do all we could to benefit the people morally and socially and for these purposes we wanted to build or to buy houses and boats in such places as we could carry on our work with vigour and in health.[73]

70. Henry M. Stanley, *How I Found Livingstone* (London, 1872), 416, 566. With more enthusiasm than truth, a L.M.S. official later said the goal of his society was "to establish itself at the point where Livingstone had last been seen by Europeans." R. W. Thompson, *British Foreign Missions* (London, 1899), 99. Stanley, however, advised against setting up at Ujiji. A. W. Dodgshun, "Journal," entry of Nov. 27, 1877, L.M.S. Archives.

71. See A. J. Hanna, "The Role of The London Missionary Society in the Opening up of East Central Africa," *Transactions of the Royal Historical Society*, 5th series, V:41–59 (1955); Hore, *Tanganyika*, 3 ff.

72. Hore to Mullens, Sept. 17, 1878, L.M.S. Archives.

73. Thomson to Mullens, Aug. 30, 1878, *ibid.*

Unimpressed, the Arabs retorted that orders from the sultan of
Zanzibar were necessary before any permanent settlement was
possible. They affirmed that the letters from the sultan brought
by the missionaries made no reference to such a settlement. The
Arabs therefore decided that until the sultan's letter arrived
the missionaries would have to live within the limits of Ujiji
where they would be under Arab protection. Thomson was
sure this was the work of Mwinyi Kheri who was acting to
prevent a European establishment.[74]

Mwinyi Kheri's reference to the authority of the sultan of
Zanzibar was not entirely sincere. The Ujiji leader had not been
appointed to office by the sultan, nor had he been confirmed in
office. The sultan, Barghash bin Said, took little interest in the
interior of Africa; as long as ivory came to his coastal markets,
and as long as no European threat materialized, Barghash left
the inland Arabs to their own devices. And generally the Ujiji
Arabs did not admit of any Zanzibar administrative jurisdiction
over themselves or their property. They often affirmed they were
free settlers on an independent territory.[75] The Arab settlers did,
of course, have a feeling of loyalty to the sultan of Zanzibar,
but they were content to apply in times of need to his nearest
representative, the Arab governor of Tabora.[76] As far as Mwinyi
Kheri and the missionaries were concerned, it is apparent that
the Arab leader only referred to the sultan for orders when he
wished to ensure delay that would serve his own interests.

Additional letters did arrive from Zanzibar but without effect-
ing any change in the Arab refusal; some of the Arabs affirmed
that even if ten letters came they would not allow settlement.[77]
The Arab attitude is understandable. The British, by their often
indiscriminate efforts to repress the slave trade on the eastern
African coast, were clearly suspect.[78] To the Arabs, these British

74. Thomson to Mullens, Aug. 25, 1878, Hore to Mullens, Sept. 17, 1878,
ibid.; Thomson to Kirk, Aug. 24, 1878, in Kirk to Salisbury, Oct. 14, 1878,
F.O. 84/1514, P.R.O.; Thomson to Kirk, Aug. 30, 1878, in Kirk to Salisbury,
Nov. 7, 1878, F.O. 84/1515, *ibid.* A later missionary visitor charged that the
sultan's letters often bore secret marks that countered his written message.
Coulbois, *Tanganyika,* 64.
75. Hore to Mullens, Feb. 18, 1879, L.M.S. Archives.
76. Hore to Mullens, April 16, 1879, *ibid.*
77. Hore to Boustead, Ridley and Co., March 17, 1880, *ibid.*
78. See Hutley to L.M.S., Feb. 11, 1881, *ibid.* For these excesses, see Nor-

missionaries bearing letters from the powerful British representative at Zanzibar could very well be agents of that power and forerunners of a serious interference in the established balance between Mwinyi Kheri and the Jiji.

Mwinyi Kheri's fears were correct. Hore, the mainstay of the mission because of the frequent deaths and departures of the other members, began to work for a firmer assertion of the authority of Zanzibar over Ujiji. Reacting to Hore's complaints, John Kirk, British representative at the sultan's court, informed Barghash that his abstention from authority at Ujiji could lead Britain to "conclude that the Sultan has no authority in these regions and no rights to be respected by us." Kirk had Barghash write to his representative at Tabora, Abdullah bin Nasibu, to order him to establish direct and effective authority over the Zanzibari subjects residing in Ujiji. Kirk also sent his own urgings, in "plain terms," to ensure that the sultan's orders would be followed.[79] In his letter to Abdullah bin Nasibu, Barghash pointed out that it was the governor's duty to protect the Europeans at Ujiji. Thus he should send men to the lake port to hoist the flag of Zanzibar and assume sovereignty. Mwinyi Kheri, if he could be trusted, could continue in office as the sultan's representative. Mwinyi Kheri also was informed by Barghash of these developments.[80]

But the proposal was clearly British inspired. Barghash as yet had no great interest in Ujiji, while, more important, Abdullah bin Nasibu certainly knew better, with his fragile power base at Tabora, than to attempt to interfere in the affairs of an independent Arab community. Mwinyi Kheri's position therefore remained secure.

Hore, however, continued to press Mwinyi Kheri. When the Ujiji leader returned from Uvira in March 1880, Hore implicitly threatened him: "I further reported to him your [Kirk's] offer of friendship and interest, dependent upon his liberal policy with regard to our settlement here, and gave him a hint as far as I deemed advisable of the probable future arrangements

man R. Bennett, "Charles de Vienne and the Frere Mission to Zanzibar," *Boston University Papers on Africa*, II, *African History* (Boston, 1966).

79. Kirk to Hore, June 21, 1880, N-7, Zanzibar Archives.

80. Barghash to Abdullah bin Nasibu, June 1880, *ibid.*; Barghash to Mwinyi Kheri, June 17, 1880, *ibid.*

for the maintenance of order and civilization in Ujiji." Hore also "reminded him that your [Kirk's] promise of friendship was no idle word as he had already seen by your letter to him." But Hore had little success. A council of Arabs in September again decided to refer the matter of settlement to Barghash.[81]

Mwinyi Kheri blamed the decision on his fellow Arabs and said he could not act. Earlier, another of the Arab leaders had said that Mwinyi Kheri was the real originator of all delays.[82] In truth, the Arab community was probably united in wishing to prevent a missionary base in their midst. Hore then left Ujiji to return to Zanzibar, stopping at Tabora to discuss the problem with Abdullah bin Nasibu. The Arab leader seemed confused as to what he should do if Mwinyi Kheri refused to cooperate. Hore advised Abdullah to act forcefully and left Tabora with the expectation that the sultan's orders would be carried out. He might not have been so confident if he had known that in the previous year Abdullah bin Nasibu had informed a British missionary that he had no authority to act in Ujiji since it was an independent territory.[83]

Without aid from Zanzibar, the L.M.S. men strove as best they could to follow their missionary calling at Ujiji. Mwinyi Kheri did not intervene in things spiritual, but he made sure nothing more was attempted. One possible outlet for the frustrated missionaries was the chance that they might be able to bypass the Arab community to deal directly with the Ha leadership. There had been some slight contact with the *abami* of Bujiji shortly after the arrival of the L.M.S., but Mwinyi Kheri knew of the resulting tentative plans to visit the *abami* and was able to prevent contact.[84] Other efforts to secure land from Abe, the *umutware munini* of Kawele, met similar failure. Abe, called by Hore "a sad drunkard," was under the influence of Mwinyi Kheri and would not violate his wishes.[85] With no success from

81. Hore to Kirk, Sept. 16, 1880, K-1, *ibid.*

82. Hore to Kirk, April 15, 1879, Q-27, *ibid.*

83. Hore to Kirk, Dec. 7, 1880, in Kirk to F.O., June 12, 1881, Q-25, *ibid.*; Dodgshun to Kirk, Jan. 27, 1879 in Kirk to Salisbury, March 5, 1879, *Slave Trade Correspondence Presented to Parliament in 1879, ibid.*

84. Hore to L.M.S., Dec. 9, 1878, L.M.S. Archives. Future efforts also failed. See Wookey to L.M.S., Jan. 26, 1881, *ibid.*

85. Hore to L.M.S., April 16, 1879, *ibid.*; Dec. 9, 1878, *ibid.*

the Jiji authorities, Hore and his colleagues then attempted to win a site at Kigoma by dealing with the local Arab leader, Mwinyi Akida, and the African leader, Mbogo. Mwinyi Akida appeared willing to secure the missionaries land, asking at the same time that they use their influence to obtain for him the post of governor of Ujiji; but he lacked the power to act counter to Mwinyi Kheri's policy.[86]

There was no alternative then but to remain at Ujiji until a location could be secured outside of Mwinyi Kheri's sphere of influence. The Arabs were tolerant and left the missionaries in peace, even when in 1883 they launched a steamer on Lake Tanganyika. But there was little likelihood of missionary success in the Muslim-dominated town. A station was founded at Mtowa, on the western shore of Lake Tanganyika, but an equal lack of success awaited the missionaries at this way station for Congo caravans.[87] At Mtowa too, the word of Mwinyi Kheri had some importance, and he was several times accused of intriguing against the British missionaries.[88] Lack of success caused the L.M.S. to end their work at Ujiji in 1883 and at Mtowa in 1885. They transferred their activities to Kavala Island, offshore from Mtowa, where they remained until 1888.[89]

Mwinyi Kheri had succeeded, by his peaceful delaying tactics, in preventing a British presence which might have damaged his interests. The threat was more dangerous than he knew: in 1880 Hore, stimulated by Mwinyi Kheri's attitude, entered into discussions with Kirk about "the desirability of your being represented in the interior." Hore's hatred of the slave trade also played a role in this request; he said, "I itch to take more energetic measures than prudence perhaps and at any rate my missionary work would justify." [90] Kirk favored the suggestion;

86. Hore to L.M.S., Feb. 26, 1880, March 10, 1880, *ibid.;* Hore to Kirk, Feb. 25, 1880, in Kirk to Salisbury, June 25, 1880, F.O. 84/1574, P.R.O.

87. At Mtowa, a missionary once told the Africans he and his fellow missionaries were the children of God. He said, "they would answer cooly, pointing to the wonderful things in and about the house — *you* are his children *indeed.*" Jones to L.M.S., Dec. 2, 1884, L.M.S. Archives.

88. Griffith to L.M.S., Dec. 27, 1879, Nov. 13, 1881, *ibid.*

89. The London Missionary Society eventually moved to work in the area now incorporated into Zambia. Robert I. Rotberg, *Christian Missionaries and the Creation of Northern Rhodesia* (Princeton, 1965), 16 ff.

90. Hore to Kirk, Aug. 17, 1880, N-7, Zanzibar Archives; Hore to L.M.S., July 20, 1880, L.M.S. Archives; Hore to Kirk, Feb. 25, 1880, N-7, Zanzibar

he knew the Foreign Office would not allow the appointment of an official where British might could not protect him, but he asked for Foreign Office approval for Hore to be his "official correspondent." Kirk thought this would be the "thin edge of the wedge" of British influence in Central Africa.[91] The Foreign Office supported the scheme, but L.M.S. policy was against the engagement of their personnel in political affairs and Hore's appointment was not sanctioned by the society.[92] Mwinyi Kheri thus escaped the danger of harboring a semi-official British agent, although Hore and others, even without official positions, did report fully to Kirk at all times. To Hore, Mwinyi Kheri was "a pushing avaricious, and unscrupulous man" and an important hindrance to a Christian missionary; nonetheless, the L.M.S. suffered no harm from Mwinyi Kheri's Arab community.[93]

The British missionaries were not the only Europeans wishing to settle in Mwinyi Kheri's Lake Tanganyika preserve. A Roman Catholic order, the White Fathers, spurred to action by the largely Protestant effort to penetrate east central Africa, sought and received permission from Rome to enter the region.[94] A party of White Fathers, led by Père Deniaud, reached Ujiji in January 1879, to investigate the possibilities of a mission station on Lake Tanganyika's shores. The Arabs — Mwinyi Kheri was then absent — gave them a cordial welcome, as did the L.M.S. missionaries. The Arabs' friendly reception of the White Fathers was attributed to the inactive political role of France in eastern Africa.[95] This was true, but the Arabs no doubt also recognized

---

Archives. The Ujiji Arabs knew Hore's attitude and had stopped the open selling of slaves. Hore to L.M.S., Jan. 10, 1879, L.M.S. Archives.

91. Kirk to Hore, March 23, 1880, *ibid.* Hore thought his appointment would assist his efforts to bring Mwinyi Kheri into line through pressure on the sultan of Zanzibar. Hore to Kirk, July 20, 1880, P-16, Zanzibar Archives.

92. Lister to Kirk, May 21, 1880, *ibid.;* Whitehouse to Hore, May 4, 1881, L.M.S. Archives.

93. Hore to L.M.S., Feb. 9, 1880, *ibid.* Hore, while acknowledging the aid of several Arabs of Ujiji in his later account of his career, made no mention of Mwinyi Kheri. Hore, *Tanganyika,* pp. VIII–IX. When the L.M.S. left Ujiji the Arabs promised to aid them in the future if they visited the port. The promise was carried out. Hore to L.M.S., Dec. 5, 1883, Brooks to L.M.S., Aug. 6, 1884, L.M.S. Archives.

94. R. P. Marcel Stoorme, *Rapports du Père Planque, de Mgr Lavigerie et de Mgr Comboni sur l'Association Internationale Africaine* (Bruxelles, 1957), *passim.*

95. For French policy, Norman R. Bennett, "Some Notes on French Policy in Buganda and East Africa, 1879–1890," *Makerere Journal,* IV:1–17 (1962).

the possibility of playing the two European groups against each other.

The White Fathers quickly perceived that Muslim-dominated Ujiji was an unlikely place for a Christian mission. Reconaissance trips were made to the north to find an Arab-free area. Père Deniaud decided to establish in Chief Rumonge's territory in Burundi in July 1879. But the settlement was made without the advance permission of Mwinyi Kheri in an area subject to his raids; when his men caused difficulties, Deniaud, accompanied by Hore in the L.M.S. boat, went to Mwinyi Kheri at Uvira. The meeting was unsatisfactory, and the mission was withdrawn from the area in November 1879.[96] Deniaud did not give up hope, however, and reestablished contact with Mwinyi Kheri. This time the talks were successful, and permission was granted for a new station in Rumonge's chiefdom.[97] According to Hore, Mwinyi Kheri was paid for allowing the mission to reopen in May 1880; he went to the Barundi "and put it to them smilingly whether they are not aware that he is their Father come to make friends with them." With the Arab leader's presence, all was quickly settled.[98] Rumonge did not prove even then to be an entirely friendly ruler, but when troubles occurred, Mwinyi Kheri answered Deniaud's appeal and dispatched his nephew, Bwana Mkombe, to reestablish order.[99]

Later, however, a crisis occurred in which Mwinyi Kheri was implicated. The White Fathers, as was their custom, purchased children from slavers to rear and educate in the Catholic faith. The local African population sought to reclaim one of the young slaves, and the quarrel ended in the death of three of the mission party — Deniaud, Augier and D'Hoop. The station was evacuated.[100] Several authors have blamed the deaths on Mwinyi Kheri and the Arabs, claiming they acted behind the scenes to stimulate this African reaction.[101] But Mwinyi Kheri does not

96. Mgr. Gorju, *En zigzags à travers l'Urundi* (Namur et Anvers, 1926), 11; Hore to L.M.S., Oct. 20, 1879, L.M.S. Archives.

97. Gorju, *Zigzags*, 11; P. M. Vanneste, "Deniaud," *Biographie Coloniale Belge* (Bruxelles, 1955), IV, 212–213.

98. Hore to Kirk, Aug. 17, 1880, N-6, Zanzibar Archives.

99. Vanneste, "Deniaud," 216.

100. *Ibid.,* 217–218; Adolphe Burdo, *Les Belges dans l'Afrique Centrale. De Zanzibar au Lac Tanganika* (Bruxelles, 1886), 469–472.

101. As Coulbois, *Tanganyika*, 71; R. Bourgeois, *Banyarwanda et Barundi* (Bruxelles, 1957), I, 201.

appear to have been guilty. He had been on sympathetic terms with the Frenchmen, and he would not have ignored the difficulties the deaths of Europeans would cause him in the future. Mwinyi Kheri wrote immediately to Zanzibar to attest his innocence, claiming, falsely, that the Frenchmen had established in Burundi without seeking his permission so that he had not had time to take proper measures for their protection. Mwinyi Kheri affirmed that he would at once lead an armed group to punish the guilty Africans.[102] His claim of innocence should be believed; he had nothing to gain and much to lose from the death of the missionaries. The punitive expedition was successful and the local African ruler was killed along with many of his people.[103]

Still the White Fathers continued to press for a station in Burundi. In 1884, they moved to Uzige to an area where Arab raiding was endemic. Here the Arabs made it very clear that they opposed the missionaries, eventually causing the White Fathers to leave to spare the African inhabitants from threatened raids. Mwinyi Kheri was held responsible in this case, and this kind of pressure is certainly in line with his usual policy of securing his interests vis-à-vis Europeans without bloodshed.[104]

In spite of these difficulties, Mwinyi Kheri generally had good relations with the White Fathers. He aided them materially when possible and had no objection to their proselytizing; once he even affirmed that his religion and that of the White Fathers differed but "a little" since they both had but one God, and that certainly the differences were not enough to raise mutual hostility. Mwinyi Kheri always considered the White Fathers under his personal protection in a way the British missionaries never were because of their frequent reports to the consul in Zanzibar, especially concerning Arab slaving activities. The French might also write, but their government's disinterest in east central Africa was clear to all.

102. Mwinyi Kheri to Barghash, 28 Cherral 1299, in Ledoulx to Ministère des Affaires Etrangères, Dec. 10, 1881, Correspondance Commercial, Zanzibar, t. 4 bis, Archives des Affaires Etrangères, Paris.

103. Griffith to L.M.S., May 29, 1881, L.M.S. Archives.

104. Coulbois, *Tanganyka*, 71–79. A L.M.S. missionary affirmed that the move to the new station had been made without Arab permission. Jones to L.M.S., Dec. 21, 1884, L.M.S. Archives.

Even while surmounting the difficulties of European penetration, Mwinyi Kheri had finally decided to accept official recognition as governor of Ujiji from the sultan of Zanzibar. Perhaps stimulated by the intrigues of Hore and Kirk, Mwinyi Kheri acknowledged the sultan's authority and hoisted the Zanzibari flag in 1881. Barghash confirmed Mwinyi Kheri in office as governor of Ujiji, Uvira and Uguha.[105] The new office led to few changes in Mwinyi Kheri's position; he had been the recognized leader of Ujiji before the appointment, and he remained so after it, without inaugurating any basic changes in policy.[106] He was so discreet a ruler in fact that a European visitor of 1883 was not even aware on meeting Mwinyi Kheri that he was governor.[107] Mwinyi Kheri continued to concentrate on his commercial concerns, spending as much time as previously at Uvira.[108]

For several years after the arrival of the L.M.S. and the White Fathers, only individual European visitors came to Ujiji, and Mwinyi Kheri was allowed to finish his career in peace. Renewed Arab activity came to Lake Tanganyika's shores in 1884, stimulated by the increasing European pressure on east central Africa, but Mwinyi Kheri was not involved. He remained governor until his death in 1885.[109]

Thus quietly closed the career of this important, albeit shadowy, leader of the Ujiji Arabs. Led into the interior to seek ivory and slaves, Mwinyi Kheri remained around Ujiji for about forty years, slowly gaining in prestige and power until he was recognized as leader of the Arab community. His position owed noth-

---

105. Mwinyi Kheri to Barghash, 28 Cherral 1299, in Ledoulx to Ministère des Affaires Etrangères, Dec. 10, 1881, Correspondance Commercial, t. 4 bis; Griffith to L.M.S., May 29, 1881, L.M.S. Archives.

106. A few "pure" Arabs were unhappy at the appointment, but they did not contest it. Wissmann, *Unter deutscher Flagge*, 234.

107. Coulbois, *Tanganyka*, 64.

108. An Arab described as the *liwali* (governor) for the Lake Tanganyika region appeared in the area in 1881. This individual, Msabbah bin Nejim el Sheheni, remained around Ujiji for some time, but he apparently did not replace Mwinyi Kheri in Ujiji or elsewhere. Heinrich Brode, *Tippo Tib* (London, 1907), 133–134, 137, 146, 218, 339; *Maisha ya Hamed bin Muhammed*, 131, 133, 161.

109. See, for example, Jones to L.M.S., Dec. 2, 1884, L.M.S. Archives. The Arabs' activity is discussed in Roland Oliver, "Some Factors in the British Occupation of East Africa," *Uganda Journal*, XV:49–64 (1951); Kirk to Salisbury, Oct. 26, 1885, E-87, Zanzibar Archives.

ing to the sultan of Zanzibar, although Ujiji was often called the sultan's most distant outpost. Sultan Barghash could only recognize Mwinyi Kheri's preeminence and appoint him his representative. The strength of the sultan's position in the interior, however, stemmed from appointments such as this one; as long as the interior Arabs looked to Zanzibar for moral and physical support, plus their essential trading goods, and as long as European intruders did not move to displace Arab predominance, independent individuals of Mwinyi Kheri's sort would well serve the sultan of Zanzibar by providing the security essential for the collection of the trading goods so necessary to the prosperity of Zanzibar.

Gungunhana

---

by DOUGLAS L. WHEELER

Assistant Professor of History
University of New Hampshire

For all his importance, both real and imagined, in the history of Mozambique, Gungunhana of Gaza has received surprisingly little biographical attention. By any account, he is a major figure of the last two decades of the nineteenth century in southeastern Africa; his relations with the Portuguese government and British commercial interests alone would make him notable, not to mention his less well-known connections with his neighbors — the Ndebele, the Shona, and the Swazi. As a figure in African history, he deserves attention. Although he was unique in his own right, he shared a similar situation with other contemporary African leaders, and his downfall was a milestone in the history of southern Mozambique.

Apart from a few short articles in Portuguese and a few pages here and there in American and English monographs, there is little written on his short but eventful reign from 1884 to 1895.[1] The most recent and comprehensive effort is more a running diplomatic history featuring Gungunhana than a detailed biographical sketch.[2] Warhurst relies almost exclusively on official and unofficial English sources, while leaving to others an examination of the extensive Portuguese material available. This approach would suggest that Gungunhana was his own master in making most decisions, that he devoted much of his energy to obtaining aid from British interests, and that he was careful not to become involved in the rebellion of 1894 or to provoke any trouble with the Portuguese.

---

1. Eduardo Borges de Castro, *Gungunhana* (Lisbon, 1896); Juliao Quintinha, *Reis Negros* (Lisbon, 1936); "Gungunhana," *Grande Enciclopedia Portuguesa e Brasileira* [hereafter *G.E.P. e B.*], (37 vols.; Lisbon and Rio de Janeiro, 1924–1960), XII:922–923; James Duffy, *Portuguese Africa* (Cambridge, 1959), 232–233.

2. Philip R. Warhurst, *Anglo-Portuguese Relations in South-Central Africa 1890–1900* (London, 1962), 78–108.

An examination of other materials suggests that the reality was different. Gungunhana was a curious mixture of suspicious intriguer, clever diplomat, and sometime collaborator. To the Chope, the Tonga, and the Shona, he was anathema. He tried to rebuild the crumbling Shangana empire in Gaza, which he inherited from his father, by means of conquest, collaborating with the Portuguese for firearms and money, and dealing with British commercial and official parties. Not unlike Lobengula of the Ndebele, whom he resembled in appearance and in fortune, the chief of Gaza was often dominated by his mother, his uncles, and his generals or *indunas*. He was obsessed by fears of dethronement. Throughout his reign, he used Portuguese aid, or planned to use it, to retain his power and to expand his authority. Driven by his aggressive retinue as much as by his own instincts, he resisted Portuguese administrative and military expansion while attempting to reconquer his hereditary enemies, the Chope.

The important events in Gungunhana's career are similar to those of other dynasties in nineteenth-century Africa: fratricides, succession disputes, royal poisonings, court intrigues, and finally exile on a distant island and impressment into the very army that had destroyed his power. Both the Portuguese and other Europeans exaggerated and even ennobled his power and character. Mozambican nationalists today often refer to him as "Emperor." For Portugal, Gungunhana's defeat was the colonial sensation of the century and was made into a legend to compensate for other less glorious episodes. It is an oversimplification, nevertheless, to explain the chief's defeat purely in military terms. Shangana power was eroded by internecine warfare in Gaza; and labor migration, epidemics, alcoholism, and the destruction of the cattle-based economy undermined the traditional African society on which it was based and combined with convulsions from nearby Rhodesia and Swaziland to bring about disaster.

Background

Mudungazi, Mundungaz, Gungunyane or Gungunhana, as he called himself after coming to power, was a son of Muzila (*circa* 1820–1884), chief of the Shangana of Gaza. The name Gungunhana is probably a Shangana corruption of the traditional

Swazi word for their king, *ingwenyama,* meaning "lion." Gungunhana was thus often called The Lion of Gaza.[3] He was the
last Shangana king of any significance to rule in southern Mozambique. and the last of a line of a Ngoni dynasty that
originated in Zululand, northern Natal, in the early nineteenth
century. The name "Shangana" is derived from the name of the
king who led Ngoni refugees from Zululand after 1819 — Soshangane (*circa* 1800–1858 or 1859). Fleeing the wrath of the
Shaka Zulu, the Ngoni regiments under Soshangane came to rest
in the Limpopo Valley. They were frequently on the move thereafter, however, and in the 1830's Ngoni forces attacked and
sacked most of the Portuguese settlements south of the Zambezi
River, thus acquiring a fearsome reputation with the feeble
Portuguese community.[4]

The Shangana state featured a supreme king and powerful
queen mothers — who had both political and religious duties —
an aristocracy, and the regimental commanders or *indunas* (lieutenants). Military power among the Shangana was founded on
the age-grade regiment or *manga,* a unit of warriors of sixteen
years or older. These *mangas,* sometimes also referred to by their
Zulu name, *impi,* worked on principles which had been developed
in Zululand. Conquering weaker groups such as the agricultural
Tonga, they created an empire based on the possession of cattle,
military organization, and royal tribute. Vassal tribes and villages under the Ngoni sway were made to pay tribute in the form
of cattle, foodstuffs, or trade articles. A unique physical mark of
the Ngoni masters was the piercing of the earlobes — a practice
which they forced subject tribes in Gaza to adopt.[5]

3. Hilda Kuper, *The Swazi. A South African Kingdom* (New York, 1963), 2.
4. Caetano Montez, "As Invasoes Dos Mangunis e Dos Machanganas,"
Moçambique (Lourenço Marques), April–June, 1937, 25–55; Rocha Martins,
História das Colónias Portuguesas (Lisbon, 1933), 267–273; Daniel da Cruz,
Em Terras de Gaza (Oporto, 1910), 270–275.
5. Information from acting director of Arquivo Histórico de Moçambique,
Lourenço Marques, in letter of July 22, 1964, to the writer. In the literature,
there is much confusion between the terms, "Landins," "Vátuas," "Chan-
gana" or "Shangaans." I will use "Shangana" here, since it is the Portuguese
term for the group in southern Mozambique which became a mixture of
Tonga and Ngoni elements as a result of the invasion from Zululand in
the early nineteenth century. "Vátua," or "those who came from the interior," was originally a Tonga or Chope term for the fierce invaders from
the south. By the late nineteenth century, the Portuguese used the term
"Vátua" to mean the Ngoni-influenced elite in Gaza. For material on the

According to oral tradition, the dynasty of Jamine was traced back to four chiefs in Zululand who never lived in Mozambique: Mucachua, Mangua Gaza, Uguagua-Macue, and Segote.[6] Then came Soshangane and his son Muzila. Each chief or king who resided in Mozambique had a "sacred village," a repository for his earthly remains. Soshangane had his Chaimite, and Muzila created his Uduengo. Later, Gungunhana built the village of Manjacaze, a town which exists today with the same name. Each village was supposed to represent the deceased king in posterity.[7]

Although some Ngoni groups swept north of the Zambezi, the forces of Soshangane and his descendants remained south of the great river in central-southern Mozambique in a region which came to be called Gaza, after Mangua Gaza, one of the clan heads in Zululand. At the peak of Shangana power under Soshangane about 1850, the area of control and influence included most of the region between the Incomati River and the Zambezi; that Ngoni control did not extend inland much beyond the edge of the Rhodesian plateau is clear. The authority possessed by the Shangana kings is difficult to assess, but the size of the region, the frequent displacement of the royal kraal, and the nomadic nature of the Ngoni cattle-based economy, makes it probable that neither Soshangane nor Muzila had more than an ephemeral allegiance from subject groups.[8]

Soshangane died in either 1858 or 1859, bringing about a serious succession dispute between two of his sons, Muzila or Umzila and Mawewe. Through the friendship and influence of a Portuguese hunter-trader, Muzila obtained the arms and aid he needed from Portuguese authorities at Lourenço Marques to defeat and expel his brother Mawewe during 1861.[9] Muzila approved

---

ethnic groupings in Mozambique, see "Vátuas," *G.E.P. e B.*, XXXIV:358; "Moçambique," *ibid.*, XVII:450; António Rita-Ferreira, *Agrupamento e Caracterização Etnica dos Indigenas de Moçambique* (Lisbon, 1958).

6. The clan of Soshangane was called "Jamine" or "Nomaio."

7. Trindade Coelho, ed., *Dezoito Annos em África. Notas E Documentos Para A Biographia Do Conselheiro José d'Almeida* (Lisbon, 1898), 383.

8. Warhurst, *Anglo-Portuguese Relations*, 79–81; António Cardoso, "Expedição As Terras Do Muzilla (1882)," *Boletim da Sociedade de Geographia* [hereafter *B.S.G.L.*], Series 7 (1887), 188–190.

9. Visconde Paiva Manso, *Memória Sobre Lourenço Marques (Delagoa Bay)* (Lisbon, 1870), 120–125.

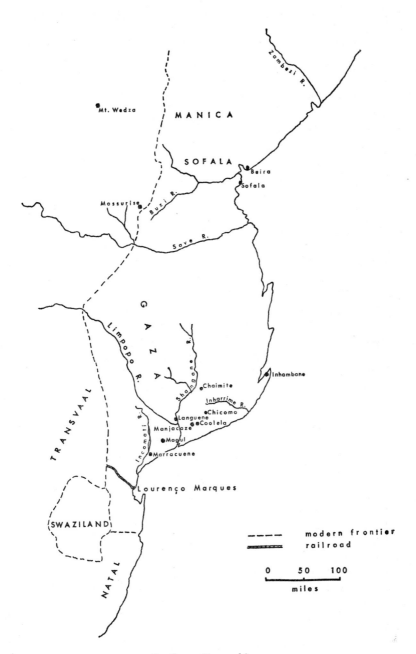

Southern Mozambique

and perhaps signed a treaty of alliance and "vassalage" with the Portuguese which later became an object of controversy. The Portuguese government thereafter claimed that the Shangana were legally vassals of the crown and that the royal heirs of Muzila were under Portuguese authority. Gungunhana was to bear the burden of this Portuguese claim in later years.

Gradually the Shangana lost their ethnic homogeneity; they intermarried with many groups of Swazi, Ronga, Tonga, Chope, Ndebele, and even Shona. By the 1870's tribesmen from such groups rose to high positions in the elite in Gaza. One example was Maguiguana (or Maguejana) the "secretary" and later chief general of the king, who rose from an obscure position as an alien cook in the royal kraal to a position of great influence over Muzila and Gungunhana.[10]

Muzila ruled Gaza from 1861 to about August 1884, when he died an apparently natural death at Mossurise on the edge of the Rhodesian plateau. He had moved his kraal north and west during his reign. Under his rule, Shangana territory was divided into sections ruled by governors or *grandes*, as the Portuguese called them. The iron law of military strength perpetuated the Ngoni authority over the agrarian populations in the interior and terrorized the cattle-keepers as well.

The power of Muzila, however, was shallow and he bequeathed to his successor several problems: increasing emigration of young men to Natal and the Cape Colony to earn European money, recurring human and cattle epidemics, the neglect of agriculture, and a dependence on hunting and raiding the neighboring Tonga, Chope, and Shona. The *mangas* of the earlier years were fast disappearing. Alien tribesmen were recruited en masse while the more eligible young men trekked southward. The emigration from Gaza and southern Mozambique that became so apparent in the twentieth century was underway by the late 1860's. Africans went to work in mines and on plantations in territory outside of Portuguese influence because, as the English consul, Frederick Elton, so caustically put it, they had learned that "the English pay for labour." [11]

---

10. Coelho, *Dezoito Annos*, 83.
11. Frederick Elton, "A Journey from Delagoa Bay," *Journal of the Royal Geographical Society*, XLII:1–49 (1872).

In late 1883, the Portuguese official António Maria Cardoso visited the failing Muzila. Cardoso noted that Muzila now ruled over a force and power which were "much less than was actually imagined." [12] The old chief busied himself only with raiding and obtaining firearms. The report of Cardoso's journey into the Mozambique interior during 1882 and 1883 provides the earliest known mention of Gungunhana. The Portuguese officer noted that three of Muzila's sons were already contending for the throne; they were Como-Como — apparently the royal favorite at the time — Mafumane, and Gungunhana. At the time, Gungunhana was losing in a struggle with Mafumane, and reportedly, he, like his father before him, asked for Portuguese aid; but it is not clear whether the Portuguese helped either party.

The best available evidence suggests that the Shangana succession system was determined by the ruling king or chief, who designated an elder favorite son.[13] The conflict came to a head during 1884: Muzila died in August and by the end of the year, Gungunhana had emerged as king or chief of the Gaza Shangana. The fate of Como-Como remains unknown. Mafumane was murdered by order of Gungunhana. Sources differ as to the method of elimination; Gungunhana either sent a force to murder Mafumane in a distant village or he invited his brother to a banquet in his kraal, had him poisoned or stabbed, and then displayed his head.[14] Whatever Gungunhana's method of assuring his royal longevity, his fear of possible usurpers persisted. The Lion of Gaza was constantly searching for two other royal heirs, Anhana and Mafabaze, both of whom escaped his grasp. Gungunhana's right to the throne was later cast in an unfavorable light by Portuguese commentators. As late as 1889 Portuguese information claimed that there remained a party of Mafumane's followers, and it was suggested that he and not Gungunhana was

12. Cardoso, "Expedição," 189; Manuel Alberto and Francisco Toscano, *O Oriente Africano Português* (Lourenço Marques, 1942), 170; St. Vincent Erskine, "A Journey to Umzila in South Eastern Africa," *Proceedings of the Royal Geographical Society*, XIX:110–134 (1875).

13. Coelho, *Dezoito Annos*, 208–209; 83; Almeida, the subject of Coelho's biography, claimed that Mafumane was quite popular and was "the rightful successor" to Muzila's throne.

14. Coelho, *Dezoito Annos*, 208–209; Rocha Martins, *História*, 285; Cruz, *Em Terras*, 116.

"a true descendant of the Zulus." Even in 1893 a Portuguese observer reported that the followers of Mafumane were still numerous.[15]

It is difficult to determine the exact date of Gungunhana's birth. The official record of his death states that he was sixty-seven years old, but this figure was based on the estimate of his age at the time of his baptism in 1899.[16] In any event, both figures were most likely guesses based on a visual assessment and perhaps Gungunhana's own estimate. An examination of photographs of the chief reveal to this writer that he *could* have been as young as forty or forty-five upon his arrival in the Azores, which would place his birth date in the 1850's. His son Godide was born in the mid-1870's and it is likely that his father was at least twenty when he sired him.[17]

There is also the problem of Gungunhana's place of birth. Coelho claims that the chief was born in the royal kraal of Muzila at Mossurise, on the Rhodesian plateau.[18] As Muzila did not occupy this area until 1858 or later, it is likely then that Gungunhana was born after this date. This writer concludes, then, with the incomplete evidence available, that Gungunhana was probably in his mid-twenties when he ascended the throne of Gaza and that he was born sometime in the late 1850's or early 1860's.

Reign, 1884–1894

By late 1884 Gungunhana was supreme at the royal kraal at Mossurise, near Mt. Selinda, Rhodesia. He promptly embarked upon attempts to conquer Chief Mutassa of Manica to the north and the Shona, or Duma as he called them, to the west. Shangana raids on the Manica mountain strongholds were repeatedly repulsed during the 1880's.[19] Gungunhana's *mangas* continued to raid sections of Shonaland throughout much of the chief's reign. In these forays, the chief and his advisers appreciated the

15. Coelho, *Dezoito Annos,* 208, 402.
16. Pedro de Merelim (pseud.), "Os Vátuas na Ilha Terçeira," *Atlantida* (Angra do Heroismo, Azores Islands, 1960), IV, 317–318.
17. Coelho, *Dezoito Annos,* 261–262, 458.
18. *Ibid.,* 402.
19. E. P. Mathers, *Zambesia* (London, 1891), 400–412.

uses of European technology. In June 1886, while conferring with a Portuguese envoy, Conselheiro José d'Almeida, in his kraal, Gungunhana learned of the military potential of the incendiary rocket and immediately requested an order of rockets to dislodge the Shona from their hills.[20] He obtained no rockets, but he did continue to plague the Shona; Gungunhana's tax collectors were observed among the Shona as far west on the Rhodesian plateau as Mt. Wedza.[21]

When it came to dealing with the Portuguese, Gungunhana knew that the collective Portuguese power was fairly weak but increasing. Although he and his advisers alternated their disdain for the Portuguese with some respect, they were willing to negotiate when it came to acquiring European weapons, especially rifles. This tendency originated with Muzila, who in 1881 had attacked the Chope in Inhambane district without much success, and who, in early 1882, traveled to Lourenço Marques to make amends to the governor.[22] There is evidence that the scanty supply of Shangana rifles was one reason for Muzila's failure. His son and successor inherited an admiration for the rifle along with a desire to acquire them for his warriors, at almost any cost or promise.[23]

What was the condition of the Portuguese presence in this section of southeast Africa? Was there any threat to the interests of the Shangana ruler early in his reign? The answer to this question seems to be in the affirmative. It is true that Mozambique in the 1880's remained a colony which enjoyed even less Portuguese interest and support than Angola in the same period. More isolated from Portugal and with less of a healthy plateau hinterland, this *provincia ultramarina* was in a wretched state. In general, the European inhabitants were either poorly paid public functionaries or impoverished traders. Nearly all the agriculture was in the hands of Africans. A handful of Army and Navy officers directed the affairs of the administration and were protected and supported by only a few hundred Angolas (Africans recruited in Angola) serving as police and sepoys in the coastal

20. Coelho, *Dezoito Annos,* 231–232.
21. Warhurst, *Anglo-Portuguese Relations,* 20.
22. Alberto and Toscano, *O Oriente,* 168–169.
23. St. Vincent Erskine, "Third and Fourth Journeys in Gaza," *Journal of the Royal Geographical Society,* XLVIII:25–28 (1878).

settlements. To finance the shaky colonial government, the Portuguese were obliged to draw annual subsidies from Portugal, give charters to commercial companies to explore for minerals, and depend upon a small volume of trade and customs at the ports. In the late nineteenth century, English money even became the major currency in the colony.[24]

If the reality of the colony was bleak, the prospects for a measure of economic prosperity were improving. In 1875, Portugal won an arbitration dispute with Britain over the possession of the southern part of the strategic Delagoa Bay. This award and the interest it aroused served to awaken some Portuguese colonialists to the potential value of that great harbor and estuary. Because of its strategic location as the natural port outlet for the Transvaal — where vast gold deposits were discovered in 1886 — some Portuguese wisely asserted that the harbor would revolutionize Mozambique's economy and would be "the center of commerce for all East Africa." [25] Increasing pressure came from the Portuguese colonial elite to develop, safeguard, and control southern Mozambique. The frontier of Gaza, the stamping ground of Gungunhana and his *mangas* and the limit of the jurisdiction of Lourenço Marques, located on the northern edge of the bay, was the Incomati River; the Shangana power, therefore, reached to within forty miles of the coveted harbor.

Portuguese activity in southern Mozambique quickened somewhat after the arrival of a public-works expedition in 1877, and especially after the beginning of railroad construction of the Lourenço Marques–Transvaal line in May 1886. The harbor town then eclipsed Mozambique town, the provincial capital far to the north, and its population burgeoned. In 1897 what had been true in practice was made official and Lourenço Marques became the capital of Mozambique.[26]

The first area over which the Portuguese and Gungunhana came into conflict was Manica and the hinterland of Sofala. The

24. Rose Monteiro, *Delagoa Bay, Its Natives and Natural History* (London, 1891), 271. Mrs. Monteiro wrote that the Portuguese then were only "the nominal holders of the country"; Colonel E. A. Azambuja Martins, *O Soldado Africano De Moçambique* (Lisbon, 1936), 8–10, 33–34.

25. Visconde da Arriaga, *Lourenço Marques* (Lisbon, 1882), 129; see also Visconde da Arriaga, *A Inglaterra, Portugal, E Suas Colónias* (Lisbon, 1882), 278–281.

26. Alberto and Toscano, *O Oriente*, 180–190.

Portuguese, Paiva de Andrada, had traveled to Manica in 1881 in order to obtain concessions from Muzila; the old chief, however, refused to grant any concessions in Manica since he considered the area his tributary holding. In 1884, the Portuguese administration created on paper "the District of Manica" and named the capital after the Goanese warlord Gouveia (Manuel António da Sousa) whose private African army was reconquering new territory south of the Zambezi for the governor-general.[27] The principal reason for Portuguese interest in Manica was the discovery of gold deposits in the area. The Portuguese planned to colonize the region and to exploit the minerals which they hoped would amount to a great deal.

In 1885 the authorities dispatched as envoy to Gungunhana a Portuguese trader, ex-soldier and old friend of Muzila, José Casaleiro d'Alegria Rodrigues. Arriving at the kraal in Mossurise, Rodrigues apparently persuaded the new ruler to send two *indunas* to Lisbon to sign an "Act of Vassalage" with the Portuguese crown. Dated "October 12, 1885, Lisbon," this treaty stated that Gungunhana willingly submitted to a number of conditions which included: obeying laws and orders from the governor-general of Mozambique; promising not to allow the rule of any other nation "in his territory"; permitting a Portuguese agent (resident-chief) to live near him and to advise him in ruling; flying the Portuguese flag in his kraals; allowing all Portuguese subjects to travel freely in his lands; permitting the mining of minerals only by individuals who have Portuguese concessions; and allowing the establishment of missions and schools.[28] In return, Gungunhana was made, by royal decree, an Army colonel and his major advisers, captains. It is not clear whether Gungunhana actually authorized his part in this treaty; he claimed later that the agreement was invalid.[29]

Whether reluctantly or eagerly, Gungunhana consented to the residency of the Portuguese agent and in May 1886, he received from the first *residente,* Rodrigues, the honorary title of colonel of the Second Line and a uniform and sword.[30] Later in the

27. Duffy, *Portuguese Africa,* 220, 231; Warhurst, *Anglo-Portuguese Relations,* 21–23; "J. C. Paiva de Andrada," *G.E.P. e B.,* XX:25–26.

28. Coelho, *Dezoito Annos,* 64–68.

29. Warhurst, *Anglo-Portuguese Relations,* 81.

30. Coelho, *Dezoito Annos,* 106; Alberto and Toscano, *O Oriente,* 175.

year, a new resident official arrived at the kraal, José d'Almeida. This observant envoy described the chief wearing this uniform at a meeting "with great joy" and to the deafening roar of his admiring subjects. There is evidence, however, that later the monarch did not fancy wearing the accompanying boots, and that he preferred to go barefoot at ceremonies carried on the shoulders of two subjects.[31]

Almeida was dispatched to obtain from Gungunhana a concession to exploit the Manica region for minerals. But the Lion of Gaza, suspecting the Portuguese entreaties, claimed sovereignty over the *prazos* or entailed estates near Sofala owned formerly by Portuguese, and refused to give concessions in Manica. The chief or his advisers stated that the Shangana had observed how the Portuguese influence had grown in the Inhambane district by treaty-signing and promises and that they feared the Portuguese would establish their power in the interior of Gaza if they gave concessions in Manica. When Almeida reminded the king of the 1885 treaty signed by his envoys in Lisbon, Gungunhana reportedly replied that the agreement was useless and that "the paper [treaty] is good only for fishing for lands."[32] In other words, the African potentate felt that the treaty was only a clever Portuguese trick to obtain lands not theirs. Furthermore, the chief refused to refrain from attacking a neighboring rival chief who supposedly was under official Portuguese protection.

The Shangana observation that there had been some successful Portuguese expansion into the interior of Inhambane was quite correct. The Inhambane district was a region in which the Portuguese had penetrated into the interior before 1870. By winning the loyalty of a nucleus of Chope and Valenge chiefs, they had laid a foundation for expansion. A former trader of French extraction, João Loforte, became an influential figure in the Chope region and armed this tribe for the Portuguese administration between 1869 and 1877. Loforte persuaded the people of the lakes (west of the Inharrime River) to resist Shangana raids and tax forays east of the Limpopo River valley. By the time of the rise of Gungunhana, over twenty chiefs in this region paid

---

31. Information from letter to writer dated July 3, 1964, from Colonel José Agostinho, Angra do Heroismo, Terçeira (Azores).

32. Rocha Martins, *História*, 294.

some sort of tribute to the Portuguese. Significantly, the Inhambane hinterland and its tribes proved to be the *bête noire* of the Lion of Gaza after 1884. The Shangana frequently fought the Chope, and their conflict weakened both sides in the face of Portuguese expansion. Gungunhana, nevertheless, found himself under pressure from the Portuguese government to stop his raids into the Inhambane district against tribes which were considered loyal.[33]

Reports on the cruelty of Gungunhana toward his subjects are numerous. Accounts vary, but even his son and heir apparent, Godide, said in exile that his father had been severe in Gaza and for the least excuse ordered the beheading of subjects or campaigns against weaker tribes. Reputedly more cruel than Muzila, Gungunhana was said to practice human sacrifice at the annual first fruits celebration, the ceremony of *inkuaia;* this celebration was to help bring good crops for his farming subjects. Gungunhana also participated in the national festival of his people each year in February and watched as all his warriors passed in review.[34]

The question arises as to how much learning Gungunhana possessed. There is little reliable evidence that the chief received any rudiments of European education until after his exile. But it is known that one of his sons, Mangua, could read, write, and speak Portuguese and helped the monarch with his correspondence. Furthermore, several sources state that a primary school teacher, perhaps Portuguese but quite possibly Goanese or Indian, lived in the royal kraal during the reigns of Muzila and Gungunhana. The dispatch of a teacher to Gaza was part of the 1861 treaty between Muzila and the Portuguese authorities, and apparently one teacher did remain in Gaza near Gungunhana until 1894 or 1895, in the dual capacity of instructor and public

33. Filipe Gastão de Almeida de Eça, *História das Guerras no Zambeze* (Lisbon, 1953–1954), II, 467–470; A. A. Caldas Xavier, "Districto de Inhambane," *B.S.G.L.*, series 7 (1887), 153–210; Coelho, *Dezoito Annos*, 207–209, 283.

34. Margaret Read, *The Ngoni of Nyasaland* (London, 1956), 60, 205; António José Enes, *A Guerra D'África em 1895* (2nd edition; Lisbon, 1945), 121–122. The *nq'waya* was a customary ceremony which apparently originated in Zululand and was taken north by the Ngoni.

functionary.[35] Just what influence this individual had in Gaza is not certain; it is clear, however, that the Lion of Gaza was fully absorbed in his own traditional culture.

With this in mind, it is understandable that Gungunhana was ignorant of many European ways and that his reaction to new things was often startling to the Portuguese who visited him. A case in point occurred during a visit of the Portuguese officer Paiva de Andrada in 1885. The hapless Portuguese failed to get an audience or any satisfaction about concessions from the chief after he had demonstrated the use of his binoculars to several *indunas*. When Gungunhana learned that this Portuguese stranger with his glasses was capable of making large things inexplicably tiny, the potentate quickly dismissed him from the kraal, declaring that the Lion of Gaza could hardly risk being changed into a "microscopic chief" by such a sorcerer. When it came to being photographed by Europeans, Gungunhana steadfastly refused until August 1890, when he reluctantly consented and the Portuguese eagerly took his picture at Manjacaze.[36]

Although the Shangana had rejected Portuguese proposals for concessions in Manica and its environs, the leadership in Gaza recognized that more pressure from the coast was to come. For some time, the Shangana elite had kept in touch with events to the south in the British territory of Natal. In 1870 and again in 1878, Muzila had sent embassies to the Natal government asking for trade, a British visitor to Gaza, and some kind of protection. The British did send a visitor, Mr. St. Vincent Erskine, but their official position as represented to the Shangana envoys was that the Gaza region was Portuguese territory. Not to be discouraged and desiring some kind of protection against increasing Portuguese pressure, Gungunhana sent envoys to Natal again in 1887 and asked for advice and guidance. The British replied that the Shangana paid tribute to the Portuguese and were therefore Portuguese subjects. Further, the British knew that the Portuguese *residente* was living at the royal kraal.[37]

Gungunhana and his advisers came to a crucial decision regarding the future of their people in 1889. Rather than remain

35. Merelim, "Os Vátuas," 314; information from letter to writer from Colonel Agostinho, July 3, 1964; Enes, *A Guerra*, 38.

36. Coelho, *Dezoito Annos*, 77, 271.

37. Warhurst, *Anglo-Portuguese Relations*, 79–82.

settled on the edge of the Rhodesian plateau at Mossurise, Gungunhana transferred his royal kraal and his court over three hundred miles southeast into the Limpopo Valley at Manjacaze. Why did he move forty to sixty thousand people from a plateau milieu southward to the valley near the coast where Soshangane founded the Gaza empire? Why did he leave the scene of his birth and childhood to venture closer to the Portuguese settlements on the coast? Was he merely trying to settle closer to British territory? The answer is to be found in the Portuguese expansion and pressure on Manica, the Shangana desire and need for better agricultural land in the fertile Limpopo River valley, and the consuming determination of the chief and his belligerent *indunas* to settle an old score with the Chope peoples settled between the Limpopo and Inharrime Rivers.[38]

It also appears that the chief reason for Gungunhana's move south was to reclaim the lands once held by his grandfather, Soshangane, and to assert his sovereignty over rebellious tribes in southern Gaza. There is some evidence that Gungunhana negotiated with the Portuguese for a free hand in the Limpopo region in return for withdrawal of Shangana influence from the Manica region; envoys from Gungunhana traveled to Lisbon in 1887 and pursued some negotiations.[39] In any event, Gungunhana invaded the Chope lands in the Limpopo Valley and drove out a number of Chope groups. The refugee Chope thus defeated fled north of the Inharrime into the Inhambane district and entered into a closer relationship with the Portuguese authorities.[40] The migration of the Shangana thousands during June of 1889, then, had the effect of devastating stretches of countryside and of dislocating other groups. Although Gungunhana was closer to the Portuguese settlements at Inhambane and Lourenço Marques and therefore potentially dangerous, the Portuguese evidently felt that this was offset by their having a free hand to expand into King Mutassa's Manica chieftaincy.

Gungunhana's invasion of Chope territory was the prelude to

38. Coelho, *Dezoito Annos*, 289; Warhurst, *Anglo-Portuguese Relations*, 82; J. T. Bent, *The Ruined Cities of Mashonaland* (London, 1893), 269; J. Mousinho de Albuquerque, *Moçambique 1896–1898* (Lisbon, 1913 ed.), 29.

39. J. Paiva de Andrada to Neves Ferreira, Dec. 25, 1889, in "Cartas de Paiva de Andrada," *Moçambique* (Lourenço Marques, 1941), 100–104.

40. Enes, *A Guerra*, 119.

the establishment of his royal kraal in the lands of the important Chope chiefs, Speranhana and his father Binguana. Both had lived near Manjacaze at Lake Suli where Gungunhana located his sacred village. During 1889 and 1890, the Chope and Shangana armies clashed several times, the best-known battle taking place at Baul (perhaps in 1890) near the coast. Both sides suffered heavy losses, but the Shangana pursued Speranhana and his army to the north; the Chope chief, however, managed to escape capture.[41]

Gungunhana's wars against the primarily agricultural Chope were a constant feature of his reign. What is more, the Portuguese often mistook Gungunhana's wars on the Chope near Inhambane as a rebellion or threat to the larger European settlements nearby.[42] In fact, the wars against the Chope diverted Gungunhana's energies from Portuguese intrusions and gave the Portuguese new African allies with whom to undermine his strength in Gaza.

It is clear that when it came to making important decisions about wars, migrations, and expansions, Gungunhana was not always his own master. As was the custom among the Swazi, neighbors of Gaza to the southwest, the "king" of the Shangana was often "ruled" by his own counsellors or nobles in the court.[43] The fame of the Lion of Gaza, often exaggerated, has obscured his circle of advisers and his numerous relatives.

One power behind the throne of Gungunhana was Maguiguana, the *induna impi omeno,* or chief of all war in Gaza, Gungunhana's greatest general. An old man by the time of Gungunhana's reign, Maguiguana is said to have been a cook for Muzila, later rising to be an *induna* and noble in the royal court. He soon became chief general through his bravery. He was not a true Ngoni or "Zulu" warrior, but a member of another group, perhaps the Chope or Valenge. It is interesting to note that Maguiguana was not allowed into the public meetings of the land-owning Shangana nobles as he owned no lands himself.[44]

41. Coelho, *Dezoito Annos,* 284.
42. *Ibid.,* 80–84; Albuquerque, *Moçambique,* 38–39.
43. Kuper, *The Swazi,* 55–56.
44. J. Mousinho de Albuquerque, *Relatório Apresentado Ao Conselheiro Correia E Lança Governador Geral Interino Da Provincia De Moçambique* (Lisbon, 1896), 41 n.

Yet by adopting Zulu customs in his youth, like other tribesmen from various subject groups in Gaza, he rose to fame and power by means of initiative and perseverance. Maguiguana acted as a force behind Gungunhana and advised him as a secretary. Significantly, the head general was one of the most uncompromising of the court advisers in opposing European activity. Envoy Almeida observed in May 1886 that Gungunhana followed "the thinking of his secretary Maguejana [sic] and of his numerous chiefs of war with whom he fears to differ, although he also fears a quarrel with us." [45] Throughout his reign, the chief of Gaza would find himself pulled between a number of conflicting forces: his aggressive aristocracy, the Portuguese, and various foreign interests.

Shortly after his move south, Gungunhana became involved in a conflict between British commercial interests and the Portuguese government. In late 1889, the Portuguese sent an armed expedition from northern Mozambique to the upper Shiré River. A British ultimatum to Portugal to withdraw forces from the Shiré and from Manica as well and to negotiate for frontier demarcation in 1890, greatly angered the Portuguese in Lisbon and in the colonies. The general effect was to cause even more energetic Portuguese expansion into Mozambique and particularly Gaza. Meanwhile, British commercial and imperial expansion, embodied in the British South Africa Company of Cecil John Rhodes, threatened Portuguese sovereignty in Gaza. Rhodes needed outlets for his settlements in Rhodesia to the west of Gaza. Besides attempting to purchase Delagoa Bay from Portugal, he wished a right-of-way for a proposed railroad to connect the Rhodesian settlements with the Indian Ocean. The shortest route would pass through the northern section of Gaza. The British South Africa Company wished to negotiate with Chief Gungunhana as he was considered the major African power in the region and as the Shangana were considered superior to the Portuguese in military power.[46]

45. Coelho, *Dezoito Annos*, 83, 133, 269, 289; Amadeu Cunha, *Mousinho. A Sua Obra E A Sua Epoca* (Lisbon, 1944), 220–221.
46. Warhurst, *Anglo-Portuguese Relations*, 83; J. G. Lockhart and C. M. Woodhouse, *Cecil Rhodes. The Colossus of South Africa* (New York, 1963), 219–221.

So began a conflict which appeared to the Portuguese at the time as a "matter of life or death for the province of Mozambique." [47] The British South Africa Company sought a concession in Gaza and wanted to influence Gungunhana against the Portuguese as well. Dr. Aurel Schultz, company physician and agent, was dispatched to the kraal of Gungunhana in early 1890 and concluded a concession dated October 4, 1890. Providing for mineral rights as well as a right-of-way to Mashonaland, the treaty was not finally approved by Gungunhana until the thousand rifles, twenty thousand cartridges, and the agreed-on annual subsidy to himself were in his hands. The treaty led Gungunhana to believe that he was dealing with representatives of Queen Victoria and not the agents of a British commercial company only recently chartered. To him, evidently, Rhodes *was* the British government. After getting promises of the above-mentioned gifts, Gungunhana was also promised "two bulls, a horse, and a mastiff" by the agents. It was not altogether a coincidence that the Gaza monarch requested almost precisely the same gifts in this concession as did his neighbor and "in-law" Lobengula, chief of the Ndebele, in his agreement with the same company.[48]

A more detailed inquiry into this concession is necessary in order to illustrate the characters of the contracting parties. While negotiating with the British agents at his Manjacaze kraal, Gungunhana insisted that "the whole coast is mine," including the Inhambane region. Determined to display his power over both José d'Almeida and Dr. Schultz, who were arguing the question, it is reported that he screamed, "Not without consulting me shall you settle this question." [49] Yet it is clear that Rhodes himself knew that the Shangana monarch could not claim the Inhambane region on the coast since his writ did not go beyond the Inharrime River. Furthermore, Rhodes knew that by an Anglo-Portuguese convention of August 1890, Gazaland was given to Portugal in return for a portion of Manica for Britain, so that the British agents had no clear right to be negotiating for concessions with a chief in Portuguese territory.[50]

47. José d'Almeida to Gov.-Gen. of Mozambique, March 9, 1891, in Coelho, *Dezoito Annos,* 324.
48. Lockhart and Woodhouse, *Cecil Rhodes,* 220–221.
49. *Ibid.,* 220.
50. Warhurst, *Anglo-Portuguese Relations,* 67–69, 71, 89–90, 93–94.

Portugal protested the Schultz concession to the British government and an armed expedition to Manjacaze under Almeida, probably the largest yet seen in that area, was dispatched in December 1890, in order to put counterpressure on Gungunhana. By then Dr. Schultz had left and the Shangana potentate awaited the delivery of the promised goods. In the meantime, however, Gungunhana acted the deliberate diplomat and did not completely alienate the Portuguese. In September, three months before the arrival of the large Portuguese force, he gave the Portuguese representatives a large ivory tusk as a symbol of respect for King Dom Luiz I of Portugal who had died in late 1889.[51]

It was at this time that Gungunhana gained his reputation as a crafty but cautious diplomat among his Portuguese opponents. Although participants in this struggle between the two expanding forces in Mozambique frequently accused the Lion of Gaza of being "insatiably ambitious," a "shrewd intriguer," and an exponent of a policy of "aggrandizement," they never accused him of being reckless and foolhardy.[52] Those who knew him well, as José d'Almeida did, respected his sagacity in internal as well as in external affairs. The Portuguese authorities believed that Gungunhana was overly fond of drink and therefore sent considerable shipments of port wine to his kraal; however, Almeida, the *residente,* observed that Gungunhana as a rule declined to drink heavily until after a morning full of visits, business, and dispensing justice. Moreover, he claimed, Gungunhana drank less than his subjects and "it is not so much for the love of alcohol, as for the display of greatness, that they drink . . . the prestige of the monarch of that large country is due, in great part, to these shows of grandeur, which all subjects envy, and which they competitively try to imitate." [53] Indeed, in August 1890, when Almeida and several Portuguese colleagues visited Gungunhana, the chief confronted a group of Banyan traders in his kraal and made it known to them that he wished the sale of alcohol in Gaza prohibited as it was such a cause of trouble among his people.[54] But in spite of this statement,

51. Coelho, *Dezoito Annos*, 276.
52. António Enes, *A Guerra*, 5–15; Enes, *Moçambique (1893)* (Lisbon, 1896), 170–175.
53. Coelho, *Dezoito Annos*, 373.
54. *Ibid.*, 274.

traders continued a profitable traffic in rum, brandy, and wines.

Although the Portuguese authorities attempted to assuage the temper of the Lion of Gaza with a steady stream of port, their conscious attempts to "inebriate his ambition," as one official put it, were rather useless.[55] The chief's determination to remain independent of Portuguese authority and to consolidate his power within Gaza remained unwavering, at least until the threat of Portuguese armed intervention materialized. In the meantime, the British South Africa Company managed to get the promised rifles to Manjacaze by February 30, 1891, in spite of Portuguese efforts to impound them. On March 2, Dr. Leander Starr Jameson, Rhodes' chief agent, arrived at the royal kraal after a grueling journey through the country ravaged by Gungunhana's migration.[56] Jameson paid the chief his first annual subsidy of £500 and the concession was thereby confirmed; Gungunhana received annual subsidies from the company for several years thereafter. One company agent, Will Longden, remained at the royal kraal until late 1893, when he was withdrawn by Rhodes after Portuguese protests.

In April 1891, Gungunhana sent two *indunas* to England to ask for British protection. This had no bearing, however, on the outcome of the political treaty between Britain and Portugal signed on June 11, 1891; the kingdom of Gungunhana was partitioned between Britain and Portugal. This treaty was a confirmation — with different frontiers — of the Anglo-Portuguese convention of August 1890.[57] Northern Gaza or Gazaland, between the Save (Sabi) River and the frontier became British territory, but the greater part of Gaza was officially recognized as Portuguese territory.[58] Thus the British South Africa Company's hopes for influence in Gaza waned, although Rhodes continued to pay Gungunhana his subsidy. Although Salisbury had earlier in 1891 apparently argued for the "neutrality" of Gungunhana within Portuguese territory and thereby recognized his strength, in April 1891 he stated emphatically that: "Gungun-

55. Enes, *A Guerra*, 11.

56. Warhurst, *Anglo-Portuguese Relations*, 86; Mousinho de Albuquerque, *Moçambique*, 29.

57. Warhurst, *Anglo-Portuguese Relations*, 104–105.

58. Duffy, *Portuguese Africa*, 219–221.

hana's independence has not been recognized by HMG [Her Majesty's Government]." [59] The fate of Gungunhana, in the realm of diplomacy at least, was sealed by the treaty of June 1891.

Although the Portuguese had now obtained international recognition of much of what they considered "the province of Mozambique," their power, prestige, and resources seemed incapable of supporting their sovereignty. The humiliation of having to bow to the British "ultimatum" of 1890, and the loss of a part of Manica and Nyasaland, coupled with the *de facto* independence of their "nominal vassal" Gungunhana in Gaza, encouraged a group of Portuguese officials to propose the destruction of the chief without delay.[60] Others, such as José d'Almeida and António Enes — who was later royal commissioner and governor-general of Mozambique — proposed a peaceful, "wait-and-see" policy. Almeida favored a policy of nonviolence, of patient and tenacious negotiation with Gungunhana and his *indunas*. His conviction that a final martial showdown in Gaza was avoidable lasted well into 1895.[61]

This policy of peace was founded mainly on a survey of respective strengths. In a report of December 1890, Almeida advised that it would be "very difficult" to defeat Gungunhana, and that it would be foolhardy even to try it for fear of a reverse and the consequent possibility that Britain might take advantage of Portuguese weakness and seize the province or an important part of it.[62] António Enes declared in an important report of 1893 that Portugal must wait and tolerate this "semi-independence" of the chief, while watching the weakening Shangana power until the right moment came to attack. Enes wrote that Gungunhana was, in his opinion, losing popularity because of the failure of his internal policy.[63] Much to the disgust of the older Ngoni and Zuluized groups, Gungunhana was apparently choosing court favorites from non-Zulu groups of the conquered tribes such as the Tonga, Chope, and Valenge. The

59. Warhurst, *Anglo-Portuguese Relations*, 91.

60. Enes, *A Guerra*, 4–11; see also F. A. Oliveira Martins, *O Ultimatum Visto Por António Enes* (Lisbon, 1948).

61. Enes, *Moçambique*, 175–178; Coelho, *Dezoito Annos*, 369–370, 384, 499, 500–511.

62. Coelho, *Dezoito Annos*, 287–290.

63. Enes, *Moçambique*, 178.

army of the Lion now was composed of great numbers of men recruited from the weaker tribes, the traditional prey of the Shangana. Enes predicted that Gungunhana would not live long because of his bouts with alcohol and food and that many sons would dispute the succession to his throne. Furthermore, his nobles were angered by his arbitrary confiscations of the cattle and women obtained in raids.

The judgment of Enes has considerable truth in it and is supported in part by later developments. Yet this European's analysis was closest to the mark when he discussed Gungunhana's policy objective: to maintain "real and practical independence" in Gaza.[64] Gungunhana had already shown how clever he was at playing both ends against the middle with British and Portuguese interests. Although he sent envoys to South Africa and to England, he also negotiated with the Portuguese through embassies at Lisbon. His character and power in Gaza seemed to the Portuguese authorities to be "an instrument of domination and . . . an element of defense against foreign greed." [65] The Portuguese, therefore, decided not to disturb him for the moment but to take the defensive precaution of constructing a protective wall of blockhouses and loyal African chiefs between their coastal settlements and the Gaza frontier. Both Almeida and Enes supported the official credence that Gungunhana would not fight a war unless cornered, and that, although his armed effectiveness was apparently decreasing in relation to theirs after 1893, it was best to avoid or postpone a decisive armed conflict.

In spite of the lack of shared trust between the Portuguese authorities and Gungunhana, the chief did show a certain affection for Almeida. During 1892 and 1893, when Almeida was not the Portuguese *residente* at Manjacaze, Gungunhana had his son Mangua, who knew Portuguese, compose a letter to Almeida (dated May 11, 1892). This short message, one of the few known examples of the chief's thoughts on paper, stated that he had rejected the entreaties of English agents to "become English"

---

64. Some modern Portuguese judgments of Gungunhana neglect the internal weaknesses in Gaza. "Gungunhana," *G.E.P. e B.*, XII:922; Enes, *Moçambique*, 176.

65. *Ibid.*, 178.

by answering that "my father was of the Portuguese and I always must be Portuguese." Apparently anxious for Almeida's return to Manjacaze, he headed the letter with the title, "My Father Muzilla." Just why Gungunhana wrote this message is unclear, though it is probable that the chief wished to maintain his Portuguese contacts and that Almeida had some influence with him.[66]

Almeida was loath to return even a slight affection or interest to Gungunhana, but in late 1893 he was drawn back to Gaza on a special mission. Almeida was a secretary and agent of the Mozambique Company, a commercial enterprise financed largely by non-Portuguese capital and chartered by the Portuguese government in 1891; it held concessions in southern Mozambique.[67] Because of the Shangana raids in Mozambique Company territory during 1892–1893, the company officials wished to reach some sort of agreement with the king of Gaza. The Mozambique Company territory included that Manica and Sofala territory north of the Save River where Gungunhana continued to have some sovereignty and influence.[68] Almeida, with his considerable experience in dealing with the African monarch, was chosen to negotiate with Gungunhana and returned for a stay at Manjacaze between October 30 and December 13, 1893.

A great public meeting or *banja* was held on November 19 that year in the kraal, and four Portuguese, including Almeida, attended, along with Gungunhana and many of his advisers and relatives. The chief apparently swore in public to uphold an agreement whereby he recognized the right of the Mozambique Company to administer without interference all of its concession territory north of the Save. Gungunhana would receive one-half of the hut tax (*imposta da palhota*) collected in that area as "compensation" for giving the company his authority and the use of his *indunas* and *mofanas* (individual soldiers) to guarantee "public order" and to help collect taxes. This agreement of fourteen articles reads like a cynical marriage of interests; included are provisions that Gungunhana provide armed tribesmen to enable the company to conquer tribes beyond its control in north-

66. Coelho, *Dezoito Annos*, 364–365.
67. Duffy, *Portuguese Africa*, 90–92.
68. Coelho, *Dezoito Annos*, 363–373.

ern Gaza. A new marriage tax was to be paid by all Africans in company territory involved in polygamous marriage. Further, the *indunas* of Gungunhana were authorized by the agreement or modus vivendi with the company to recruit from among the Tonga all labor necessary for public services.[69]

Almeida felt that this 1893 agreement could be a stepping-stone toward controlling Gungunhana and eventually establishing a kind of co-administration with the Shangana. Other Portuguese, nevertheless, maligned the agreement as an appeasement of a bloodthirsty autocrat. Envoy Almeida reasoned in retrospect that the Mozambique Company had little choice, since neither the Portuguese administration nor the company had an army worthy of the name, and the Shangana *impis* had been supreme in this region for half a century. According to Almeida, who certainly had no illusions about the weakness of the chartered company employing him, it was actually illegal to use an army in any part of Gaza, according to Article 2 of the 1891 charter of the Mozambique Company as well as Article 2 of the 1885 Act of Vassalage of Gungunhana, both of which recognized that in Gaza the chief had complete jurisdiction as well as the right to govern and to collect taxes.[70]

Why did Gungunhana become a party to this modus vivendi? Although he swore to it at the public *banja,* he did not sign it as he did the Schultz concession of 1890 for reasons stated by Almeida: "Gungunhana never signed it, nor does he sign any paper, because he cannot read it, nor does he trust a reading given to him, even though the reader might be his own son Mangua." [71]

Extremely cautious with all such agreements, the chief nevertheless informally consented to the 1893 modus vivendi apparently because he was uncertain of further monetary support from Rhodes and believed that a partnership with the Mozambique Company might increase his wealth and prestige more than an arrangement with the Portuguese government, his nominal suzerain.

A week after the modus vivendi was agreed upon, one aspect

69. *Ibid.,* 374–376 for text of *modus vivendi.*
70. *Ibid.,* 377–379.
71. *Ibid.,* 381.

of Gungunhana's power was tarnished: some eight hundred of the thousand rifles given to him by Rhodes' agent for the concession were destroyed in a hut fire near Manjacaze. Who was to blame? Certainly envoy Almeida had an excellent motive for such an act and later gained a reputation for preventing arms from falling into the chief's hands. The evidence implicating Almeida, however, is scanty. Almeida's writings would lead us to believe that he had nothing to do with the occurrence, which he termed a "providential fire." [72]

Gungunhana was angry and Almeida left the royal kraal under a dark cloud. The chief made two requests of the departing Portuguese envoy: a gift of a thousand rifles from the king of Portugal, and the surrender to him of the son of Anhana — an heir of Muzila and rival of Gungunhana — who was hiding somewhere to the west. Despite Almeida's parting gift of ten oxen, two ivory tusks, and three lion skins, the Lion of Gaza insisted upon the guns and the rival claimant. Later, Gungunhana asserted that Almeida had promised these things when leaving, but it seems unlikely that the Portuguese representative would do so under the circumstances. It is more probable that the Shangana leader misconstrued Almeida's parting words.[73]

The loss of the rifles caused some commotion in the royal kraal during and after December 1893; hostility toward the Portuguese grew stronger. During the following year, Gungunhana made several requests of the authorities for rifles and gave the excuse that he needed them to defeat his major enemy still at large, the Chope Chief Speranhana. Furthermore, some of the remaining two hundred rifles of the 1891 concession had been lost in an earlier war against the Chope. Obtaining no satisfaction, the chief then sent a letter in December 1894 to José d'Almeida, asking him to return to Gaza to confer.[74]

As events approached a final confrontation between the two conflicting forces, conditions in adjacent territories aggravated the

72. *Ibid.*, 406–417.

73. Coelho, *Dezoito Annos,* 377. The American consul in Mozambique wrote later that by law all fire arms in Mozambique had to be licensed for a fee equivalent to $20 and that there was a strict ban on arms importation. Hollis to Uhl, August 7, 1894, *Despatches from U.S. Consuls in Lourenço Marques, Mozambique 1854–1906*, roll 2, T-171, National Archives, Washington, D.C.

74. Coelho, *Dezoito Annos,* 413–414.

situation. That the Shangana maintained close links of blood, marriage, and diplomacy, and perhaps even trade, during the late nineteenth century with their neighbors, the Ndebele and Swazi, there can be no doubt. The Shangana contacts with the Ndebele were perhaps the most important of all. A sister of Muzila had married Lobengula in the 1870's, and an older sister of Gungunhana's also became a wife of the Ndebele king sometime before 1887.[75] The Ndebele war of 1893 with the armed forces of the British South Africa Company spread waves of confusion and despair and drove Ndebele refugees in several directions from Rhodesia. During 1894–1895 Portuguese authorities reported that a considerable number of Ndebele were fleeing defeat on the plateau and had streamed into the Limpopo basin. Apparently, some of these displaced Ndebele warriors settled in lower Bilene through an arrangement with Gungunhana in early 1895.[76]

The tales of European power and victory and of African terror and defeat must have had their effect in Gaza. Stories of the Ndebele rout to the west undoubtedly disheartened certain groups among the Shangana. A similar reversal of Swazi fortunes to the south occurred in 1894 and encouraged confusion and despair. The British government handed over the protectorate administration to the Boers of the Transvaal Republic, and this later led to more Swazi rebellions and unrest.[77] There were Swazi elements among the Shangana in Gaza. The various crises were part of the gradual disintegration of traditional African power in southeast Africa; the neighbors of the Shangana fought out the armageddons of their tribal independence and succumbed to European domination. At a time when the frontiers in that region were non-existent or only recently drawn, Gaza felt the tremors of approaching disaster through the tribulations of its neighbors. In June 1895, the American consul at Mozambique Island wrote Washington that ever since the Ndebele war of October to December 1893, Africans south of

75. *Ibid.*, 232–233, 324.

76. *Ibid.*, 457–458. Gungunhana's intertribal diplomatic contacts also reached the Swazis, for in 1890 the chief was planning a marriage with "a princess of Swaziland." *Ibid.*, 274.

77. Kuper, *The Swazi*, 9–11; R. P. Stevens, "Swaziland Political Development," *The Journal of Modern African Studies*, I:328 (1963).

the Zambezi were "in a state of unrest." [78] His broad generalization was being borne out in fact.

As the Shangana grievances and apprehensions mounted, so did the impatience of the Portuguese administration. In the Lourenço Marques district, trouble had been brewing for over a decade as petty African chiefs struggled among themselves for supremacy.[79] In 1894 a war began in this district which eventually drew Gungunhana into it. There is little reliable evidence that Gungunhana was involved in the original outbreak of hostilities in 1894 as the Portuguese later claimed.[80] It is true that there was a minor battle between several of Gungunhana's *indunas* and a Portuguese detachment some thirty miles inland from Beira on the Buzi River in June 1894, but this was not decisive in leading to general hostilities;[81] it was merely one episode in a worsening situation. In the Magaia region, some fifteen miles north of Lourenço Marques, the Portuguese had supported Chief Mobvesha against Chief Mahazul for the throne vacated by the death of Chief Mapunga in 1890. A conflict was the result. Mahazul resisted Portuguese pressure, protested an increased hut tax as well as the Portuguese decision in litigation (*milando*) over the succession, and sent a party of nobles to a public meeting at the Portuguese post at Angoane. On or about August 22, 1894, fighting broke out there as the Africans resisted the arrest of several of their number by Angolan troops (under Portuguese orders) at the post.[82]

Within weeks, the peoples north of Lourenço Marques, led by Chief Mahazul and his neighbor chief Matibejana of Zixaxa, were on the warpath, determined to capture and sack the town. The first attack on Lourenço Marques, which was poorly defended by only a few companies of Angolas and a handful of white Portuguese officers, came on October 14. Reinforcements

78. Hollis to Uhl, June 28, 1895, *Despatches*, roll 2.

79. Alberto and Toscano, *O Oriente*, 172; Coelho, *Dezoito Annos*, 461; Carlos Selvagem, *Portugal Militar* (Lisbon, 1934), 614–616; Marcello Caetano, ed., *As Campanhas de 1895 Segundo Os Contemporáneos* (Lisbon, 1945), 41–46.

80. Selvagem, *Portugal*, 615; Mousinho de Albuquerque, *Moçambique*, 39–40; Henrique Galvão and Carlos Selvagem, *O Império Ultramarino Português* (Lisbon, 1952–1953), IV, 69; "Gungunhana," *G.E.P. e B.*, XII:922–923.

81. Hollis to Uhl, June 28, 1894, enclosing Report of C. Andrews, June 23, 1894, from Lourenço Marques, *Despatches*, roll 2.

82. Caetano, *As Campanhas*, 43–47.

arrived from Lisbon and Luanda in mid-November 1894: some eight to nine hundred troops of the Second Chasseurs battalion and three hundred *Angolas*. The Portuguese still were not strong enough to take the offensive and remained in a defensive position behind barricades, blockhouses, and barbed wire. Another serious attack by the forces of the petty chiefs came on January 7, 1895, and the authorities of the besieged town of about 3,500 inhabitants feared for the future of Portuguese sovereignty. Either out of magnanimity or shrewdness, Cecil Rhodes, long the Portuguese bête noire, offered aid in putting down the revolt in late December 1894; his offer was refused by Portugal. But thereafter he paid Gungunhana's annual subsidy directly to Portugal by agreement.[83]

Gungunhana and the Campaign of 1895

The 1895 Campaign, or the first Gaza campaign of 1895 as it is sometimes called, has become a legend in Portuguese historiography. More heroes and more books have emerged from this episode than out of any other colonial campaign in Portuguese Africa's long past. Woven into the fabric of national tradition, the campaign inevitably has suffered distortions. Not a single campaign but several distinct episodes spread over a period of sixteen months, it actually began in 1894 and was not decided ultimately until 1897, when the last Shangana regiments were smashed by Portuguese forces. Phases of the campaign took months when they could have been decided in minutes, as were many of its ephemeral skirmishes.[84]

This campaign was crucial to the Portuguese because it confirmed their rule in southern Mozambique and boosted national confidence at a time when Portugal was experiencing a moral crisis. One "hero of Africa," a participant in the campaign, Joaquim Augusto Mousinho de Albuquerque, looked back on

83. Warhurst, *Anglo-Portuguese Relations,* 106; Alberto and Toscano, *O Oriente,* 204–205.

84. João de Azevedo Coutinho, *Memórias De Um Velho Marinheiro e Soldado De África* (Lisbon, 1941), 359. A fairly comprehensive survey of the 1895 campaign is contained in J. Teixeira Botelho, *História Militar e Política dos Portugueses em Moçambique De 1833 Aos Nossos Dias* (Lisbon, 1936), 71–72 ff.

the critical years 1894–1895 and claimed that Portugal had nearly lost the province of Mozambique. António José Enes, the organizer of the campaign, later wrote that the victories of 1895 were due to "moral forces," and had restored the prestige of Portuguese authority in Africa, proving for posterity that his generation was still "Portuguese" in the sense of national pride.[85]

But until the latter part of 1895, victory was not assured to the Portuguese. Many foreign observers in Mozambique at the time felt that the Portuguese would lose the war and that, especially after the Jameson Raid, there was a chance that Great Britain might intervene and take over Delagoa Bay. The American consul, Hollis, exaggerated the strength of Gungunhana as well as the weakness of Portugal, and even after the end of the 1895 campaign, he refused to believe that Gungunhana was beaten.[86]

In early 1895, when over three hundred European soldiers were laid up with fever in the Lourenço Marques hospital and after the Portuguese had suffered a reverse near the town, it appeared that the African forces were paramount.[87] When several whites were murdered along the Incomati River and further attacks made on Lourenço Marques, the Lisbon government replied to the frantic requests of the colonial administration and decided to dispatch a strong military expedition to Mozambique. At last, the excuse to defeat Gungunhana, the reluctant vassal, had come. Appointed head of the entire operation was António Enes, who was named royal commissioner. He arrived in Lourenço Marques during January 1895, and he grimly set out to solve a problem which he had studied for at least four years: the future of Chief Gungunhana of Gaza. The report of the American consul on the serious mood of the day is suggestive: "There were no ceremonies when the Governor departed, or when the Commissioner arrived, which is something unusual." [88]

Shortly afterward, on February 2, 1895, a Portuguese force, which included two hundred *Angolas* out of about eight hundred

85. Mousinho de Albuquerque, *Moçambique*, 73; Enes, *A Guerra*, 128, 467–478.

86. Hollis to Uhl, June 28, 1895, December 31, 1895, *Despatches*, roll 2.

87. E. F. Knight, *Madagascar in War Time* (London, 1896), 4; Hollis to Uhl, April 6, 1895, *Despatches*, roll 2; Enes, *A Guerra*, 36.

88. Hollis to Uhl, January 14, 1895, *Despatches*, roll 2.

and fifty troops under Major José Ribeiro, met and dispersed a
dawn attack by three thousand Vatua (Shangana) warriors (mostly
under the command of Chiefs Mahazul and Matibejana) at Marracuene, near the Incomati.[89] Even now, it is not known how
many of the warriors at Marracuene were under the sway of
Gungunhana. For the first time in this area the Africans learned
the effects of the deadly European machine guns. But, although
the skirmish was considered a heartening Portuguese victory
and the sign of a beginning offensive, the royal commissioner felt
that the war could not continue without a major reinforcement
from Europe. As he wrote to his daughter, "It seems the war is
over, which is fortunate, since I certainly cannot continue it with
such decimated troops." [90]

The war, however, was not over, although Marracuene saved
Lourenço Marques from further African attacks from the north.
The Lisbon government, encouraged by the victory, expedited
the dispatch of several European battalions totaling two thousand
European troops in infantry, artillery, and engineer units.[91]

Early in 1895 at the royal kraal at Manjacaze, Gaza, there were
as yet no hostilities. The Portuguese *residente* during part of
this period was Navy Lieutenant Joaquim Judice Bicker, who
had several years of experience in Gaza but was not especially
popular with Gungunhana. Nonetheless, at a meeting with the
chief on February 26, 1895, Bicker managed to extract "promises"
from the Lion not to attack Inhambane and to send *indunas* to
Lourenço Marques to parley for peace.[92]

Veteran negotiator José d'Almeida returned to Mozambique
in January 1895, reluctantly cutting short his recuperation from
malaria. In the meantime, in November 1894, Almeida had been
attacked in the Lisbon press and accused of being a poor administrator in Gaza and somehow to blame for the troubles there.[93]
He returned to Gaza both as an official of the Mozambique Company and as a special envoy of the Portuguese royal commissioner,
Enes. His mission was to try to bring Gungunhana to terms as a
vassal of Portugal, but, failing that, at least to prevent the chief's

---

89. Galvao and Selvagem, *Império,* IV, 66; Selvagem, *Portugal,* 618–619.
90. Caetano, *As Campanhas,* 39–40.
91. Enes, *A Guerra,* 17.
92. "J. Judice Bicker," *G.E.P. e B.,* IV:69; "José d'Almeida," *Ibid.,* II:57.
93. Coelho, *Dezoito Annos,* 411–412.

interference in the revolt in the Lourenço Marques district.[94]

When Almeida reached Manjacaze and the Portuguese residency on March 16, 1895, he learned of persistent rumors of war between Gungunhana and the government; he reported that the chief was in what he termed an anxious and vacillatory state of mind. He found that earlier, in September 1894, Gungunhana had been informed of the arrest and imprisonment of two petty chiefs in southern Mozambique. After the government had termed them rebels and sent them to exile in the Congo (northern Angola), Gungunhana had asked that their families be protected in his village.[95] Thus, the monarch of Gaza demonstrated that he would protect neighboring chiefs from the Portuguese administration and would therefore stand in the way of the gradual extension of Portuguese rule into the interior. The Portuguese policy of deporting political undesirables became especially oppressive to African society in early 1895, and this worsened racial relations. As a Swiss missionary communicated to António Enes at the time: "These deportations had had an unhappy echo throughout the entire country." [96]

Even in March and early April 1895, however, a full-scale war between the two forces, African and European, was not certain. (Although Enes confided to his daughter in March that such a campaign if fought would be over by August or September after only one month of combat once reinforcements arrived, the royal commissioner still had to convince other Portuguese leaders that an invasion was necessary.[97] When he submitted his April operations plan, the campaign against Gungunhana was still only an "aspiration." Enes' plan of April 3 outlined a scheme of maneuver for the conquest of Gaza and the defeat of Gungunhana. There would be three columns of troops: the major one, the so-called "Northern Column," would strike inland from the port of Inhambane, create a base at Chicomo on the frontier of what was considered Gungunhana's territory, and then attack the kraal at Manjacaze with over a thousand troops. Of the other two smaller columns, one would patrol the Limpopo River with

94. Enes, *A Guerra*, 120–126; Coelho, *Dezoito Annos*, 433.
95. *Ibid.*, 419; Caetano, *As Campanhas*, 48–49.
96. Junod to Enes, Feb. 23, 1895, in Caetano, *As Campanhas*, 45.
97. *Ibid.*, 89.

steamers and the other would patrol the Incomati. Thus, the three columns would act as three pincers to form a *cordon sanitaire* and surround the African *impis*. The Incomati column would control the area between the river and the Limpopo, while the Limpopo force would have the mission of preventing any landing of reinforcements or arms for Gungunhana from the outside.[98]

Enes' April operations plan included a deceptive scheme. Believing that Gungunhana would bluff and remain reluctant to fight, Enes planned to circulate the information that the large Portuguese expedition coming to Lourenço Marques was formed only to stop attacks on crown lands and not to attack Gungunhana in his royal kraal. Enes reasoned that Gungunhana's location at Manjacaze, so close to the coast and to Portuguese settlements, made a Portuguese attack and envelopment more feasible than if the chief had remained in the interior at Mossurise. Indeed, in 1889, Almeida, on the occasion of Gungunhana's move south, had predicted that the new location in the Limpopo Valley would favor the government in the event of a future campaign.[99] And so it did.

The royal commissioner's plan to deceive, however, fooled no one, least of all Gungunhana, who apparently feared the worst from the beginning of the trouble. The chief learned from his own spies and from foreign visitors to his kraal that he was likely to be attacked. Within less than a week after the Enes plan was agreed upon, Almeida wrote from Manjacaze that "several days before" Gungunhana had asked him if the Portuguese were preparing to make war on him. Several Indian traders, as well as an English couple fluent in Zulu, the Fels, had informed him that a large "*impi* of whites," as Gungunhana put it, was gathering at Lourenço Marques and Inhambane to attack him from the south and also through Chicomo to the east. Almeida was enraged but tried in vain to quiet the fears of the chief. He told him that the European troops were not to be feared and that they would attack only the rebel chiefs.[100]

The two rebel chiefs in question, Mahazul and Matibejana, had fled with their followers into Gungunhana's territory across

98. *Ibid.*, 63–65.
99. Coelho, *Dezoito Annos*, 209.
100. *Ibid.*, 459–460.

the Incomati after the defeat at Marracuene in February. Gungunhana was disturbed by the news of the battle of Marracuene, and he evidently considered the two rebel chiefs his vassals and therefore offered them asylum in Gaza. There is evidence that Protestant missionaries — the Wesleyan mission and the Anabaptist Roman Swiss mission with stations in Lourenço Marques and near Manjacaze — had some influence over Gungunhana's decision to offer asylum and over the rebels and their followers during 1894–1895.[101] The Swiss missionaries especially — Messrs. Junod, Berthaud, and Liengme (a medical doctor) — tended to support Gungunhana in giving refuge to Mahazul and Matibejana (sometimes referred to familiarly as "Zixaxa"). Dr. Liengme remained in the kraal at Manjacaze as a missionary and doctor from late 1893 through the last major battle of the campaign in 1895. It is likely that some of the rebel followers were catechists and neophyte Christians. In any event, Gungunhana protected and sheltered the chiefs because Matibejana was a personal friend and because he believed that rejecting the rebels would jeopardize his traditional authority in Gaza and beyond.[102]

Meanwhile at the Portuguese residency in Manjacaze, Almeida kept a close watch on developments. On April 16, the second son of Gungunhana, Carlos Fernando Machado Mangua, died very suddenly in the royal kraal. The evidence which Almeida privately gathered suggests that it was a case of murder by poisoning. This incident followed closely the alleged poisoning of the boy's uncle, Makidame, the Shangana governor of Inhampura; Makidame apparently was poisoned for disloyalty to Gungunhana. The heir and first son of Gungunhana, Godide, appeared to be the murderer of Mangua, the only member of the Shangana elite with the rudiments of a Portuguese education and pro-Portuguese leanings. Almeida concluded that Godide was to blame for the demise of Mangua as they had been seen quarrel-

101. "Crónica Geral," *Portugal em Africa* (Lisbon), III:138–140 (1896); Coelho, *Dezoito Annos,* 497–498; Caetano, *As Campanhas,* 41–46; Mousinho de Albuquerque, *Moçambique,* 95–96. During his fight against the Portuguese, Gungunhana is said to have visited a mission station (Gikuki) near Inhambane and used lead from the mission printing press for bullets. Information from Per Hassing, Boston University, in a letter to the writer, Aug. 28, 1964.

102. Enes, *A Guerra,* 249–251. Enes described Matibejana as "intelligent, bold, ambitious." According to Enes, he joined Mahazul in revolt only because he felt his region would have to be defended against Portuguese attack. *Ibid.,* 37.

ing in public frequently. Almeida thought it was an ill omen for future Afro-Portuguese relations.[103]

What Gungunhana thought of the death of his son is not known. There was a funeral ceremony at Manjacaze, but little more was heard of the incident. The chief was occupied now with affairs of state as he began to send envoys in several directions to obtain the allegiance of various chiefs in the Lourenço Marques and Inhambane districts. Attempting to marshal strength for the impending conflict, in May 1895 Gungunhana also sent out tax collectors, who reportedly demanded over a pound in gold from huts in one region in order to fill the royal treasury.[104] As the situation worsened vis-à-vis the Portuguese, Gungunhana continued his policy of warring on the neighboring Chope. In March 1895 he ordered the mobilization of five of his *mangas* to fight the Chope chiefs.[105]

The army, led by Maguiguana but controlled by Gungunhana, consisted of approximately six *mangas* altogether, each *manga* composed of two to three thousand men. A partial order of battle and the names of each *manga* were as follows: Zibancua; Zimpafumana; Mabanga; Zinhone-Mochope (commanded by Molungo and consisting of loyal Chope); Izincumande (estimated at about a thousand men); and Maiache.[106] Although these regiments maintained traditions brought from Zululand in the early nineteenth century, later tribal intermixture and the hiring of auxiliary troops had weakened the *esprit* of the units. The importation of alcohol and the migrations to South Africa had also taken their toll. The name of each *manga* signified an outstanding characteristic of the warriors: "Zimpafumana" meant "the tall men," and men of the Zinhone-Mochope were known as the "white birds," from the white feathers on their shields.[107] The total strength of the army was perhaps twenty thousand.[108]

103. Coelho, *Dezoito Annos,* 460–462.

104. *Ibid.,* 473–475.

105. *Ibid.,* 458, 467–468.

106. *Ibid.,* 261–262, 458.

107. Aires D'Ornellas, *Cartas D'Africa. Campanha do Gungunhana. 1895* (Lisbon, 1930), 90–92.

108. Selvagem, *Portugal,* 623; Mousinho de Albuquerque, *Moçambique,* 39–40. Mousinho acknowledged that the size of the Shangana army had been exaggerated by Portuguese observers; some estimates, he noted, were as high as two hundred thousand.

In the meantime, the Portuguese expeditionary forces were gathering on the coast. In mid-April, Colonel of Infantry Eduardo Galhardo, commander of the "Northern Column," arrived at Lourenço Marques, and within two months several Portuguese battalions and supporting units had arrived from Lisbon. Galhardo had no previous campaign experience in Africa.[109] In mid-June he established a base camp at Inhambane and then marched inland with a force of about eight hundred Europeans and four hundred Angolas to a camp at Chicomo. Small units of cavalry and artillery moved with the infantry into Chicomo while the amphibious columns on the Limpopo and the Incomati began to patrol the river banks.

At the royal kraal at Manjacaze, Gungunhana negotiated with envoy Almeida to preserve the crumbling peace. Portuguese press reports as well as private campaign reports popularized an image of Gungunhana at the time sitting on a throne in his kraal, with a scepter in hand, drinking port from "a silver cup." [110] Almeida's colleagues on the coast at Lourenço Marques kept strict control of the news of the negotiations. As the American consul at Mozambique Island reported in June 1895: "The government is very careful that nothing but official news shall be promulgated, and the only newspaper in Lorenzo [*sic*] Marques has been suppressed." [111]

Almeida attempted to convince Gungunhana that the so-called "promise" to supply him with a thousand rifles and the heir of Anhana was no longer feasible; but little progress was made during Almeida's mission to Gaza from March to late May 1895. Gungunhana was now quite anxious to establish definitely the frontiers between Gaza and Portuguese territory and to affirm his independent jurisdiction. During Almeida's absence in 1894, according to the report of one *residente,* Gungunhana began to claim that his dealings with the British South Africa Company were invalid, that he had ceded concession land to no one, and

109. "Galhardo," *G.E.P. e B.,* XII:69–70.
110. "Paiva Couceiro," *ibid.,* XX:20–22. It is probable that this "silver cup" was an apocryphal version of the inscribed silver cup ("To Gungunhana from Queen Victoria") which Gungunhana reportedly received from the Queen of England through his envoys in 1891. No such silver cup was found in Gungunhana's treasury upon his capture. J. Mousinho de Albuquerque, *Livro Das Campanhas* (Lisbon, 1935), I, 60–61.
111. Hollis to Uhl, June 7, 1895, *Despatches,* roll 2.

that the coveted subsidy each year from Rhodes had been not for a concession but to "repay him for the tribute he had received" before 1889 from his former vassal, Mutassa of Manica.[112]

Gungunhana found that Almeida opposed his attacks on the Chope. Although he could do little to prevent these actions, part of an old tradition among the Shangana elite and their age-grade regiments, Almeida did try to stop supplies of firearms from getting into the hands of the chief. On two occasions before June 1895, he acted decisively: once discouraging the sale of several hundred rifles by an English trader, and later disguising a shipment of two Nordenfeldt machine guns and ammunition sent through Manjacaze on the way to a military post at Inharrime.[113]

During the first week of June, Almeida traveled to Lourenço Marques, accompanied by several of Gungunhana's *indunas,* to confer with António Enes, the royal commissioner; Gungunhana had promised Lieutenant Bicker in late February that he would send envoys to meet with the Portuguese government. The *indunas* claimed that they wanted peace, but Enes refused to see them in person and conferred only through Almeida. Enes' reason for this and for refusing to take a gift of tribute (*saguate*) was that Gungunhana had been a disloyal vassal of Portugal by harboring the rebel petty chiefs in Gaza.[114] The negotiations were further complicated by the enmity between Almeida and Enes; the royal commissioner had no confidence in his envoy, whom he facetiously referred to as "the chartered tamer of the lion of Gaza." [115] Enes claimed that Almeida wished to save Gungunhana from defeat and final humiliation by persuading him to obey the Portuguese government with regard to surrendering the rebels but that he was not doing a very good job of dissuading the chief from his independent path. Hence, the *indunas* of Gungunhana left Lourenço Marques without seeing Enes or getting any satisfaction from their claims for peace.

Several weeks later, Enes was visited by two Swiss missionaries, Junod and Liengme, who came to discuss the approaching conflict. Liengme claimed that all the Shangana chiefs — except for

112. Coelho, *Dezoito Annos,* 401–402.
113. *Ibid.,* 470–480.
114. Enes, *A Guerra,* 238–246.
115. *Ibid.,* 247.

a few hotheads like Manhune (and perhaps Maguiguana) — wanted peace. The missionary asserted that requiring Gungunhana to surrender the rebels was an unchristian and immoral act since they were now "guests" of the chief and he could not break his word. Enes feared Liengme's influence over the chief in Gaza but Almeida wrote him later that the missionary had no influence at Manjacaze.[116] Enes ended the interview by stating that the government would not back down from its position.

After these fruitless conferences, Enes assumed a tougher position and on July 14 issued his "Conditions with which the submission of Chief Gungunhana will be Accepted." The foremost and *sine qua non* condition — one which Gungunhana would never completely fulfill — was the surrender of Mahazul and Matibejana "to be duly punished." In the remaining fourteen conditions the authorities demanded: an annual tribute of £10,000 to the government, Gungunhana's recognition of Portugal's right to establish military posts and garrison troops in Gaza, an end to war between Gungunhana and vassal chiefs of the crown (mainly the Chope), the placing of African armed forces at the disposal of the government, and last, that if Gungunhana failed to obey the king of Portugal, he would "lose the right to rule the lands of Gaza thus causing the Chiefs of these lands to meet and to choose his successor." [117]

Gungunhana's acceptance of these conditions would have been tantamount to the loss of that "real and practical independence" which Enes in 1893 had acknowledged as the chief's major objective. Gungunhana was presented this official document of conditions on August 8 at his kraal by Almeida, who had returned on his second mission. After the document was read, the Lion of Gaza refused steadfastly to hand over his subject chiefs but still claimed that he did not want war with Portugal. A week later, Gungunhana stated his terms to Almeida: Portuguese withdrawal from the frontiers of Gaza and acceptance of the *saguate* (tribute) from the Shangana; in return, Gungunhana would hand over several important *indunas* (rebels) to Portugal, but not Mahazul and Matibejana. The chief claimed he was willing to pay £1,000 in gold as tribute.[118]

116. *Ibid.*, 249–251; Alberto and Toscano, *O Oriente*, 211.
117. Coelho, *Dezoito Annos*, 504–505.
118. *Ibid.*, 516–518; Enes, *A Guerra*, 310–311.

Still, the African leader did not plan to put all his eggs in the Portuguese basket, and he cast about for support and protection from other quarters. Somehow he contacted the British consul at Lourenço Marques to ask permission to send another embassy of *indunas* to Natal. Although advised against this step by the consul, he dispatched several envoys to Pretoria and Natal, as well as to Cape Town, with gifts of ivory tusks, hoping to gain some kind of protection or alliance.[119] These African ambassadors returned to Gaza in late September 1895, after a long journey of two months. The official response from Boer and Briton alike was disappointing; nothing was promised.[120] The last hopes of Gungunhana were dashed and he now realized that his time was growing short.

But until the ambassadors to Cape Town returned, Gungunhana hoped that he could enlist British aid, at least to protect him from the military expeditions now camped on his frontiers. Clearly, this idea temporarily bolstered the negotiating position of the chief at Manjacaze. Others in his party, however, apparently felt that war was inevitable.[121] Although refusing to hand over the rebels, Gungunhana stated on August 19 that he would pay the tribute demanded in the "Conditions" as well as accept the establishment of military forts. He also declared that he would soon be forced to obtain the protection of "the flag of other whites" if the king of Portugal continued to treat him so poorly.[122]

The evidence suggests that the Shangana leader was sincere in asking for peace but that the surrender of the rebels to Portuguese punishment conflicted with his traditional code. Yet Gungunhana was not merely stalling for time in order to strengthen his army, for apparently until the very last he felt he could avoid

119. Enes, *A Guerra*, 459; Coelho, *Dezoito Annos*, 522.
120. Warhurst, *Anglo–Portuguese Relations*, 106–107. According to Almeida's report, the Shangana embassy returned to Gaza before Gungunhana's fall. In late March, Gungunhana told Almeida that he intended sending envoys to England to treat with the government about the question of the rifles he needed. Coelho, *Dezoito Annos*, 522. Apparently, the chief never dispatched these ambassadors.
121. Enes, *A Guerra*, 310–311; Ornellas, *Cartas*, 85. Lieutenant Ornellas wrote home that many Africans in late June 1895 considered war inevitable and were not deceived by Portuguese maneuvering.
122. Coelho, *Dezoito Annos*, 522.

a final hostile confrontation. Certainly, the chief was prepared to resist the Portuguese invasion momentarily since his army had been reunited for months. What some observers did not realize was that Gungunhana's forces were losing strength gradually because of famines and diseases which afflicted the waiting warriors. Demoralized by the waiting, the hardship, and the fear of the European army, some deserted. Others left to tend their farming as it was the harvest season. Contrary to certain Portuguese assertions, the chief of Gaza was not stalling for time to gather strength, but was actually witnessing a growing demoralization among his forces as he attempted to negotiate a peace and avoid general war. Because of this policy, Gungunhana fell out with Maguiguana and Manhune, who tried to dispel all fear of the Portuguese expedition and to commit the Shangana to a full-scale war.[123]

Meanwhile, the Portuguese expedition at Chicomo languished in inaction too. Decimated by fever, lacking proper transport, and anxious to attack Manjacaze, Galhardo's army was on the verge of mutiny. Galhardo's lack of popularity and decisiveness aggravated the situation. Less than fifty miles separated Chicomo and the kraal of Gungunhana, and officers like the dashing cavalry leader Mousinho de Albuquerque proposed a quick cavalry attack and an end to the long and difficult negotiations which were producing nothing but delay.[124]

The royal commissioner wrote that peace negotiations were effectively finished on August 15;[125] a kind of negotiation, however, continued into September and later. On August 28, Enes sent Gungunhana a message to the effect that if he refused to hand over the rebels to the forces at Chicomo, he himself would be treated as a rebel.[126] Previously Gungunhana had angrily told Almeida that the Portuguese forces (the Incomati column) had disembarked and had invaded the Cossine region, considered part of Gaza and his territory; Chief Matibejana was residing in this district at the time. Almeida wrote Lourenço Marques and com-

---

123. *Ibid.*, 520. Almeida reported to Enes by telegram on August 10: "We do not think that Gungunhana wants to gain time, since he is entirely prepared to offer us tenacious resistance in case we enter his lands."

124. Caetano, *As Campanhas*, 290–300, 313–314.

125. Enes, *A Guerra*, 310–311.

126. Coelho, *Dezoito Annos*, 523.

plained that his position as negotiator with Gungunhana had been compromised by the Portuguese aggression and that peace was now impossible.[127]

Portuguese and Shangana forces clashed in a skirmish at Magul to the west of Manjacaze on September 8. A body of about two hundred and seventy-five Portuguese and several Angolas engaged two or three *mangas* (about six thousand warriors) of Gungunhana. While the Portuguese suffered the loss of only five dead and twenty-three wounded, the Africans lost several hundred men.[128] The historian searches in vain for the evidence that "moral forces" won this battle. As one Portuguese participant so aptly put it, the European superiority on this battlefield and during the campaign in general was founded firmly on the possession of "one of the best European rifles." [129]

The battle of Magul helped undermine the power of Gungunhana by spreading terror and fear among the population. A number of petty chiefs in and around Gaza began to side openly with the Portuguese government against the chief. A week after Magul, Almeida ended peace negotiations and retired to Inhambane. His companion, Lieutenant Ornellas appointed by Enes to see that Almeida did not "appease" Gungunhana, later wrote that the royal commissioner had deliberately undermined the negotiations in order to ruin Almeida.[130]

Yet other forces, even more deadly in the long run than the Portuguese armed intrusion, were at work in Gaza during late 1895. Shangana strength and the will to resist were weakened by diseases and scourges which gathered momentum in the time of troubles. As in wars before and since, disease and famine followed the warriors and their families. Hence, the smallpox that raged among the Ndebele in 1893–1894 probably entered Gaza with the refugees. Southern Mozambique itself, beginning about 1890, was visited by a series of scourges: rinderpest, smallpox, locust plagues, and later, during 1895, a famine. The parasitic boring worm prevalent in Angola, *pulex penetrans,* became more common in Gaza because of the presence of infected Angolan

127. *Ibid.*, 499, 511, 523; Caetano, *As Campanhas,* 158–160.
128. Selvagem, *Portugal,* 620–623.
129. Ornellas, *Cartas,* 97–98, 291–295, 305.
130. *Ibid.*, 291–295.

troops in the Portuguese expedition and in garrisons on the coast[131]

Although Gungunhana sent envoys to the Portuguese again on September 20 to ask for peace, he received no definite reply. It is probable that by this time, even had he been willing to surrender the rebels, the Portuguese would have attacked. Colonel Galhardo wanted to attack Manjacaze in early October to end the war, but he refused to advance westward the few miles without more carts and oxen from Inhambane. Fearing the unfavorable effects of the approaching rainy season, Enes urged Galhardo to stop delaying his march.[132]

Gungunhana hastily gathered his forces to fight the Portuguese. After his *mangas* fought several skirmishes in late October, he received intelligence that the European army was now advancing from Chicomo. Galhardo had with him five hundred and seventy-seven Europeans and five hundred African auxiliaries, accompanied by thirty-eight carts. Gungunhana's forces, numbering somewhere between ten and fifteen thousand warriors, marched out to meet the Portuguese. Apparently one-fourth to one-fifth of the Africans were armed with rifles, as the Portuguese later found about three thousand rifles on or near the battlefield.[133] Where did the chief obtain these rifles? Although the Portuguese prevented many firearms from getting into Gaza, their control over the interior was not yet complete; Indian traders in Bilene supplied Manjacaze with arms and gunpowder in 1895.[134]

At Lake Coolela, not far from Manjacaze, on the morning of November 7, the two opposing forces again met in battle. Some eight *mangas* charged the Portuguese lines in the classic Zulu

131. Cruz, *Em Terras,* 214–216; Caetano, *As Campanhas,* 162, 273; Hollis to Uhl, Dec. 31, 1895, *Despatches,* roll 2; Mousinho de Albuquerque, *Moçambique,* 211.

132. Coelho, *Dezoito Annos,* 520 n.

133. Selvagem, *Portugal,* 623; Caetano, *As Campanhas,* 355–357; Ornellas, *Cartas,* 113–114; "Moçambique," *G.E.P. e B.,* XVIII:320.

134. Mousinho de Albuquerque, *Livro Das Campanhas,* I, 44–45. One Portuguese report identified one of these traders as an African who was educated in India and who knew how to read and write Gujerati. Reportedly, he had several trading posts in Gaza and supplied Gungunhana with arms and gunpowder during the 1895 campaign and was a "dedicated friend" to Gungunhana.

half-moon or "horn of the bull" formation and at one point came within yards of breaking the European lines. But the traditional fighting machine, with little training in the use of their rifles, was mowed down by the Portuguese rifle and machine gun fire. The firing lasted only forty minutes, and within an hour the power and prestige of the Lion of Gaza were hopelessly undermined. While the Portuguese force advanced and suffered fewer than forty-five casualties, the Africans fell by the thousands and broke into an disorganized retreat and flight.[135]

Coolela was the Waterloo of Gungunhana. The little allegiance his mercenary regiments, Chope and Tonga, had before this severe reverse vanished in minutes. Gungunhana packed up his treasury, mounted an ox cart, and fled northward with some followers from his kraal. When the Portuguese expedition reached Manjacaze on November 11, they found that the chief had escaped; only women remained in the royal kraal. After burning the place to the ground, Galhardo turned and marched back to Chicomo and the coast.

The administration at Lourenço Marques felt that the war was over. Within three weeks of Coolela, the main body of the Portuguese expeditionary force was embarked on vessels and on the way back to Lisbon. Enes, who had been following the campaign from Inhambane, returned to Lourenço Marques and left for Lisbon on or about December 16.[136] The rainy season had already begun in southern Mozambique, and it was generally agreed by the administration that military operations would cease in Gaza until the following March or April. Gungunhana had been decisively defeated, his kraal destroyed, and his *mangas* dispersed. Although the Lion of Gaza had escaped, Royal Commissioner Enes was not especially anxious to capture him; indeed, Enes believed that Gungunhana would never surrender, so he left for Lisbon almost reconciled that the chief would resist capture and perhaps trek to another colony.[137]

Where was Gungunhana? The Portuguese heard reports that he had traveled northward, but for nearly a month his exact whereabouts were unknown. One of the "heroes" of Coolela,

---

135. Selvagem, *Portugal,* 623.
136. Enes, *A Guerra,* 459, 466.
137. *Ibid.,* 464.

Mousinho de Albuquerque, was named military governor of Gaza on December 10, and he decided to pursue Gungunhana from the post of Languene, about seventy miles up the Limpopo. On December 12, Albuquerque learned from informants that Gungunhana was at Chaimite, a tiny village three days' march northeast of Languene. There were rumors that the chief was gathering a new army to fight again and that he was being advised by several itinerant English hunters and traders. These rumors, probably untrue, nevertheless served to urge Albuquerque into action at a time when the other Portuguese authorities in Mozambique counseled caution.[138]

There is evidence that Gungunhana may have been planning to seek refuge in Transvaal. Apparently he hesitated. Meanwhile, the chief had retreated to the sacred village, the resting place of his grandfather's bones — Chaimite. He went to worship, to call forth as only he knew how as the heir of the Shangana throne, spirits which might aid him in his plight. Although his own sacred village, Manjacaze, had been destroyed by the European intruders who had invaded Gaza, Gungunhana evidently believed that retirement to Chaimite, the resting place of Soshangane, would both protect and inspire him. Fittingly, he returned to the spiritual home of the first of his dynasty to try to insure that he himself would not be the last of the line.[139]

Gungunhana's pursuers began to march on December 26. The force consisted of two officers and forty-seven European soldiers, and over two hundred African auxiliaries, who were not allowed to carry rifles. Albuquerque reached the village of Chaimite only two days later, having attracted to his rearguard a following of over fifteen hundred African warriors — more observers than participants in anticipation of meeting Gungunhana. As the Portuguese approached Chaimite, several of Gungunhana's former *mangas* surrendered and joined the procession. Practically no resistance was encountered during the march. Surprisingly, however, Albuquerque learned that Gungunhana's network of spies and informers was still very much in operation, and it was clear that the Lion of Gaza was still greatly feared in the countryside through which the Portuguese force passed. As Albuquerque

138. Mousinho de Albuquerque, *Relatório*, 3–25, 51.
139. Mousinho de Albuquerque, *Livro Das Campanhas*, I, 43–47.

admitted: "The fear he still inspires among them today is incredible." [140] The Portuguese officer wrote later that he feared
that his small force might well meet the fate of the Wilson Patrol
in the Ndebele War two years before.[141]

The chief of Gaza was willing to negotiate for some kind of
settlement until the very end. Gungunhana wanted to parley
despite his decisive defeat at Coolela. On December 13 an embassy from his camp arrived at Languene and brought along
Chief Matibejana one of the rebels sought by the government.
Evidently, Gungunhana hoped that by offering Matibejana he
could delay or even prevent the Portuguese from attacking or
pursuing him. The Portuguese put Matibejana into custody
and did not execute him, as the African envoys from Gungunhana had expected they would. The Portuguese officials told
the envoys to return to Gungunhana and tell him to surrender
the other rebel, Mahazul.[142] Gungunhana thereby learned from
his envoys that his pursuers would parley no longer — the Lion
of Gaza must have known then that his own surrender would
be the next Portuguese demand.

On December 28, Albuquerque entered the village of about
thirty huts, and protected by the African troops outside the pali-
sade around the huts, he met no resistance as he sought the chief.
Gungunhana's bodyguard had rifles but did not use them as Albuquerque went up to Gungunhana, pushed him to the ground,
and told him that he was no longer chief of the Shangana
("Nguni") but a coward ("Tonga"). Gungunhana was to receive
no more royal Zulu greetings, the *bayete*,[143] but was now des-
picable in the eyes of his own people in Chaimite as well as
those of the procession. In the enclosure the Africans beat their
shields with their assagais to applaud the Lion's final degradation
before Albuquerque.[144]

The Portuguese leader then ordered the summary execution of
two of Gungunhana's advisers and nobles: Manhune and Queto,
an uncle. Both of them were reputed to have incited the chief
to war. The "Chief of all War," Maguiguana, had escaped.[145]

140. Mousinho de Albuquerque, *Relatório*, 51.
141. *Ibid.*, 29–30.
142. *Ibid.*, 35–45.
143. *Ibid.*, 37–38.
144. Enes, *A Guerra*, 460–471.
145. *Ibid.*, 249–250; Mousinho de Albuquerque, *Relatório*, 37–38.

Would the Portuguese shoot Gungunhana too? The old mother of Gungunhana, Impiucazamo, a queen mother as well as a sorceress, feared this and pleaded on her knees with Albuquerque to spare her son.[146] But Albuquerque had not planned to execute the king of Gaza; he was too great a prize and potential exhibit to destroy. Gungunhana was shackled in irons by his captors and led away toward the river, where he was placed aboard a steamer and taken to Lourenço Marques as a prisoner of the governor-general of Mozambique.

Capture, Exile, and Death

Gungunhana's capture by the Portuguese did not put an end to African resistance in Gaza. Several Shangana chiefs, such as Cuio and Ingoiura, continued to rule, while groups of Africans remained armed with firearms which they had obtained from Banyan traders in Gaza as well as from across the Transvaal frontier.[147] More important, a number of Gungunhana's followers believed that the Lion of Gaza was still in Mozambique as a prisoner of the Portuguese in Lourenço Marques. The escaped Maguiguana, martial heir of Soshangane, began a full-scale revolt in Gaza in 1897. Known as the second Gaza campaign, or the revolt of Maguiguana, the rebellion again began at Chaimite, the "sacred center" of the Shangana tradition, and it fed upon the widespread African grievances against Portuguese taxation and Portuguese confiscation of Gungunhana's large cattle herd. Albuquerque later claimed that this campaign was more difficult and more "decisive" than the one with Gungunhana. When the old but brave Maguiguana fell at Macontene in August 1897 close to the Transvaal border to which he was fleeing, the Gaza dynasty of Jamine was effectively finished.[148]

There was an irony to the capture of Gungunhana which, in retrospect, magnified the sensational and mystical aura of the

146. Cunha Amadeu, *Mousinho,* 222. She was killed by Maguiguana during the 1897 revolt for refusing to conjure against the Portuguese.

147. *Ibid.,* 219–221.

148. Selvagem, *Portugal,* 632; Mousinho de Albuquerque, *Moçambique,* 83, 221; Cruz, *Em Terras,* 14; Royal Navy Intelligence Division, *A Manual of Portuguese East Africa* (London, 1920), 505; "Gaza," *G.E.P. e B.,* 339 ff. There is a great deal of printed material on the revolt of Gungunhana's chief general, who is also worthy of biographical attention.

event for the public. Albuquerque's bold action was inconsistent with the winter operations plan of the government; Enes had left for Lisbon and did not learn of the chief's capture until January 11, 1896, in a telegram from the queen of Portugal herself.[149] On December 31, not knowing that Gungunhana had been taken three days before, the new governor-general issued a communiqué to Albuquerque ordering him to cease all offensive operations in Gaza until the end of the rainy season in 1896. The governor clearly feared a reverse that might arise out of pursuing the chief into Gaza. Albuquerque, however, was already on the Limpopo returning to Lourenço Marques with his celebrated captive, and he learned of this contradictory order only when he landed.[150]

The treasury of Gungunhana and his immediate worldly possessions were also captured by the Portuguese and delivered to Lourenço Marques. Substantial but not extraordinary, the royal booty consisted of £2,072 in English gold, eight diamonds (three large and five small) in a glass, seventeen tusks of ivory, and a number of English coins.[151]

Gungunhana and his party, "traitors to the fatherland, who dared to raise arms against it" (Albuquerque), were handed over to the governor-general by their captors on January 6, 1896, in a ceremony at Lourenço Marques. Accompanying the ex-ruler of Gaza were seven of his wives, an uncle, Molungo, his son and heir, Godide, and Chief Matibejana of Zixaxa, with three of the latter's wives. They were soon embarked on a Portuguese steamer and arrived in Lisbon on March 13, 1896. There the African prisoners were transferred to the fortress of Monsanto, a prison and garrison in the suburbs of Lisbon.[152]

149. Enes, *A Guerra*, 466.
150. Mousinho de Albuquerque, *Relatório*, 69–70.
151. Mousinho de Albuquerque, *Livro Das Campanhas*, I, 60–61.
152. For nearly all the material on the exiled years of Gungunhana, the author is especially indebted to Colonel José Agostinho of Angra do Heroismo, Terceira, Azores Islands, for his extraordinary generosity and kindness. During a personal visit of the writer to Angra, as well as in correspondence, Colonel Agostinho related his childhood experiences involving Gungunhana and gave the writer a great deal of useful information. The writer also thanks Senhor Joaquim Gomes da Cunha (pseud., Pedro de Merelim) for his article in the local publication, *Atlantida* (1960). See also Pedro de Merelim, "Os Vátuas," 308; Azevedo Coutinho, *Memórias*, 340. Albuquerque was named governor-general of Mozambique the day Gungunhana arrived in Lisbon.

In June of that year the Portuguese authorities decided to move the prisoners to the Azores Islands, some nine hundred miles west of Portugal in the Atlantic. The reasons for this transfer were several: the greater isolation of a mid-Atlantic location would preclude any escape and return to Mozambique; and the island climate and environment would allow the exiles to live in greater comfort and freedom than was feasible in Lisbon. Furthermore, there was a royal precedent. The exiled Portuguese King Afonso VI (1643–1683) had lived in the fortress on Terceira Island for five years. Terceira was thus considered a more amenable place of exile than Portugal.[153]

The authorities ruled that each of the four Africans could take along only one female companion; but the ten wives present banded together and refused to leave the fortress of Monsanto unless they all could go.[154] As a result, the women remained in Lisbon and the four men left without them. As the Portuguese cavalry escort came to fetch the prisoners, they grew frightened that they were about to be shot, and Gungunhana sat resolutely on the floor of his cell and refused to budge. He was forcibly removed to the carriage and taken to the wharf.

The steamer *Zambeze* landed at Angra do Heroismo on June 27. Located on the southern coast of the island of Terceira, the town of Angra faced on a bay and was defended by the fortress of São João Baptista, built under the Spanish domination in the seventeenth century. The African prisoners were marched to the fortress, put under the charge of four Portuguese army sergeants, and soon afterwards posed for their photograph; Gungunhana appeared indifferent but annoyed, while the older Molungo was clearly dejected. All were barefoot but only Molungo and Gungunhana wore the characteristic Zulu head ring, symbolic of nobility among the Shangana.[155]

Gungunhana lived the rest of his life in exile on Terceira making no attempt to escape. A Portuguese who knew him describes him in his own words as a man preoccupied with memories of his days in Gaza:

> He was a silent man, who rarely addressed anybody and always answered any questions with few or no words. He passed most of

153. "Afonso VI," *G.E.P. e B.*, I:503–505.
154. Merelim, "Os Vátuas," 308–309.
155. *Ibid.*, 308–311.

his time making small *tcheetshas* [baskets] he gave or sold to visitors, sometimes murmuring native songs, war songs, hunting songs, as Godide interpreted them to me (*Elephant killed my father,* or something alike). He resented his present condition and he was very happy when I, still a little boy, told him: *Gungunhana inkossi lama Monte Brasil* (G., King of Mount Brasil).[156]

The four Africans were officially enlisted in the Portuguese army unit garrisoned in the fortress, the 10th Chasseurs (*Caçadores*), and each man received the daily pay of a "Second Sergeant" of 260 *réis* (about 37 cents), along with their food and clothing. Housed in three small houses just inside the western entrance to the fortress, the prisoners at first were restricted to the garrison grounds and were guarded by Portuguese sergeants. Later they were allowed to go into the town of Angra and pass their time in the wooded peninsula, called Monte (Mount) Brasil, which was especially reserved for them as a hunting preserve.

During the first three years of his exile on Terceira, the Gaza ruler had extensive contacts with Catholic priests. On April 16, 1899, at the Cathedral of Angra do Heroismo, the four African exiles were baptized by the authority of the governor of the Fortress. The baptismal certificates in the parochial archive of the cathedral provide the historian with some useful if questionable biographical data. Thus Gungunhana's age is recorded as sixty years; Molungo is listed as seventy; Godide as twenty; and Matibejana as thirty.[157]

By 1899 Gungunhana had acquired, at least superficially, the outward characteristics of a Portuguese. On the day of his baptism, he posed for his photograph with his companions and appeared dressed in a conventional suit, hat, and holding a cane. His expression in this photograph is visibly more pleasant and

156. Quoted from an annotation by Colonel Agostinho made in July 1964 to Merelim, "Os Vátuas." Agostinho, when accompanying the chief on hunting expeditions in the wooded preserve (Mount Brazil), told the African: "Gungunhana is King of Mount Brazil." Apparently, Gungunhana was pleased by the young boy's flattery. Often when Gungunhana went out from his fortress abode, a crowd of little boys followed him and the chief would shoo them away in his own language. Colonel Agostinho today, nearly sixty-five years after knowing Gungunhana, is recording what he remembers of the chief's language.

157. *Ibid.,* 315.

relaxed than his visage in the pictures taken of him during 1896. Instead of "Gungunhana," he now had the Christian name of "Reinaldo Frederico Gungunhana." Portuguese teachers, perhaps military personnel, spent time with the royal exile trying to make him learn to read and to write Portuguese. Reluctant to learn, Gungunhana did, nonetheless, practice the art of calligraphy by copying a number of Portuguese essays on military discipline. Several of these curiosities, written between December 1899 and February 1900, survive.[158]

Undoubtedly, the Lion of Gaza missed his wives who remained behind in Lisbon. But much of his time was spent in hunting rabbit on Monte Brasil next to the fortress with his two younger companions. After heavy banquets of rabbit and wine, the Africans were known to visit a brothel in the town. Especially during the first few years of his exile, the African leader was a celebrated and familiar figure on the island. The townspeople of Angra popularized him, and one Portuguese youth even wrote and produced a local operetta entitled, "Gungunhana in the Azores." Even before the exiles arrived on the island, too, in late March 1896, one rage in haberdashery there was a hat "à Gungunhana." [159]

Hunting in the "great forested spaces" and indulging in some of the pastimes he enjoyed in Gaza filled his last days with some comfort if not satisfaction and joy. Preoccupied with memories of Mozambique, reliving vicariously his victories and his defeats, he kept to himself much of the time. A young Portuguese boy,

158. The manuscript is in Portugal at the library of the Sociedade de Geografia, Lisbon, in the Secção do Reservados, Res. Pasta A, no. 15, *Cartas do Gungunhana. Provas caligraficas de Reinaldo Frederico Gungunhana, feitas no Castelo em Angra do Heroismo em 1900.* Samples copied by both Godide and Matibejana are also on deposit here. The essays Gungunhana copied were oaths of allegiance to the Portuguese Army, his conqueror, and to military duty and discipline. The chief's handwriting is extremely regular and symmetrical. Ironically, Gungunhana persisted in his misspelling of "Portuguese" throughout. Samples of the celebrated exile's handwriting were apparently in some demand in Portugal during his lifetime. In the Lisbon daily, *O Século,* June 12, 1900, an item mentioned the penmanship lessons of the African exiles. Old Molungo refused to learn to write. The writer has in his possession a postcard with a photograph of the four exiles dated "January of 1904" which bears the signature "Gungunhana." It is very likely that this photograph was the last one taken of the chief.

159. Merelim, "Os Vátuas," 314.

friendly and intelligent, sometimes accompanied him hunting and the elderly African enjoyed hearing himself called a king in his own language even though he was now a monarch of only a wooded peninsula on an alien island.[160] The fair climate of the island and his generally tranquil life served to lengthen his life, which many Portuguese had considered to be over in the 1890's.

At nine o'clock in the evening of December 23, 1906, Mudungazi, Gungunhana, or Reinaldo Frederico Gungunhana, died in a bed in the Hospital da Boa Nova in Angra do Heroismo. The cause of death was recorded as a cerebral hemorrhage; he was thought to be about sixty-seven years old.[161] He had lived in the fortress of São João Baptista for ten years and twenty-seven days. His body was buried in one of the two cemeteries on the island; five years later, his remains were transferred and deposited in a common ossuary, as was the custom of the inhabitants of Angra. No physical monument to his memory remains on the island.

Epilogue

Gungunhana ruled for a little more than eleven years in southern Mozambique and a small part of what is now Rhodesia. His influence reached in the west to among the Shona and Ndebele, in the south to the Swazi, and in the north to perhaps a hundred miles north of the Save River. His writ was feared and respected in much of what now composes the modern districts of Gaza and Inhambane. Gungunhana's position in African history is significant. A study of his reign suggests that African intertribal relationships in this era and region were close and far-reaching, and that, like other traditional leaders in tropical Africa, his powers of decision-making were circumscribed by those of his advisers and by a net of traditional obligations; it is clear that internal weaknesses within Shangana

160. Letter, Colonel José Agostinho to writer, July 3, 1964.

161. Merelim, "Os Vátuas," 317–318. The first to die of the four exiles, Gungunhana was survived by his son, Godide (died 1911), Uncle Molungo (died 1912), and Matibejana, who lived until 1927. Matibejana fathered a child by a Portuguese woman in the village of Angra; today the son of Matibejana resides in Angra and makes his living as a cabinetmaker.

society were almost as much to blame for the final defeat by Portugal as the superiority of Portuguese firepower.

That Gungunhana remained in power as long as he did and that he achieved paramountcy in Gaza at all were significant facts in themselves. Threatened by usurpers and harassed by his retinue, the Lion of Gaza was something less than a lion when it came to opposing the wishes of old veterans like Maguiguana.

Always the bush politician, sometimes the statesman, Gungunhana was only a straw warrior when it came to fighting. Perhaps his gravest error — or was it the error of his aggressive counsellors? — was to move his kraal and people into the lower Limpopo Valley, so close to the Portuguese settlements. The perennial war policy against the Chope kept his generals happy but distracted attention from the growing Portuguese menace on the coast and helped to undermine his strength. Gungunhana was a lucid tactician but not a strategist; he was a shrewd but not a brilliant bargainer. He could not appreciate the significance of the Anglo-Portuguese alliance which precluded his being saved by Britain. To the last day of his reign, he apparently believed that he could prevent Portuguese conquest by bluffs, threats, or by actually making an alliance with "other whites."

To say that Gungunhana was "more inclined to intrigue than to warfare," or, what is an earlier interpretation, that "he always preferred intrigue to decisive action," is to misunderstand his basic dilemma and to underestimate his statesmanlike abilities.[162] Gungunhana feared a full-scale war with Portugal because he knew it would probably mean an end to that "real and practical independence" which he so treasured. Caught between the traditional Ngoni (Zulu) belligerence of his generals and the Portuguese determination to crush him, between war or surrender, and between deportation (he had seen other chiefs deported in Mozambique) and relegation to the status of a puppet ruler in Gaza, he chose a middle path. But in António Enes, Gungunhana found a bargainer with no bargains to offer — only the surrender of his independence. The chief feared displeasing both extremes of opinion (his generals or the Portu-

162. Duffy, *Portuguese Africa*, 232; Royal Navy Intelligence Division, *A Manual*, 499–500.

guese government); this was, as Almeida aptly put it, "the hesitation in which he agonizes." [163] What is more, a study of the
1895 campaign shows that with the exception of men like Enes
and Albuquerque, the Portuguese seemed more inclined to intrigue and indecision than the king of Gaza.

Gungunhana had a profound sense of Shangana rights and
tradition. He knew the boundaries of Gaza and the legacies of
his ancestors. Gaza was his home. As Almeida described this
phenomenon: "No one could or should expect that Gungunhana
would abandon this country completely, taking from it all his
people, because such an act would go against his traditions and
those of his nation, quite proud and warlike, who still vividly
remember the bloody battles that brought these peoples under
his rule." [164] Yet, despite the force of tradition behind him —
an uncompromising tradition — Gungunhana sought to compromise with Portugal (and other European interests) in order
to maintain a kind of independence.

Enes wrote in final judgment of the monarch of Gaza: "The
so-called vatua [*sic*] empire really was a power, and if it fell
so rapidly and so easily, it was only because its chief was very
able in his building it up, but had none of the qualities essential
for defending it." [165] It would be more accurate to say that Gungunhana in 1895 was not in the "circumstances" essential for
remaining independent in Mozambique. Indeed, Gungunhana
fully appreciated the European technology that would keep him
in power, but he lacked the warriors trained to use it. His intelligence system was quite remarkable and the Portuguese did
not fool him as to their intention. He also appreciated the
worth of formal treaties and that they enabled the signatories
to go "fishing for lands." [166]

Cornered between various conflicting forces, he was attempting
to compromise with an opponent who was through bargaining.
Gungunhana could not be expected to understand that the disjointed but ultimately successful campaign to defeat him would
become a kind of psychological *revanche* for Portugal's unfortu-

163. Coelho, *Dezoito Annos,* 83. This is described in Portuguese as "o
estado de oscillação em que se agita."
164. *Ibid.,* 377.
165. Enes, *A Guerra,* 128.
166. Rocha Martins, *História,* 294.

nate past. Furthermore, he could not deal effectively with forces which now gripped his people: alcohol, disease, famine, and demoralization. In the end, he retreated before naked force.

His was not "the greatest empire that the negro race [*sic*] has created in Eastern Africa," [167] but it remained an enduring influence in southern Mozambique for over a generation. Gaza oral tradition records the fear and respect felt for the Lion among the Chope even after his exile (see Songs). The belief that Gungunhana was still a prisoner in Mozambique played a part in the serious revolt which erupted two years after his fall at Chaimite. Despite the patent exaggerations of his power and influence, he was in fact "an extraordinary tyrant." [168] Gungunhana was the most famous African monarch in Mozambique in modern times. His victories and defeats, his oppressions and kindnesses, and his name kept old men talking and musicians singing long after he died, a dispossessed exile on a distant and mysterious island.

Gungunhana in Oral Tradition, Inhambane District, Mozambique (recorded ca. 1940; translation by Douglas Wheeler).[169]

[Chopi] *Song from Zavala, Inhambane*

> Combatemos contra o Gungunhana,
> E ficámos vencidos. Mas os portugueses
> nos salvaram.

> (We fought against Gungunhana,
> And we were conquered. But the Portuguese
> saved us.)

Song from Zavala, Inhambane (*chorus*)

> Combatemos; mas ficámos vencidos.
> Ficámos sem mulheres
> Porque os vátuas as levaram.
> Somos uma povoação de solteiros.

> (We fought; but we were conquered.
> We were without women

---

167. Coelho, *Dezoito Annos*, 383.
168. Cruz, *Em Terras*, 107.
169. Amadeu Cunha, *Mousinho*, 438–440.

Because the Vátuas carried them off.
We were a village of bachelors.)

Song

Vamos ver se vamos para o Transvaal
Para fugirmos ao Gungunhana.
Mas êles não deixam
Mandam-nos voltar para trás.

(Let us go see if we can go to Transvaal
To flee to Gungunhana.
But they do not let us
They order us to turn back.)

Lobengula

by PER HASSING

Professor of World Christian Missions
Boston University

The Zulu, who lived on the southeast coast of Africa in what is now Natal and Zululand, were welded together by the remarkable Chief Shaka at the opening of the nineteenth century. About 1820, one of his *indunas* (generals), Mzilikazi, broke away from Shaka during a disagreement and fled north with his followers; Mzilikazi and his people were thereafter known as the Ndebele. They settled for a while in the Marico Valley of what is now the Transvaal.[1]

While Mzilikazi's group lived in the Marico Valley they had contacts with Europeans; Robert Moffat of the London Missionary Society, who was stationed at Kuruman in Bechuanaland, visited Mzilikazi in 1829 and 1835. The result of the visits was a fascinating friendship which lasted for life. In 1836, Mzilikazi concluded a treaty of friendship with the government of the Cape Colony.

In 1837, the settlement was attacked by a Zulu army and was also defeated in a battle with the Boers; the result was that the Ndebele resumed their wandering, which ended about 1838 in the settlement north of the Limpopo River in what is known as Matabeleland.

During the years of wandering, the original Zulu stock became considerably mixed with members of other tribes. A large number of outsiders — men, women, and children — had, over the years, been incorporated into the tribe, so it was by no means pure Zulu. During the years, three strata of Ndebele society became recognizable, the *Zansi,* the *Enhla,* and the *Holi.* The *Zansi* were mostly descendants of the original adherents of Mzilikazi who had fled from Shaka. Included among the *Zansi*

1. Hilda Kuper, A. J. B. Hughes and J. van Velsen, *The Shona and Ndebele of Southern Rhodesia* (London, 1955) has been used for the social organization of the Ndebele, their historical background, and the spelling of African names.

were other Nguni who had been incorporated into the Ndebele
tribe during the years of wandering. The *Enhla* were of Sotho
stock who had come into the tribe during Mzilikazi's stay in
the Transvaal. The *Holi* were of Shona and other origins, and
were neither Nguni nor Sotho. They became the most numerous
group but were not regarded as full members of the tribe and
constituted a servile group in the social scale.

The tribe was born in battle when Mzilikazi fled from Shaka
and lived on war and pillage as it moved farther into the

Rhodesia

interior. Raiding was a way of life and continued even after the settlement in Matabeleland; the Ndebele economy was a war economy, and Lobengula did nothing to change it. Every year during the dry season the warriors raided the neighboring tribes; their tactics aimed at surprising their victims (usually early in the morning) killing those considered useless and capturing the rest together with their domestic animals, mostly cattle. The captives and cattle were presented to the chief. The raids were cruel and brutal, and the memory of them lingers to this day among the Shona people. The Ndebele reputation for blood, lust, and tyranny derived from these raids.[2]

The Ndebele group had been brought together by Mzilikazi and was in a very real sense his creation. The central place given to the chief in the Zulu tradition was reinforced among the Ndebele by the conditions under which the tribe lived and grew during the years of wandering and by the strong personality of Mzilikazi himself. The dominant role of the chief continued after the settlement in Matabeleland, where the tribe occupied a small territory around Bulawayo. Scattered around the territory were centrally located towns in which the chief placed his wives and his trusted *indunas*. Each of the towns had its own *impi* (regiment) and was visited by Mzilikazi from time to time.

The Succession: 1868–1870

Mzilikazi died on September 6, 1868, at the village of Ingama near the present site of Bulawayo. He was buried among the granite boulders in the Matopo hills, overlooking his kingdom. The death of the chief caused considerable uneasiness in the tribe because of uncertainty about his successor. In a tribal council, the late chief's trusted *induna*, Umcombate, was chosen as regent. During the sixteen-month interregnum, while the succession was being decided, the Ndebele remained loyal to the

2. For description of raids, see Frederick Courteney Selous, *Travel and Adventure in South-East Africa* (London, 1893), 101–105; W. A. Elliott to London Missionary Society [hereafter L.M.S.], October 5, 1885, L.M.S. Archives, London (microfilm copy held by the Boston University Library).

tradition that there should be a legitimate chief. The choice was soon narrowed down to two men, Nkulumana and Lobengula.

Nkulumana was the son of Mzilikazi by his principal wife, Umoaka. The name was given him in honor of the missionary Robert Moffat, Mzilikazi's good friend, whose mission station in Bechuanaland was called Kuruman. Nkulumana was probably born about 1828. After Mzilikazi's death Nkulumana was absent from Matabeleland. There are two versions of his story.

One version recounts that when the Ndebele tribe was seeking a place to settle, they separated into two groups, one under Mzilikazi going north to the Zambezi River, the other under the *induna* Gundwane, reaching what is now Bulawayo and Matabeleland. Hearing nothing about the chief and his section of the tribe for about two years, the group under Gundwane chose his son Nkulumana as their chief. But just before his installation, Mzilikazi appeared and proceeded to execute all those responsible for the plot, including Nkulumana. A Sotho named Gwabaio was ordered to kill Nkulumana, which he did. This execution was witnessed by Nkulumana's servant, Gualema. Gwabaio and Gualema were still alive and testified to the truth of the story before a tribal council in August 1869.[3]

The other version held that Nkulumana was sent away by Mzilikazi, according to Zulu custom, in order to be kept safe and out of tribal squabbles until the time came for him to inherit the chieftainship. For years no one seemed to have knowledge of Nkulumana's whereabouts, but there was a rumor that a man by the name of Kanda, working in the garden of Theophilus Shepstone, secretary for native affairs in Natal, claimed to be Nkulumana. But Shepstone wrote a letter to William Sykes, missionary of the London Missionary Society in Matabeleland, saying that Kanda disclaimed being the heir of Mzilikazi. One of Umcombate's first acts as regent was to send a party to Natal to find Nkulumana; the party returned reporting that Kanda was not the true Nkulumana because he was ignorant of events that the true son of Mzilikazi would have known.[4] Yet, David Erskine, colonial secretary to the Natal government, wrote to

3. J. P. R. Wallis, *The Northern Goldfields, Diaries of Thomas Baines* (London, 1946), 683–684.
4. *Ibid.,* 340, 684–685.

Thomas Baines that there was no doubt that Kanda was Nkulumana.[5]

In his youth Nkulumana belonged to the regiment of Zwongendaba, led by Mbiko, who in his youth had been honored for bravery. This section of the tribe refused to believe that Nkulumana was dead. Mbiko remained loyal to him and charged that Umcombate was senile and unable to exercise proper judgment, a charge which the Europeans present in the country denied. Persistent rumors that Nkulumana was alive kept a section of the tribe restless for his return.

The other possible heir to the chieftainship, Lobengula, was Mzilikazi's son by a minor wife, Fulata, a Swazi woman. This fact was not in his favor, as he was not considered by some of the Ndebele to be of pure Zulu stock. Lobengula was the favorite of Umcombate, who encouraged him to accept the chieftainship. But Lobengula was rather reluctant to accept Mzilikazi's position until he was quite certain that Nkulumana was not alive and that a majority of the tribe accepted this as fact. Lobengula was afraid that if he were not dead, Nkulumana might return to win the loyalty of the tribe.

In the end, the majority party under Umcombate agreed to install Lobengula as the new chief. But when Lobengula heard of their plan he became so perplexed that he hurried to the missionary at Inyati, Thomas Morgan Thomas, asking his advice. Umcombate, however, sent for the stubborn chief-elect; Lobengula was brought to Mhlahlanhlela on January 22, 1870, where he was prevailed upon to accept the position. He was installed on January 24, 1870; about nine thousand warriors of the various Ndebele regiments were present to dance and pledge their loyalty. Ten white men also attended. One of Lobengula's first official acts was to supervise the slaughter of the cattle brought to him by the many regiments as tribute, for ceremonial sacrifice and for the feast to follow.

There was no doubt that the new chief had been freely chosen by a majority of the *indunas*, or that he had done everything

5. *Ibid.*, 245. The best analysis of the succession crisis is Richard Brown, "The Ndebele Succession Crisis, 1868–1877," *Historians in Tropical Africa, Proceedings of the Leverhulme Inter-Collegiate History Conference, University College of Rhodesia and Nyasaland, September 1960* (Salisbury, 1962), 159–175.

in his power to find the rightful heir to Mzilikazi's position; but he still faced two threats to his power before it could be considered safe. The first challenge came from the Zwongendaba regiment under Mbiko, who openly opposed Lobengula's right to rule. Mbiko continued to claim that Nkulumana was the true heir and that he was alive in Natal. Lobengula was very patient and tolerant, allowing them to flout his authority openly. He was very reluctant to take steps that would lead to the killing of many of his people and perhaps cause a permanent division within the tribe. In the end, however, he had no choice but to assert his right to rule. Either he was the chief whom all acknowledged, or there would never be peace and unity among the Ndebele. Lobengula tried to reconcile Mbiko, but was re-buffed with scorn. He therefore rallied his forces, led them into battle himself on June 1, 1870, and routed his enemy. Mbiko, with about 250 of his followers, was killed, while more than 100 were wounded. Lobengula demonstrated his magnanimity by pardoning those willing to acknowledge his authority and by allowing missionaries to look after the wounded of both parties.[6]

This attack on the rebels, undertaken as reluctantly as the assumption of the chieftainship six months earlier, confirmed Lobengula in his position. The *indunas* and the mass of the Ndebele would now remain loyal to him until the end.

A new threat came from Kanda, Shepstone's employee. Kanda changed his mind and claimed to be Nkulumana, the true heir of Mzilikazi. Shepstone wrote to Lobengula on May 27, 1871, telling him about Kanda's intention to travel to Matabeleland to claim the chieftainship, adding that on his way Kanda would visit the president of the Transvaal.

Shepstone claimed to be neutral in the dispute between Loben-gula and Kanda, but his claim cannot be taken very seriously. First, he had written to Sykes that Kanda was *not* Nkulumana and thereby influenced the choice of the tribe. But in his letter of May 27, 1871, to Lobengula he wrote about Kanda's "right of birth"; the whole letter gives the impression that he supported Kanda's claims, his protestations to the contrary notwithstand-ing. He also furnished Kanda with a wagon for his journey

6. Sykes to L.M.S., June 10, 1870, L.M.S. Archives. This letter is an ex-cellent source written on the spot nine days after the event.

and facilitated his meeting with the president of the Transvaal. Both Shepstone and the Transvaal president were interested in placing at the head of the powerful Ndebele tribe a friendly man indebted to them.[7]

Various groups turned to Kanda at this time. After Lobengula's victory over the Zwongendaba regiment in June 1870, some of the defeated elements fled to the south seeking Nkulumana. Among those who had found his way to Natal was Mzilikazi's oldest son, Mangwana. Lobengula stated that he was guilty of incest, having had intimate relations with one of his father's wives; the crime was punishable by death. The defeated Ndebele faction thought they had found a rallying point in him. In addition, Macheng, chief of the Mangwato, a tribe in Bechuanaland, wanted to help Kanda in order to have a friendly, rather than unfriendly, chief as his neighbor.

Lobengula rejected Kanda's claim very convincingly in a letter to Shepstone.[8] When Kanda moved north, probably in June 1871, he received some military support from Macheng and met Lobengula's *impi* on the Shashani River. But Kanda's efforts failed. All the Ndebele living in Matabeleland supported Lobengula. Although some might have liked another chief, they could only lose in the event of hostilities; the only safe course was to remain loyal to the new chief. That Kanda, in order to achieve his object, had sought the help of the Transvaal Boers and the Mangwato, both traditional enemies of the Ndebele, would not enhance his standing in the tribe. It would certainly not attract those who might still have some doubts about Lobengula. The choice had been made, and it now mattered not whether Kanda was the real Nkulumana or an impostor. When Lobengula's *impi* met Kanda's forces, the issue was soon settled in Lobengula's favor.[9]

Both in the case of Mbiko's defiance and Kanda's claim to the chieftainship, Lobengula had acted with firmness and good judgment. He was now securely in command of the Ndebele tribe.

7. Wallis, *Northern Goldfields,* 613–615.

8. *Ibid.,* 683–687.

9. Thomson to L.M.S., May 1, 1872, L.M.S. Archives; Brown, "The Ndebele Succession," 172–173.

The Peaceful Years: 1871–1887

Lobengula was a man of about thirty-four years when he became chief. J. B. Thomson, a missionary of the London Missionary Society, a man with some medical training, saw him first in May 1870, and estimated him to be about thirty years of age; he described him as five feet, nine inches in height, "with a very good natural face," very affable and fond of a joke. Another observer estimated his height to be from five feet, eleven inches to six feet.[10] Lobengula almost always made a favorable impression on visiting Europeans. Sidney Shippard, the deputy commissioner for Bechuanaland, described him as he first saw him in October 1888:

> A few minutes after I had taken my seat near his waggon a curtain was drawn aside, and the great man appeared and deliberately stepped over the front box of his waggon and sat down on the board before the driver's seat. He was completely naked save for a long piece of dark blue cloth rolled very small and wound around his body, which it in no wise concealed, and a monkey skin worn as a small apron and about the size of a Highland sporan. In person he is rather tall, though considerably shorter than Khama [chief of the Mangwato] and very stout, though by no means unwieldly. His countenance reminded me of Mr. George French Argus' portrait of the Zulu Chief 'Mpanda. His colour is a fine bronze, and he evidently takes great care of his person, and is scrupulously clean. He wears the leather ring over his forehead as a matter of course. Altogether he is a very fine-looking man, and, in spite of his obesity, has a most majestic carriage.
>
> Like all the Matabele warriors, who despise a stooping gait in a man, Lo Bengula walks quite erect with his head thrown somewhat back and his broad chest expanded, and as he marches along at a slow pace with his long staff in his right hand, while all the men around shout out his praises he looks his part to perfection.[11]

Another man who knew Lobengula for six years also gave a very favorable description of him:

10. Thomson to L.M.S., May 3, 1870, L.M.S. Archives; Neville Jones, *Rhodesian Genesis* (Bulawayo, 1953), 11.
11. Shippard to Robinson, Oct. 20, 1888, *Parliamentary Papers* [hereafter P.P.], C. 5918 (1890), 124.

I have seen Lobengula laughing and enjoying jokes and talks. He was nearly always approachable . . . Only once have I ever seen him lose his temper and only twice when he was afraid of his power to control his people.

I never knew or saw Lobengula take spirits of any kind and only once a sip of champagne on St. Patrick's Day, 1890. I never saw him under the influence of drink of any kind and there was never any heavy beer-drinking at the king's kraal. Indunas wanted to keep their heads clear when at the king's and they drank very little.[12]

Lobengula performed the rituals which tradition required of him, such as sacrifices to the spirit of the ancestors and for rain and abundant crops. One observer, Baines, suggested that Lobengula really did not believe in them, but did it only for the sake of his people. Lobengula is reported to have said: "We do not believe that the killing of an ox or burning particular herbs makes rain, but these are the means by which we ask it, just as you ask it by reading in your book and saying prayers." [13] The Ndebele leader discussed theology with missionaries from time to time, indicating a faith in God as creator and sustainer of the universe. It hardly seems necessary to ascribe these beliefs to the influence of missionaries who lived with him for little more than a decade. He probably accepted these beliefs because they coincided with his own.

And it does not seem reasonable to say that he performed the rituals faithfully merely because of the beliefs of his people. It would be highly questionable to imagine a deep psychological and mental separation between the people and Lobengula. The more probable assumption is that he was an expression and representative of his people. To think otherwise would seem to imply an unwillingness to accept Lobengula as a man on his own terms. The Europeans liked and respected him, and there might have been an unconscious effort on their part to make him over in their own image rather than accept him on his own — African — terms. There must have been an inner consent on his part to witchcraft, especially since so many of his people lost their lives on account of suggestions made by the diviners at the court. The punishment for witchcraft was very

---

12. Jones, *Genesis*, 9–10.
13. Wallis, *Northern Goldfields*, 322.

severe; not only the person concerned, but the whole family, village, and even the domestic animals were destroyed.

A celebrated case of witchcraft was that of Lobengula's sister, Umcencene, also called Nini, Nyina, or Lena. He had shared his childhood with her, and she had his confidence in an unusual measure. When Lobengula one day asked one of his diviners, Zondo, why he had no children despite his many wives, Zondo answered that they were being bewitched by Umcencene. She was subsequently killed on order of Lobengula. The missionary, Thomas, stated that "she was strangled, and buried in a cave not far from her father, the late king." [14] But Father Croonenberg, a Jesuit missionary recently arrived in the country, stated that she was hanged and her remains devoured by jackals and vultures.[15] There is, however, a strange aspect to this story as it is known that Lobengula left six sons at his death, some of whom must have been born before Umcencene's execution in April 1880.[16]

Why did Lobengula order the execution of his own sister? Was it because he believed she was the cause of his having so few children, or did he sense that her influence on him was a source of dissatisfaction among his diviners and *indunas?* It seems plausible that the former reason, which is supported by the sources, is the true one; yet one cannot be sure that the white men in Bulawayo really understood all that went on.

Because of the annual raids of the Ndebele on their neighbors, Lobengula's involvement in punishment for witchcraft, and the cruelty with which some known offenders against Ndebele law and custom were punished, Lobengula himself has been described as cruel and tyrannical.[17] This is questionable, however. Raids were a part of the system under which the Ndebele lived, while a killing, following charges of witchcraft, would have been carried out for reasons of state. When a public scapegoat had to be found and sacrificed, the reasons (as in the case of Lotje

14. *Ibid.*, pp. XXXII–XXXIII.

15. M. Lloyd, trans., *Diaries of the Jesuit Missionaries at Bulawayo, 1879–1881* (Publication No. 4 of the Rhodesiana Society, Salisbury, 1959), 51.

16. Hugh Marshall Hole, *The Making of Rhodesia* (London, 1926), 332 n.

17. John Smith Moffat to Colenbrander, June 23, 1892, P.P., C. 7171 (1893), 35–36; Carnegie to L.M.S., May 4, 1886, L.M.S. Archives; Wallis; *Northern Goldfields*, 665.

discussed below) were the same which in a modern democratic state would have required the resignation of a prime minister. It should also be remembered that Lobengula treated the remainder of the Zwongendaba dissidents with great leniency; and he was logical and reasonable in his attitude toward Nkulumana. And he refrained from killing Mzilikazi's widow, who was guilty of incest. When it was discovered that a white man had brought syphilis into the tribe, his first inclination was to have both the man and the Ndebele woman killed; but he was persuaded to take other measures.[18] A missionary once reproached him for his severe punishments and told him how offenders were dealt with in England. He replied: "What, give the wrongdoers shelter, blankets and food! Why, within a few days all my subjects would be inside!" [19]

Lobengula's relations with the missionaries in his country were always good. The first L.M.S. missionaries had arrived in Matabeleland in 1859, a decade before Lobengula became chief. Robert Moffat, the senior missionary at Kuruman in Bechuanaland had been Mzilikazi's friend while he lived in the Transvaal, and Lobengula never forgot that Robert Moffat had earned his father's trust. He frequently attended services in Bulawayo, although he never became a Christian, nor did he encourage his people to become Christians. As long as Lobengula lived the visible results of the labor of the missionaries were nil. Some of them told Lobengula plainly that his people resisted Christianity because they were afraid of punishment. Would it be better for them to leave the country and go elsewhere, the missionaries asked? But Lobengula did not want them to leave, maintaining that his people did not tell the truth and were too lazy to learn. Understandably, the Ndebele attitude was that as long as their chief did not lead the way, they dared not become too friendly with the missionaries.

When Jesuit missionaries arrived in 1879, Lobengula's first reaction was that he had enough missionaries; the people did not want to learn, and the L.M.S. representatives had achieved nothing. He did, however, allow the Jesuits to stay, but they left in 1889, concluding that it was useless to remain as long as

18. Wallis, *Northern Goldfields*, 555, 689–690.
19. *Ibid.*, pp. XXXIII.

Lobengula ruled. He had not even allowed them to introduce a simple plow. Still, his relations with the missionaries were honorable, and he protected them and never retracted a promise once given. He always kept them under his eyes in Matabeleland, however, and never allowed them to work among the Shona.

He had a similar attitude toward other Europeans in his country. He expressed his basic outlook in an early letter to Shepstone: "I am a friend of white men. I am opening my country to them and I hope in years to come that lasting friendship and advantageous intercourse will be established between us." [20] But, although this was his basic attitude, as the years went by it became increasingly difficult for him to maintain it in the face of increasing European activity.

In 1863 Mzilikazi had granted permission for John Lee to settle with his family at Mangwe near Bulawayo. Two years later Henry Hartley received permission to hunt in the country. In 1866 gold was discovered in Mashonaland. The following year gold was discovered at Tati. These events brought other Europeans to the country. During the interregnum (1869) John Swinburne and Thomas Baines were looking for gold and concessions, but Umcombate delayed a decision until Lobengula was installed, so that Mzilikazi's heir would receive "a clean country." A few months after Lobengula's accession, John Lee was appointed his representative at Mangwe to receive and forward all applications for entry.[21]

Lobengula allowed traders, hunters, gold and concession seekers, travelers and missionaries entry into the country freely, always receiving them with honor and keeping the promises he gave. He protected them against his more turbulent warriors and treated them freely to his hospitality. While it is true that some of them felt Lobengula caused them needless delays, they forgot that he had other interests and problems in governing his tribe. There can be no legitimate complaint against his treatment of the incoming Europeans.

Lobengula became quite furious in 1877 when the French missionary Francois Coillard was found trying to begin work among the Nyai people. The Paris Evangelical Missionary

20. Wallis, *Northern Goldfields*, 686.
21. *Ibid.*, 547–548, 562–563.

Society was looking for an additional field of labor and was under the impression that the Nyai were independent, while in fact they were Lobengula's subjects. Coillard innocently entered Lobengula's territory without a permit to enter and establish his work. He would have been in a dangerous position if the L.M.S. representatives in Matabeleland had not intervened on his behalf.[22]

More serious was the tragedy of Captain Robert Paterson and his party a year later. A wealthy, but rather haughty young man named Richard Frewen had traveled in Matabeleland in 1877. He had hoped to be able to go beyond the Zambezi, but he failed to do so because of various circumstances, including difficulties with his Ndebele servants. Frewen accused Lobengula of wrecking his expedition and threatened him with the vengeance of the British government. Lobengula, already upset over the Coillard incident, did not want any trouble from the young man and ordered him out of the country. On his return to Pretoria Frewen complained to Theophilus Shepstone, then administrator of the Transvaal, that Lobengula was hindering the traders and hunters in Matabeleland. Because of his connections he also gained the ear of the high commissioner for South Africa, Sir Bartle Frere.

As a result of this affair, in 1878 Shepstone sent an official mission, led by Captain R. R. Paterson and Lieutenant T. G. Sergeant, to investigate the complaint. The group reached Bulawayo in August, but by then the Ndebele were suspicious because of Frewen and his threat of government intervention, and because of Shepstone's former association with Nkulumana. It did not help matters that the two officers were tactless, and that the letter they brought from Shepstone was undiplomatic. The *indunas* were furious. When the two men wanted to go on to the Zambezi, Lobengula advised them to go back to Pretoria and return in another year. But they persisted, and Lobengula finally allowed them to proceed. Lobengula, hearing that they had engaged Morgan Thomas, the son of the London Missionary Society missionary as a guide, advised the father that young Thomas should not go.

22. C. W. Mackintosh, *Some Pioneer Missions in Northern Rhodesia and Nyasaland* (Livingstone, 1950), 6.

When Paterson's party reached a spring three days from the Zambezi, all three Europeans perished along with their African servants. Lobengula said they had drunk poisonous water, but refused to let white men bury the bodies. Morgan Thomas' brother, David, later made an investigation; he believed they were murdered, although Thomas Morgan Thomas exonerated Lobengula. It was widely believed, however, that Lobengula, upon pressure from his *indunas,* had ordered their deaths. The suspicion has lingered to this day, and, although it is impossible to be sure, it seems reasonable to believe that Lobengula gave the order.[23]

During this early period of his reign, Lobengula was asked for and gave various concessions involving land and mining rights. Earlier, under the interregnum, Umcombate had given Thomas Baines a tentative concession on behalf of the company he represented. Lobengula confirmed it verbally on April 9, 1870. Baines was very cautious about this since he knew how sensitive the Ndebele were, both in regard to land and to a written document; in the end he asked for and received a written concession dated August 29, 1871.

In giving the concession, Lobengula made it quite clear that he merely granted permission to dig for gold and in no way gave Baines ownership of the land or the right to alienate it. The written agreement was explicit on this point: "In making this grant I did not alienate from my kingdom this or any other portion of it, but retained intact the Sovereignty of my dominions." In the course of the negotiations Lobengula added what may have been a premonition: "Yes, you may promise fairly now, but in future time, when you are strongly established, you may forget your promise and exceed the liberty I have given." [24] Sir John Swinburne, who had been seeking a concession on behalf of the London and Limpopo Mining Company at the same time as Baines, received the so-called Tati Concession granted to Captain Levert on April 29, 1870. Lobengula thought that he had granted permission to dig for gold, but Levert's interpretation was much more liberal — claiming that the concession turned the whole area over to the company,

23. Edward C. Tabler, *Zambezia and Matabeleland in the Seventies* (London, 1960), 128–130.
24. Wallis, *Northern Goldfields,* 561, 695.

with rights to keep out competitors. This troubled Lobengula. He apparently had thought that people would come, dig for gold, and then leave, much as they came to hunt for elephants. He made a very telling remark to Baines about this: "I gave Mr. Levert a cow to milk and he might have milked her dry; but now he wants not only the milk, but claims the cow as if he won her by conquest." [25]

Therefore, when John Boden Thomson of the L.M.S. applied to Lobengula for a second mission station to be called Hope Fountain, Lobengula was more cautious. He explained carefully that he gave the society liberty to occupy the site "as a Mission Station through its representative, as long as they like under me as a chief, and that no trader is to build on it." [26]

These and other negotiations over land grants and mining concessions should have warned Lobengula about the pitfalls and difficulties of dealing with Europeans; but when the crucial test came in 1888 there is little to indicate that Lobengula had learned from his earlier encounters with Europeans.

Intertribal relations were of great importance at that time in Central Africa. Lobengula had varied experiences with his neighboring tribes and their chiefs. The Shona-speaking people to the east and southeast of Matabeleland consisted of small units of related tribes with no chief comparable in strength to Lobengula. He regarded them as "his dogs" and their territory, Mashonaland, as a hunting ground for his warriors. The Mangwato to the south were traditional enemies of the Ndebele, but the last raid against the Mangwato had taken place in 1862 before Lobengula's accession. Macheng's unsuccessful plot with Kanda against Lobengula has been mentioned. The territory between the Macloutsi and the Tati Rivers was claimed by both Lobengula and Khama, Macheng's successor as chief of the Mangwato, but neither pressed the claim out of respect for the power of the other. Nevertheless, verbally Lobengula showed little respect for Khama. The boundary between the territories of Khama and Lobengula was never settled, yet Lobengula resented it when Khama agreed with Sir Sidney Shippard on a

25. *Ibid.*, 556.
26. Thomson to L.M.S., Dec. 2, 1870, L.M.S. Archives; Wallis, *Northern Goldfields*, 556.

northern boundary. Who was Khama to give him, Lobengula, "a line"?

The Lozi of Barotseland, led then by Lewanika, were another traditional enemy of the Ndebele. The Ndebele had been raiding the fringes of Lozi territory, but Lobengula became uneasy about the mounting pressure from the Europeans in the south. He made an effort to conciliate Lewanika by sending a delegation to the Lozi chief in 1882, proposing a defensive alliance against the white menace. But it so happened that F. S. Arnot, a Scottish missionary, was staying at Lewanika's court. When Arnot's advice was sought, he suggested that Khama, the Christian chief of the Mangwato, was a better man to deal with than Lobengula, so Lobengula's proposed alliance came to naught.[27]

The Beginning of the End: 1888–1890

While Lobengula was looking after the interests of his people, settling their daily affairs, and dealing with the Europeans who came into the country, Europe had started in earnest "the scramble for Africa." The contenders for Matabeleland were the Boers and the British, with Portugal and Germany trailing behind. By declaring a protectorate over Bechuanaland in August 1885, Great Britain had become Lobengula's neighbor. The South African Republic and Lobengula had the Limpopo River as a common boundary.

In March 1882, Piet Joubert, commandant general of the South African Republic, sent a letter of friendship to Lobengula.[28] In July 1887 Pieter D. C. J. Grobler was sent to Bulawayo to sign a treaty of friendship with Lobengula. According to this treaty, the South African Republic was given jurisdiction over its subjects living in Lobengula's territory, the right to regulate the influx of Europeans into Matabeleland and to send a consul to Bulawayo. On his way back, Grobler was killed in an incident with some of Khama's people near Baines' Drift on the Limpopo.[29]

27. Mackintosh, *Pioneer Missions*, 10.
28. Colonial Office White Book [hereafter C.O.], 369 (1889), 213.
29. For the Grobler treaty see, P.P., C. 5918 (1890), 29; C.O. 369 (1889), 169–172.

There was a question for some time as to whether Lobengula had in fact signed such a treaty. In the beginning Moffat doubted it, and it has been called "a forgery of the grossest type." But, there can be no doubt that there was such a treaty; Lobengula admitted signing it to Sidney Shippard.[30] Lord Salisbury, however, ruled that the South African Republic had no right to enter into such a treaty according to the London Convention of 1884, which supposedly regulated the Transvaal boundaries.[31]

When the treaty became known to Cecil Rhodes, whose ambition it was to extend British rule in Africa from the Cape to Cairo, he sprang into action.[32] He persuaded the British high commissioner, Sir Hercules Robinson, to send a message to John Smith Moffat, assistant commissioner for Bechuanaland, instructing him to negotiate another treaty with Lobengula. (Moffat had left the service of the London Missionary Society in 1879 and had entered the civil service.) Part of his duty as assistant commissioner was to cultivate friendly relations with Lobengula, with a view to a possible British protectorate extending to the Zambezi.[33] He was then in Bulawayo on a friendly mission to Lobengula.

Moffat received his instructions at the end of January 1888, and worked very quickly. On February 11, Lobengula signed the so-called Moffat treaty. It gave Great Britain an option on Lobengula's territory; that is, Lobengula promised not to cede any land to, or enter into any agreement with, any power without the prior consent of Her Majesty's Government.[34]

Lobengula could justify both the Grobler and Moffat treaties because he understood the Grobler treaty to be just a confirmation of an earlier 1853 treaty between Mzilikazi and the Transvaal Boers; under this treaty, protection was offered to those Boers who were permitted to enter the country.[35] As far

30. P.P., C. 5524 (1888), 2; Hole, *Rhodesia*, 62; C.O. 369 (1889), 171.
31. C.O. 358 (1889), 14.
32. There have been many studies written concerning Cecil John Rhodes, including some very recent ones. The present writer has found the most dependable one to be Basil Williams, *Cecil Rhodes* (London, 1921).
33. P.P., C. 5237 (1887), 33–34.
34. For the text of the treaty see P.P., C. 5524 (1888), 13.
35. C.O. 369 (1889), 169–172.

as the Moffat treaty was concerned, it must have appeared harmless to him because he did not intend to cede his country to anyone. Who wanted it anyway? He was safe from Khama and Lewanika. He had heard about the Portuguese on the eastern borders of his kingdom, but he had never seen them. The Boers were feared and remembered from Mzilikazi's time in the Marico district, but they had never really bothered the Ndebele in Lobengula's time. Only the British remained. If they wanted to keep out any of the others, he was content to let them do so.

But perhaps there were other thoughts in his mind? His proposed agreement with Lewanika had come to naught. The Zulu power had been broken in Natal where even the mighty Cetewayo had been forced to give in to the British; Khama had accepted a treaty with Great Britain. Lobengula was well aware of his own position, as he demonstrated by his remarks to Baines when he gave him his concession. He remarked later in the year to Shippard that he knew that he was the fly which one day would be caught by the British chameleon. Did Lobengula merely give in to the inevitable or did he hope to play the Boers against the British and thereby enhance his chances of survival?

While Moffat was negotiating with Lobengula, Cecil Rhodes sent John L. Fry to Bulawayo to negotiate a concession. He was in Bulawayo from February 10 to March 1, but he failed in his efforts for two reasons. Fry was quite inadequate for the task, and he chose an interpreter, Usher, who was not highly respected in Bulawayo by Europeans or Africans. It is difficult to understand why Rhodes sent a man like Fry; perhaps it was only an effort to gain time.[36]

Soon Rhodes sent another party to Bulawayo consisting of Charles Dunell Rudd, one of Rhodes' financial partners in Johannesburg; James Rochefort Maguire, an Irish lawyer friend of Rhodes' from his Oxford days; and Francis Robert Thompson, a South African who served as a linguist. They left Kimberley on August 15, arriving in Bulawayo on September 20, 1888. This was a highly competent and impressive party, but they also re-

---

36. P.P., C. 5237 (1887), 33; Ivor Fry, *Reminiscences*, 5 (written in 1938), Ms. in National Archives of Rhodesia and Nyasaland [hereafter NARN], Salisbury.

ceived some additional support before they obtained their objective. The Rudd party had a number of interviews with Lobengula. At the outset they presented Lobengula with one hundred gold sovereigns. They also told him that they were not like other concession seekers, since they did not want land, but only permission for about ten men to dig for gold. In return they promised Lobengula a thousand rifles, a hundred thousand rounds of ammunition, a gunboat on the Zambezi, and an allowance of £100 sterling every new moon.[37]

In Bulawayo at that time were at least four other groups of rival concession seekers, plus a group of interested individual traders and hunters. There was considerable intrigue between these groups causing a great deal of tension. The *indunas*, especially the young warriors, became excited and nervous, wanting nothing but to wipe out all white people in Bulawayo. One of the *indunas*, Lotje, favored the Rudd party.

When the tension was at its height the deputy commissioner for the Bechuanaland protectorate, Sir Sidney Shippard, escorted by Major Goold-Adams and sixteen members of the Bechuanaland Border Police, arrived. They were in uniform. There was uncertainty in Bulawayo about the reason for their coming and the Ndebele thought that an *impi* was approaching. Both Moffat and Helm, senior missionary of the London Missionary Society, had to reassure Lobengula that no *impi* was coming and that the confusion had risen because of the administrator's unusual escort.[38]

At the first interview with Lobengula on October 18, Shippard had with him his assistant, Moffat, his aid, Goold-Adams, Bishop G. W. H. Knight-Bruce, C. D. Helm and David Carnegie. Knight-Bruce, Anglican bishop of Bloemfontein, was returning from a long journey in Mashonaland. Carnegie and Helm were missionaries of the London Missionary Society at Hope Fountain. Helm acted as interpreter. No such imposing and influential group had ever had an audience with Lobengula. It could

37. Francis Robert Thompson, *Matabele Thompson* (London, 1936), 101, 178; Constance E. Fripp and V. W. Hiller, *Gold and the Gospel in Mashonaland, 1888* (London, 1949), 219, 227.

38. "Matabele" Wilson, *Diary*, Typewritten Manuscript, 56, Ms. in NARN; Helm to L.M.S., Oct. 11, 1888, L.M.S. Archives.

not fail to make an impression on him and on everyone living in Bulawayo .

In his conversation with Lobengula at this and subsequent interviews Shippard discussed the boundary with Khama, the disputed territory near Tati, the Grobler treaty, and the incident that had led to Grobler's death on the banks of the Limpopo. Shippard also stressed that "the English like to make money by trading and mining, but do not in general covet land," and although a protectorate had been exercised over Khama's country for three years, "the English had not deprived Khama or his people of any land whatever." The only threat to Lobengula and his people, Shippard noted, were the Transvaal filibusters who were seeking to destroy the Ndebele, and to seize their land and cattle. Shippard continued, saying that "though we do not covet the land of the Amandabele for ourselves, we do not wish to see the Boers gaining possession of it," and "any concession seeker who says he is asking for mineral grants on behalf of the Queen's government is speaking falsely." But nearly all of these reassurances proved to be false and even Shippard felt the hollowness of his remarks; he added to his report of the interviews: "if only he [Lobengula] could trust the English, but there's the rub." [39]

Shippard left on October 22. Moffat left a few days later. The visit influenced Lobengula; it could hardly be mere coincidence that only five days after Shippard's departure Maguire drew up the terms of the concession in preparation for the final audience with the chief. This took place on October 30, 1888, in the presence of some one hundred *indunas* and headmen. Rudd made it quite plain that he wanted a concession covering the whole country or none at all. At one point he threatened to leave unless Lobengula gave in. Sitting on an old brandy case in the midst of his goat *kraal*, Lobengula had his final meeting with Rudd, Maguire, and Thompson, with Helm serving as interpreter. He appeared "much hustled and anxious," but signed the paper ceding mineral rights to his whole kingdom. The document was signed by Rudd, Maguire, and Thompson; Lobengula added his mark; Helm and J. G. Dreyer, the transport driver for the Rudd party, signed as witnesses. No *indunas* signed as

39. C.O. 369 (1889), 170.

Lobengula said it was not necessary. In addition, Helm endorsed the concession, testifying that it had been properly explained to Lobengula and his council of *indunas* according to the constitutional usages of the Ndebele people.[40] In addition to the written agreement there were certain verbal pledges binding Rudd to deliver the first installment of rifles before any white employee or machine was introduced, and binding all miners engaged to fight in the defense of the country if called upon.[41]

Rudd left Bulawayo as soon as the concession had been signed, leaving Thompson and Maguire to look after Rhodes' interests. But now Rhodes' rivals started to work on Lobengula, informing him that he had signed away his country, and asking if he really knew that there was a queen in England? Lobengula was consequently persuaded by E. A. Maund, representing the financier George Cawston of London, a rival of Rhodes, to send two of his most trusted *indunas,* Babyan and Umjete, to London; Maund and Johan Colenbrander acted as guides, and the journey was paid for by the money received for the Rudd concession.[42] The party arrived in London on February 27, 1889.

But the excitement would not die down in Bulawayo, as Rhodes' rivals continued their pressure on Lobengula. Now suspicion fell on the missionaries. W. F. Tainton, whom Moffat had described as an able linguist, had been approached by the Rudd party to be their interpreter. He had been unable to act since he was out of favor with the chief at that time. Tainton now told Lobengula that the South African newspapers said that he had sold his whole country. So on January 18, 1889, the chief sent for Helm, requesting that he read the concession to him. This Helm did, giving the same interpretation as before: that the concession said nothing about land, only about the minerals in the land; that no power was given except to do what was necessary to remove the gold. Helm maintained that it was nonsense to say that the grantees could do whatever they liked in the country. They would not bring in more than ten white men to work and they were subject to the laws of the land.[43]

40. Fripp and Hiller, *Gold and the Gospel*, 201–202, 219–220.
41. C.O. 369 (1889), 210–211.
42. Wilson, *Diary*, 65, 217–218.
43. Helm to L.M.S., March 29, 1889, L.M.S. Archives.

A little more than a month later, on March 12 while Helm was at the chief's *kraal,* he was again asked to read the concession, this being a favorite African method of verifying that the same answers were given each time a question was asked. At this meeting the *indunas* and the other Europeans were present. Thompson was also cross-examined. Both he and Helm assured the assembly that Rudd had asked for the right to dig for gold and that no land was asked for. Helm offered to give a written statement to this effect, but the other white men present refused.[44]

The next day Helm was accused by the *indunas* of interfering with the trade by preventing traders from giving a fair price for their cattle. Helm denied this. He was also accused of interfering with the chief's mail. He denied the charge but admitted that he served as postmaster. The following day, March 14, he went home to Hope Fountain.

In the meantime the chief had sent for the two missionaries, W. A. Elliott and Bowen Rees, from Inyati, forty miles away. They arrived in Bulawayo on March 15. They knew, of course, of the Rudd concession, but were unaware of the strained feelings at the court and of the cross-examination of Helm. They were led into the chief's presence together with a number of Rhodes' rivals. They were asked to read the concession to the chief. There was no disagreement about the first half, but these two missionaries differed from Helm in the interpretation of the second half. They said no one could mine the land without having power over the land. One *induna,* Umhlaba, asked a pertinent question: "if the mining rights of a like tract of country could be bought anywhere else for a similar sum?" [45]

Various interpretations have been published concerning this meeting. This writer has found no basis in the original documents for the sensational form this case has been given by J. H. Harris, nor is there any basis for the charge that Helm changed his mind. Stuart Cloete did not grasp that there were two different pairs of missionaries involved. Helm has been criticized for not having left any records behind, and even for writing out the concession and willfully misguiding Lobengula. But no evidence has been found to throw doubt on Helm's integrity, and

44. Wilson, *Diary,* 65, 217–218.
45. Elliott to L.M.S., March 27, 1889, L.M.S. Archives.

the statement that there are no records of the events is obviously untrue.[46]

After the meeting Elliott and Rees went to Hope Fountain to consult with Helm and Carnegie. Then all four went together to Lobengula, explaining their differences of opinion, but stating that they would stand or fall together. But this only left Lobengula and the *indunas* with a feeling of having been cheated.

A few weeks later, on April 2, 1889, Leander Starr Jameson arrived in Bulawayo. He was a Kimberley doctor who had joined Rhodes and was to play an important role in the subsequent history of Rhodesia and South Africa. He came to deliver the first half of the promised rifles and to give relief to Maguire who was bored with his long stay at Bulawayo. Lobengula at once liked Jameson, especially since the doctor rendered him medical services.[47]

Jameson left on April 12, taking Maguire with him. But the tension in Bulawayo was not relieved for long; Rhodes' rivals continued to sow suspicion in the mind of Lobengula. Thus, on April 23, Lobengula wrote to Queen Victoria repudiating the concession and charging Maguire with leaving the country without his permission.

In the meantime the Ndebele in Bulawayo looked forward to the return of Babyan and Umjete; they arrived on August 7. They told Lobengula that they had been well treated, having seen the queen in audience. The emissaries had met many influential people, seen the vaults of the Bank of England, and observed military maneuvers at Aldershot. They brought two letters from London: one from Knutsford, the colonial secretary, dated March 26, 1889, consisted of a few paternalistic remarks

46. J. H. Harris, *The Chartered Millions* (London, 1920), 67–68; Stuart Cloete, *Against These Three* (New York, 1947), 219; Wilson, *Diary*, 103; J. E. S. Green, *Rhodes Goes North* (London, 1936), 100; Sarah Gertrude Millin, *Rhodes* (London, 1952), 117–118. For a full treatment of Helms' part in the concession negotiations, see Per Hassing, "The Christian Missions and the British Expansion in Southern Rhodesia, 1888–1923" (unpubl. diss., American University, 1960), 77–81.

47. Many sources describe Lobengula's ailment as gout. This may be doubted in light of modern medical knowledge. Dr. M. Gelfand in his book, *The Sick African* (Cape Town, 1944), 281, has stated: "Gout is probably not encountered in the Native. I have never seen a case or even an x-ray film of the bones or joints that was the least suggestive of this disease."

which looked innocent enough on paper, but which increased the tension in Bulawayo. He advised Lobengula to consider carefully the granting of land: "A king gives a stranger an ox, not his whole herd of cattle, otherwise what would other strangers have to eat?" [48] The second letter, from the Anti-Slavery and Aborigines Protection Society, was similar in tone: "As you are now being asked by many for permission to seek for gold, and dig it up in your country, we would have you be wary and firm in resisting proposals that will not bring good to you and your people." [49] Both of these letters advised against exactly what Lobengula had done. The colonial secretary's letter even talked about the giving away of land, and Lobengula was not conscious of having granted any land.

The two letters threw Bulawayo into great commotion. An answer dated August 19, 1889, was sent to the queen, asserting: "The white people are troubling me much about gold. If the Queen hears that I have given away my country, it is not so . . . I thank the Queen for the word which my messengers give me by mouth, that the Queen says I am not to let anyone dig for gold in my country, except to dig for me as my servant." [50]

This letter could have been awkward for Rhodes' schemes. Maguire had stated that the earlier letter of April 23, from Lobengula to the queen, was forged because neither Moffat nor a missionary had attested it. But the letter of August 10 was witnessed by Moffat and was sent through the regular channels; however, it was late in arriving. The letter of April 23 had reached London in one month and three and one-half weeks; in the case of the letter of August 10, it appears probable that someone had interfered with Her Majesty's mail, as it took three months and one week to reach London. When it did reach London, Queen Victoria had already signed the document giving a royal charter to the British South Africa Company which eventually became the owner of the concession and prepared to move into Lobengula's territory.

The letters from England caused Lobengula and his *indunas* to hold a long, excited, council meeting to which no white man

48. P.P., C. 5918 (1890), 164.
49. Hole, *Rhodesia*, 84.
50. P.P., C. 5918 (1890), 235.

was admitted. In the course of the meeting Lobengula must have turned on his *induna,* Lotje, making him a scapegoat since he had supported the Rudd application. The next day, September 10, Lotje was killed with his wives and children, slaves and cattle, fowls and dogs, and his *kraal* was burned.[51] This was an ignoble act. Lotje had been one of Lobengula's most intimate advisers.

The situation in Bulawayo was now critical. Thompson fled in panic. One of the Ndebele regiments had come to dance before the chief, asking permission to throw all the Europeans out of the country. Anything might happen, and no one understood this better than Rhodes who sent Jameson, Thompson, and two others back to Bulawayo; they arrived on October 17.

While Jameson was in Bulawayo another group of visitors arrived on January 27, 1890. They were the envoys of Queen Victoria, five officers and men of the Royal Horse Guard in full uniform, coming to announce the granting of the royal charter to the British South Africa Company. The envoys delivered a letter from the queen, dated November 15, three days prior to the arrival in London of Lobengula's letter repudiating the Rudd concession. It was a strange letter contradicting the previous letter from the colonial secretary. It opened by declaring that the queen had confidence in Moffat as her servant, that she had investigated the affairs of Matabeleland, and that

> wherever gold is, or wherever it is reported to be, there it is impossible for him [Lobengula] to exclude white men, and, therefore, the wisest and safest course for him to adopt, and that which will give least trouble to him and his tribe, is to agree, not with one or two white men separately, but with one approved body of white men, who will consult Lobengula's wishes and arrange where white people are to dig, and who will be responsible to the Chief for any annoyance and trouble caused to himself or his people. If he does not agree with one set of people there will be endless disputes among white men, and he will have his time taken up in deciding their quarrels.

The letter went on to tell of the queen's approval of the Rudd concession and that Lobengula would be well advised to let Dr. Jameson settle all the disputes among the Europeans; yet, "this

51. Carnegie to L.M.S., Feb. 14, 1890, L.M.S. Archives.

must be as Lobengula likes, as he is King of the country, and no one can exercise jurisdiction in it without his permission." The letter also promised that Rudd, Maguire, and Thompson would carry on work "without in any way interfering with their *kraals,* gardens or cattle." In return, the queen trusted that Lobengula would let them "conduct their mining operation without interference." [52]

Lobengula told the envoys that "the Queen's letter had been dictated by Rhodes," and that he did not want any such letters from her again.[53] Lobengula could only have wondered how the same queen could have written both of the letters he had received from her, of March 26 and November 15. During the next four years he probably wondered if she really meant what she had said in her last letter about his royal jurisdiction in his own territory.

In yet a later letter Knutsford informed Lobengula that his letter of August 10 had arrived after the granting of the royal charter, but that the men employed by the company "will recognize him as King of the country and will have such powers as he entrusts to them." [54]

During this time Jameson had been using all his personal influence, diplomacy, and persuasive power to get Lobengula to agree to "give" Rhodes' men the road to Mashonaland. This was no mean task, since Lobengula kept to what he had been told when he put his hand to the concession; that is, that only a hole was wanted for ten men to dig in. It appears to this writer that there was little in the events that could lead Lobengula to trust the white men. Therefore, he wanted them to come to Bulawayo so he could show them where to dig. He could not understand why so many had to come or why there had to be an *impi.* Had not the queen herself said that the white men would consult Lobengula's wishes about the digging? Why did the white men not obey the queen? Maybe the queen had not told the truth? When Lobengula finally "gave the road," without saying where, Jameson left Bulawayo on February 13.

While the negotiations proceeded, Rhodes had been recruiting and organizing his expedition into Mashonaland. The members

52. P.P., C. 5918 (1890), 233.
53. Wilson, *Diary,* 205.
54. P.P., C. 5918 (1890), 239, 288, 307.

of the expedition consisting of military and civilians were so chosen that they came from many parts of South Africa and Great Britain and had sufficient skills to set up an embryo community. If they were massacred by the Ndebele there would be many voices from many communities clamoring for revenge.

The hunter Frederick Selous was to be the guide. He had been led to believe that Lobengula had promised to send men to cut the road through the wilderness. When they did not turn up, Selous rode on to Bulawayo to ask for them. He was told by Lobengula that he had never "given the *impi* the road" and he wanted to see Rhodes in Bulawayo. Lobengula added: "I am tired of talking with Rhodes' messengers and the bearers of his words: their stories don't all agree." [55]

Selous was forced to return with the disappointing message. Rhodes never went to see Lobengula, but Jameson and Selous arrived on April 27; and on May 2 they were permitted to leave, not with a positive permission to reenter, but only with an absence of refusal.[56] Lobengula and Jameson never met again.

The expedition left Kimberley on May 6. While it was on its way to Mashonaland there was intense excitement in Bulawayo. Lobengula, of course, could not understand why an *impi* was advancing into his country when he had given permission for ten men to dig for gold. And why did the *impi* not come the usual "missionary road" to Bulawayo?

The missionaries had been advised by Jameson to leave Bulawayo. Lobengula was reluctant to let them go. He had said that there would be no war as long as the missionaries stayed.[57] Lobengula finally gave them permission to leave on June 13. Before they left he insisted that they inspect the guns so they could inform Rhodes they were where he had left them, thereby showing that Lobengula had never really accepted them.[58]

The Ndebele harvested their crops in a hurry, preparing for the worst. Lobengula sent two messages, one to the commander of the Bechuanaland Border Police at Macloutsi asking: "What white men have I killed that you are coming to seek? Why can-

55. Selous, *Travel and Adventure,* 360.
56. *Ibid.,* 361.
57. Carnegie to Doyle, May 5, 1890, L.M.S. Archives.
58. Elliott to L.M.S., June 12, 1890, *ibid.*

not two people live together in one country?" [59] The other was
sent with Johan Colenbrander (now an employee of Rhodes)
to Fort Tule; it was addressed to Jameson and asked the expedition to stop. But when the messengers arrived, the expedition
had already left. When they caught up, it was too late. Lobengula sent several letters to Sir Henry Loch, the high commissioner,
but received no satisfaction. He finally sent his most trusted
induna, Umjete, to Cape Town. Helm went with him at Rhodes'
expense. Loch assured Umjete that there would be no war and
that the expedition had only gone to dig for gold.[60]

The Ndebele regiments were very anxious for a fight, wanting
to halt the expedition by force, which they probably could have
done successfully at an early stage. Lobengula, however, kept
them back by reminding them that the white men were too numerous to kill as new ones would come to take the place of the
few lost.

John Smith Moffat remained at his post in Bulawayo. The
expedition arrived without mishap at the small hill, Harare, on
September 12, 1890. There they hoisted the Union Jack and established Fort Salisbury, where Rhodesia's modern capital now
stands.

The End: 1891–1893

For Lobengula affairs were now very complex. He had to deal
with the representative of the British South Africa Company in
Bulawayo, and with Jameson in Mashonaland, behind whom
was Cecil Rhodes. He also had to deal with the queen's representative in Cape Town, Sir Henry Loch.

Acting as if the country belonged to them, the Chartered Company proceeded to govern Mashonaland according to the South
African Order in Council of May 9, 1891. One of the order's
main features was that the whole of the company's territory was
declared a British protectorate, something Lobengula had never
agreed to. The members of the expedition proceeded to peg out
and occupy 3,000-acre farms in Mashonaland. However, the Rudd

59. Elliott to L.M.S., June 12, 1890, *ibid.*
60. Helm to L.M.S., Aug. 11, 1890, L.M.S. Archives; C.O. 392 (1890), 307,
312.

concession gave no direct power over the land, although it did say that Lobengula had agreed to grant no concessions of land or mining rights without the consent of the concession holders. The uncertainty of the Rudd concession regarding land gave an opportunity to the German financier Eduard A. Lippert of Johannesburg to interfere. Through one of his subordinates, Renny Tailyour, a concession covering exclusive land rights over Mashonaland and Matabeleland for one hundred years was negotiated with Lobengula. Lippert offered it to Rhodes for sale. Rhodes, not believing it to be genuine, told Lippert to go back to Lobengula to obtain a concession properly attested by Moffat.

Official instructions were now issued to Moffat. Moffat detested this deal immensely, feeling it to be immoral. But he was a civil servant and had to obey his order or resign. He justified his actions as follows: "If I did not feel that the Chief is quite as deceitful as those who are going to try conclusions with him, I do not know if I could sit still and let this go on, but as it is only a contest of knavery on both sides I can sit still and hope I shall not be brought into any partnership with either side." [61] The net result was that Lippert got his concession on November 17, 1891. He sold it to Rhodes for £12,630 in cash and shares.[62]

Lobengula had no right to make this sale according to the Rudd concession, but he may have felt justified in acting as he did because the Europeans in Mashonaland had taken so much more than he had given. Perhaps Lobengula felt that he was fighting a losing battle and might as well get what he could out of a lost cause. Lobengula had not, however, relinquished his power over Mashonaland and the Shona tribes. As far as he was concerned, the white people were only in Mashonaland to dig for gold, and, as a convenience, he let them be governed by Jameson. In order to maintain his overlordship, Lobengula continued to allow his *impi* to raid the Shona chiefs, to collect taxes and tribute, to settle quarrels, to kill, and to enslave as before.

During 1891 Lobengula's *impis* moved apparently aimlessly around the country, mainly to keep the warriors busy. A raid was conducted north of Fort Salisbury in which a chief, Loma-

61. Moffat to Loch (confidential), Oct. 7, 1891, NARN.
62. C.O. 426 (1892), 30. For the text of the Lippert concession, P.P., C. 7171 (1893), 8–9.

gundi, was killed.[63] In 1892 a similar raid was conducted against Chief Chibi south of Fort Victoria. On September 10, the postal cart was stopped and robbed, the *impi* threatening to kill the man in charge. On another occasion a transport rider was attacked and robbed between the Nuanetsi and Lundi rivers. On April 13, 1893, two traders from Fort Victoria were robbed and one of them died from injuries.[64] Jameson protested in vain against these raids. Even though mainly directed against the Shona, they were greatly disturbing to the European settlers.

Then two Europeans, Edkani and Shackleton, were found prospecting far inside Lobengula's territory without his permission. They were robbed by the Ndebele. Lobengula was angry; he succeeded in getting back the stolen goods, but told Jameson that such occurrences could only lead to serious difficulties between the two parties. The comment of Johan Colenbrander, now an employee of the Chartered Company in Bulawayo, was: "He [Lobengula] is trying to pull straight; therefore they [the whites] ought from their side help him in cases of this sort all they can." [65]

Here was the real issue. Lobengula regarded himself as the ruler of the country. The queen had acknowledged that in her letter. The Rudd party had told him they only wanted to dig for gold. He could live side by side with the whites in one country. What he did with the Shona people, "his dogs," mattered not. But where was the boundary between him and the whites? What was the difference between the prospecting of Edkani and Shackleton and other prospecting? Was there a division of territory?

In November 1891, the London Missionary Society missionary W. A. Elliott gave an interesting account of the question. At that time the boundary was the Umzwezwe River, but it represented an advance on the line drawn a few months earlier. Elliott speculated on what would happen when a further advance was made by the company.[66] In 1893 Jameson maintained that the

---

63. For a description of the terrible results of this raid, see Isaac Shimmin to Wesleyan Methodist Missionary Society, Sept. 28, 1893. Wesleyan Methodist Missionary Society Archives, London.

64. British South Africa Company, *Report 1892–1894,* 17.

65. P.P., C. 7171 (1893), 44.

66. *The Chronicle of the London Missionary Society* (March 1892), 71.

boundary was the Shashi and Umnyaniti rivers; Lobengula denied ever having agreed to a boundary line.

Then in early May 1893, came the so-called Victoria incident. Some Shona under a minor chief, Gomalla, cut some five hundred yards of the telegraph wire to Salisbury. Gomalla refused to give up the culprits but accepted a fine which he paid in cattle. He then sent word to Lobengula that the white men had taken Lobengula's cattle. An angry Lobengula sent a long letter to Jameson asking for an explanation and admonishing him not to punish unless he had the real culprit.[67] In the end the cattle were returned and a new effort was made to find the real offenders.

A little later Lobengula sent an *impi* to near Fort Victoria to punish the people of Chief Bere for cattle theft. Before dispatching the *impi*, Lobengula sent a message on June 26 to Jameson, saying that the *impi* had strict orders not to interfere with white settlers as he had no hostile intentions against the whites.[68] This order was obeyed to the letter, but only to the letter. The *impi* burned Shona *kraals* near Fort Victoria, killed and enslaved people, and drove away cattle. Finally, on Sunday afternoon, July 9, they killed nine Shona in the streets of Fort Victoria.[69]

Jameson, who was informed by wire, at once sent a friendly message to Lobengula asking him to keep the *impi* on his side of the boundary line. He also told Captain Lendy, officer in charge at Fort Victoria, to get rid of the *impi* without collision, informing him that Lobengula was "very anxious and, in fact frightened of any trouble with the whites." Jameson also reminded Lendy that a war would, from a financial point of view, throw the country back "till God knows when." A friendly message was also sent from Loch to Lobengula.[70]

Jameson went to Fort Victoria and had conferences with the *indunas* on July 17 and 18, concerning the purpose of the raids. The *induna* Manyow told Jameson that they had come on the chief's order and intended to stay until their purpose was accomplished. Manyow said that Mashonaland was part of the

---

67. P.P., C. 7171 (1893), 42–44.
68. *Ibid.*, 50, 54. This message reached the Colonial Office on July 12, 1893.
69. *The Zambesi Mission Record*, IV, No. 48 (1910), 71. Letter from Father Prestage dated Fort Victoria, July 12, 1893.
70. P.P., C. 7171 (1893), 50–52.

Ndebele kingdom to which Lobengula had never ceded his governing rights and that the Europeans had only permission to search for gold and precious stones. Since the days of Mzilikazi the Ndebele had always sent their *impi* to assert their overlordship over the Shona, and the right to kill those who refused to pay the annual tribute had never been questioned.

Finally, at about noon, Jameson told the *indunas* to be across the Tokwe River in an hour's time. After lunch some of the Ndebele were still in the neighborhood and Jameson ordered Captain Lendy to carry out his orders. "If you find they are not moving off, drive them as you heard me tell Manyow I would, and if they resist and attack you shoot them." [71] Lendy found the Ndebele a few miles from the settlement, at a distance variously reported from three to seven miles. As the Ndebele did not move quickly enough, the European force opened fire, killing about thirty, including Lobengula's nephew. There is no doubt that the Europeans fired first. A commission of inquiry a year later made that quite clear.[72]

When Lobengula heard of the affair he is reported to have executed the warrior who brought the news as a bearer of evil tidings. He also sent some telling messages to Jameson:

> You did not tell me that you had a lot of the Amaholi cattle hiding with you, together with their owners; and that when my indunas claimed them from Captain Lendy, he refused to give up either cattle or men, and told my induna that the Amaholis and their cattle did not belong to me any longer, and then turned his cannon on to my people. Are the Amaholis then yours, including their cattle; did you then send them to come and steal my cattle? Captain Lendy said you had bought them for money; where then did you place the cash? Who did you give it to? Let my cattle be delivered to my people peacefully. I wish you to let me know at once. I thought you came to dig gold, but it seems that you have come not only to dig the gold but to rob me of my people and country as well; remember that you are like a child playing with edged tools. Tell Capt. Lendy he is like some of my own young men; he has no holes in his ears, and cannot or will not hear; he is young, and all he thinks about is a row, but you had better caution him carefully or he will cause trouble, serious trouble between us.[73]

71. Ian Colvin, *The Life of Jameson* (London, 1922), I, 257.
72. P.P., C. 7555 (1894), 12.
73. P.P., C. 7171 (1893), 66–67.

Later on he wrote to Moffat: "you know very well that the white people have done this thing on purpose. This is not right, my people only came to punish the Amahole for stealing my cattle and cutting your wires." [74] The basic question was not settled. Who had jurisdiction over the country? Who "owned" the Shona?

The Europeans were excited. As early as July 27, a force sufficient for the invasion of Matabeleland had been raised. On August 14, the notorious Victoria agreement was signed by Jameson and the volunteers, promising each volunteer a farm of six thousand acres, fifteen mining claims and five alluvial claims, and an equal share of the loot — cattle — after one-half had been taken by the company. This done, war became inevitable and as Major Goold-Adams expressed it: "Jameson will not be able to keep the Salisbury and Victoria people much longer inactive, they will either do something to bring on a row or will leave the country." [75]

In this tense atmosphere High Commissioner Loch tried to call for a restrained and reasonable attitude and did what he could to keep the peace. It was made clear by the imperial government that any offensive move would be deprecated, unless the Europeans were actually attacked; it would under no circumstances be implicated in any situation without giving consent prior to the event. Loch wanted to give Lobengula every opportunity to control his armies and requested him to keep them away from the white settlements. He invited Lobengula to send one of his *indunas* to talk the matter over, maintaining, however, that there could be no question of delivering the Shona over to Ndebele punishment. Lobengula again sent Umjete. After an interview Loch was convinced that the Ndebele would never accept a boundary or give up raiding of Mashonaland.[76]

Another effort for peace was made on October 1, when Loch asked Lobengula to send two envoys to "talk over matters so that there may be peace." But the next day Loch received a wire from Jameson about border incidents twenty-five miles from Fort Victoria in which the Ndebele had fired on a company patrol. On October 5, it was reported that an Ndebele advance guard had

74. *Ibid.*, 67.
75. P.P., C. 7196 (1893), 38. Harry C. Thomson, *Rhodesia and its Government* (London, 1898), 254.
76. P.P., C. 7196 (1893), 16, 31, 46, 75.

fired on the Bechuanaland Border Police. It was then that Loch authorized Jameson to proceed according to his best judgment.[77] It will probably never be determined whether or not the reported firings actually took place; but because of the nature of the sources it may be doubted.[78]

Jameson was ready. There was no ultimatum even though Lobengula had all but asked for one when he wrote: "if the white people want to fight, why don't they say so?"[79] The High Commissioner had asked for envoys of peace, yet on October 6, a column left Fort Victoria, meeting the Salisbury column on October 16. The total force consisted of two hundred and fifty men from Salisbury, four hundred from Fort Victoria, plus five hundred Shona levies. At the same time the Bechuanaland Border Police moved up from Tati. The company did not want any chaplain to go with the forces, but Knight-Bruce, who was now Anglican bishop of Mashonaland, went along anyway.[80]

There were three main battles in the campaign. The first on October 25, near the Shangani River; the second on November 1, near the Imbembesi River; the third on November 2, between the Bechuanaland Border Police and a Ndebele force under Gambo on the Singuisi River. The Ndebele fought bravely, but lack of cohesion and unified command within the tribe contributed to the success of the British forces. There was some evidence that the guns Lobengula had received from Rhodes were used in the battles. Lobengula left his royal *kraal* on October 23 after firing it. When Jameson moved into Bulawayo on November 3, the British forces found the two Europeans, Fairbairn and Usher, unmolested and safe. Lobengula had kept his word.

What had happened to Loch's invitation to send *indunas* to parley for peace? His letter was delivered in Bulawayo on October 14. By then the columns were already on their way. Even so, three *indunas* were dispatched immediately with a trader, James Dawson, as guide. They came to the imperial camp at the Macloutsi River where Colonel Goold-Adams, an imperial officer

77. *Ibid.*, 46, 79–80.
78. F. W. T. Posselt, *Upengula the Scatterer* (Bulawayo, 1945), 80.
79. P.P., C. 7196 (1893), 73.
80. Jones, *Genesis*, 83; Shimmin to Hartley, Wesleyan Methodist Missionary Society Archives; *The Times*, Jan. 31, 1894.

directly responsible to Loch, was in charge. There was some confusion in the camp, and Dawson seemed to have failed to deliver a proper report. The three *indunas* became frightened; two tried to run away, but they were shot on the assumption that they were spies. The whole affair is almost incredible, and it is even more incredible that a later commission of inquiry found Goold-Adams quite guiltless.[81] Two envoys who had come on the express invitation of the high commissioner were shot inside the imperial camp in the belief that they were spies. By comparison, Lobengula stands out as a man of honor.

Helm, the missionary, who refused to be convinced by Jameson and Goold-Adams that it had all happened in good faith, summed it up very well:

> How can one look a Matabele in the face again. We have for years been talking to them about their cruelty in warfare and killing people without cause. And here the first time they come in contact with the English under the Command of an English Officer of standing all our talk is belied.[82]

As if this were not enough, on the next day, two Ndebele post runners from Bulawayo were shot on their way to Tati. They were carrying Her Majesty's mail.

But Lobengula's tragedy was not at an end. Toward the end of November Lewanika sent his forces to prevent Lobengula from crossing the Zambezi, and on November 26, two messengers from Lobengula reached Bulawayo asking that the force under Major Forbes be withdrawn so that he could come in and talk. His message was not received in good faith, the messengers being sent back with Loch's earlier message regretting the shooting of the *indunas* at Macloutsi.

Knight-Bruce offered to go alone, unarmed, towards Lobengula's camp in an effort to reach him and start negotiations for peace but was refused permission by the military command.[83] Major Forbes and Major Wilson were sent instead with armed forces to try to capture Lobengula. Their two forces were separated by the swollen river and the result was the total annihilation of Wilson's patrol on the Shangani River.

81. P.P., C. 7555 (1894).
82. Helm to L.M.S., Oct. 23, 1893, Jan. 12, 1894, L.M.S. Archives.
83. *The Times*, Jan. 31, 1894.

While pursued, Lobengula made a last effort to bring peace.
From the beginning he had been told that the white man's greatest desire in life was gold and precious stones. Neither land nor
cattle but gold was the desired treasure. Where there was gold
the white man could not be kept out, he had been told by Knutsford, the colonial secretary. So in the end Lobengula thought
that perhaps peace would come if he gave away what the white
man wanted. He therefore sent two messengers with a bag of
gold (perhaps containing one thousand gold sovereigns) to Jameson as a last peace offering. But even this was not to be. The
messengers, perhaps fearing the fate of Lobengula's other envoys,
did not go to Bulawayo, but gave the bag and the message to
two troopers, who stole the gold and suppressed the message.[84]
The troopers were later sentenced to fourteen years' imprisonment but were released on a technical point.[85]

Did Lobengula want war? All available evidence points to a
negative answer. He had sent his *impi* towards the Zambezi in
June with the intention of raiding Lewanika's territory. When
the Victoria incident occurred, the *impi* had returned with smallpox and was quarantined. Lobengula had sent his *impi* near
Fort Victoria to punish the Shona in order to avoid a clash with
the Europeans. No European was attacked, not even after the
Europeans had killed a number of the Ndebele. Before Lobengula knew about the killing of his men, he expressed regret that
the *impi* had gone too close to Fort Victoria.[86] Bowen Rees, the
last missionary to leave Matabeleland, as late as August 19, reported on Lobengula's peaceful intentions. Helm also came to
the conclusion that Lobengula would have come to terms if he
had been given the opportunity.[87]

Jameson may not have wanted the war at the time when the
dry season was coming to an end, but both Jameson and Rhodes
sooner or later wanted an end to the Ndebele power; so did the
European settlers.[88] In this they were supported by several,
though not all, missionaries — Anglican, Methodist, and Roman

84. C.O. 461 (1895), 192, 194, 254, 241.
85. *Ibid.*, 293.
86. P.P., C. 7555 (1894), 12; *ibid.*, C. 7171 (1893), 49–50, 65.
87. P.P., C. 7196 (1893), 18; *The Times*, Nov. 15, 1893; Helm to L.M.S., Jan.
12, 1894, L.M.S. Archives.
88. Colvin, *Jameson*, I, 267.

Catholic. The Europeans took advantage of the situation that had developed, and to the end refused to consider a compromise.

On February 16, 1894, news reached Bulawayo that Lobengula had died. Some believed that he died of smallpox, others that he took poison, and still others that he actually crossed the Zambezi and lived for years in the region of Lake Nyasa among the Ngoni people who were also an offshoot of the Zulu tribe.[89] It is impossible for this writer to evaluate the relative merit of these versions of Lobengula's death; there is, however, a rumor that the Rhodesian government knew the whereabouts of Lobengula's grave, but refused to disclose it for political reasons.

Conclusion

Lobengula was, throughout his career, torn between opposing forces. He very reluctantly accepted the chieftainship, but once installed as chief he established his position by logical and reasonable actions, as in the cases of the Zwongendaba and Nkulumana rebellions.

Lobengula was torn between the missionaries and the Ndebele tradition. He respected the missionaries, trusted them as interpreters, letter writers, and advisers. He was fond of them personally. Within certain limits he gave them freedom to teach and preach. Yet, Lobengula discouraged his people, at least by his example, from becoming too closely associated with the missionaries. From his point of view it may well have been a reasonable attitude; if Lobengula had permitted them to introduce the plow, for example, it would have led to a fundamental break with the established tradition of the tribe: the men handled the cattle — which the women were not allowed to touch — and that the women hoed the fields — which was work below the dignity of men.

The gospel the missionaries preached was incompatible with much of the Ndebele tradition. Lobengula could not have accepted it without opening a floodgate to change which he would not have been able to control. So he kept the forces out by refusing personally to submit. Thus no one else dared to take

89. C.O. 461 (1895), 135; Williams, *Cecil Rhodes,* 177; *The Zambesi Mission Record,* II, No. 23 (1904), 350; Posselt, *Upengula,* 112–114.

the first step. This method was successful because the missionaries did not use force to gain their goal.

Lobengula was also torn between the young warriors of his tribe on the one hand and all the European forces represented by traders, concession seekers, and officials on the other. He seemed to have liked the company of Europeans; the testimonies are unanimous in this respect. He kept his word to them, even when he had reason to break it. Lobengula knew European discipline and power, and he tried to come to terms with the new forces without allowing them to break up his own power and his tribe. But he failed because the incoming Europeans were not prepared to yield.

In addition, his warriors would not be restrained. At an early date they wanted to destroy all the white people in the country. They were quite right; it would have been "a mere breakfast" for them. But Lobengula knew that this would only postpone the day of reckoning, so he sent them raiding in other directions — to the Zambezi and even as far away as Lake Ngami. But the warriors were not willing to change their life. So the clash he tried to avoid came in the end. The result was his own downfall.

Was Lobengula weak? Some support can be given this contention. He never seemed to solve the dilemmas he faced, he only postponed them, trying to placate both sides and finding a scapegoat when things became unpleasant. He did not make a fundamental decision for or against white encroachment, for or against the missionaries, for or against the old Ndebele system of war and raiding. He could have fought the Europeans at an early stage or led his people to an adjustment to the new forces as Khama and Lewanika did.

Or could he? Was he perhaps a prisoner of his own people? Did he see that on the one hand the Europeans would never give in until they had gained all, and on the other that his proud people would never become a peaceful, pastoral, and agricultural people like the despised Shona?